INTERNATIONAL POLITICAL ECONOMY SERIES

General Editor: Timothy M. Shaw, Professor of Political Science and International Development Studies, and Director of the Centre for Foreign Policy Studies, Dalhousie University, Nova Scotia, Canada

Gary McMahon (*editor*)
LESSONS IN ECONOMIC POLICY FOR EASTERN EUROPE FROM
LATIN AMERICA

Juan Antonio Morales and Gary McMahon (*editors*)
ECONOMIC POLICY AND THE TRANSITION TO DEMOCRACY
The Latin American Experience

Paul Nelson
THE WORLD BANK AND NON-GOVERNMENTAL ORGANIZATIONS
The Limits of Apolitical Development

Archibald R. M. Ritter and John M. Kirk (*editors*)
CUBA IN THE INTERNATIONAL SYSTEM
Normalization and Integration

Ann Seidman and Robert B. Seidman
STATE AND LAW IN THE DEVELOPMENT PROCESS
Problem-Solving and Institutional Change in the Third World

Tor Skålnes
THE POLITICS OF ECONOMIC REFORM IN ZIMBABWE
Continuity and Change in Development

Howard Stein (*editor*)
ASIAN INDUSTRIALIZATION AND AFRICA
Studies in Policy Alternatives to Structural Adjustment

Deborah Stienstra
WOMEN'S MOVEMENTS AND INTERNATIONAL ORGANIZATIONS

Larry A. Swatuk and Timothy M. Shaw (*editors*)
THE SOUTH AT THE END OF THE TWENTIETH CENTURY
Rethinking the Political Economy of Foreign Policy in Africa, Asia,
the Caribbean and Latin America

Sandra Whitworth
FEMINISM AND INTERNATIONAL RELATIONS

Disaster and Development in the Horn of Africa

Edited by

John Sorenson
Lecturer in Sociology
Brook University, Ontario

First published in Great Britain 1995 by
MACMILLAN PRESS LTD
Houndmills, Basingstoke, Hampshire RG21 6XS
and London
Companies and representatives
throughout the world

A catalogue record for this book is available
from the British Library.

ISBN 0–333–60799–6

First published in the United States of America 1995 by
ST. MARTIN'S PRESS, INC.,
Scholarly and Reference Division,
175 Fifth Avenue,
New York, N.Y. 10010

ISBN 0–312–12538–0

Library of Congress Cataloging-in-Publication Data
Disaster and development in the Horn of Africa / edited by John
Sorenson.
    p.   cm. — (International political economy series)
Includes bibliographical references and index.
ISBN 0–312–12538–0
1. Africa—Northeast—Social conditions.   2. Africa, Northeast-
-Economic conditions.   3. Disaster relief—Africa, Northeast.
I. Sorenson, John, 1952–   .   II. Series.
HN788.A8D57   1995
306.'0963—dc20   94–5130
                                                          CIP

10   9   8   7   6   5   4   3   2   1
04   03   02   01   00   99   98   97   96   95

Printed and bound in Great Britain by
Antony Rowe Ltd, Chippenham, Wiltshire

To Alemseghed Asghedom
and the Eritrean Relief Association in Canada

Contents

Acknowledgements

This book originates in the practical activities undertaken by members of the Eritrean Relief Association in Canada (ERAC) to provide a better life for people in the Horn of Africa. ERAC was founded by Eritrean refugees and immigrants but came to involve other Canadians as well; as part of an international network, it provided humanitarian assistance to Eritrea, helped Eritrean refugees in Sudan and earned a reputation as one of the most efficient relief operations in Africa.

In Canada, ERAC understood that its efforts depended in large part on providing information and creating networks with other organizations. As part of its development education work, ERAC organized a conference at the University of Manitoba in Winnipeg, 29 and 30 May 1992, co-sponsored by the University's Disaster Research Unit (DRU). Although only three of the speakers from that conference have contributed chapters to this book, it represents a continuation of ERAC's efforts to encourage discussions about the future for the Horn of Africa. In this respect I would like to thank all the members of ERAC-Winnipeg who worked to make the conference a success.

In particular, I would like to thank Alemseghed Asghedom for his tireless work in organizing the conference and for his encouragement on this project. Like many other Eritreans in the diaspora, he has made constant efforts to assist those affected by war and famine in the Horn, spending long hours as a volunteer in support of relief and reconstruction activities. That such humanitarian efforts were made by refugees in the difficult process of attempting to build new lives makes them all the more admirable and inspiring. As the recipient of the Canadian International Development Agency's Development Education Award in 1994, Alem made his first visit back to Eritrea after many years abroad, seeking to create new means to assist with reconstruction. I would like to dedicate this book to him and ERAC and wish them every success in their efforts, which seem to embody all the best principles of international development.

I also thank Araia Desta, Laraine Black, Paulos Gebreyesus and Sherry Phillips of ERAC-Ontario and Joe Froese of ERAC-Saskatchewan as well as Dr John Rogge of the DRU for their support of the 1992 conference. I am also grateful to Tim Shaw for his insightful comments which helped to improve the manuscript.

I would like to acknowledge the support of the Social Sciences and Humanities Research Council of Canada for a grant which has allowed me to complete this project and continue my on-going work related to the Horn of Africa.

Finally, special thanks go to Atsuko Matsuoka for her constant encouragement and support.

JOHN SORENSON

LIST OF TABLES AND FIGURES

Tables

Figures

List of Abbreviations

AAPO	All-Amhara Peoples' Organization
AFTA	ASEAN Free Trade Area
ARDU	Afar Revolutionary Democratic Union
ASEAN	Association of Southeast Asian Nations
CCIC	Canadian Council for International Cooperation
CIDA	Canadian International Development Agency
CILSS	Comité permanent Inter-états de lutte contre la Sécheresse dans le Sahel
COEDF	Coalition of Ethiopian Democratic Forces
COMESA	Common Market of Eastern and Southern Africa
ECA	(UN) Economic Commission for Africa
ECOWAS	Economic Community of West African States
ECOMOG	ECOWAS Monitoring Group
EDU	Ethiopian Democratic Union
EEZ	Exclusive Economic Zone (200-mile limit)
ELF	Eritrean Liberation Front
ENPA	Eritrean National Peace Alliance
EPDM	Ethiopian Peoples' Democratic Movement
EPLF	Eritrean People's Liberation Front
EPRDF	Ethiopian People's Revolutionary Democratic Front
EPRP	Ethiopian People's Revolutionary Party
EU	European Union
FAO	(UN) Food and Agriculture Organisation
FRUD	Front pour la Restauration de l'Unité et de la Democratie
ICOD	International Centre for Ocean Development
IFIs	International Financial Institutions (IMF and IBRD)
IFLO	Islamic Front for the Liberation of Oromia
IGADD	Intergovernmental Authority on Drought and Development
IMF	International Monetary Fund
ITTIHAD	Islamic Union Party
KPDM	Kafa Peoples' Democratic Movement
LWF	Lutheran World Federation
MEISON	All Ethiopia Socialist Union
MULPOC	Multinational Programming and Operational Centre (ECA)
NAFTA	North American Free Trade Agreement
NGO	Non-Governmental Organization

NICs	Newly Industrializing Countries
NIDL	New International Division of Labour
NIDP	New International Division of Power
NIF	National Islamic Front
NUEW	National Union of Eritrean Women
OAU	Organization of African Unity
OCAPAC	Oceans and Coastal Areas Programme Activity Centre (UNEP)
OLF	Oromo Liberation Front
OPDO	Oromo People's Democratic Organization
PAC	Partnership Africa Canada
RRC	(Ethiopian) Relief and Rehabilitation Commission
RRP	Rassemblement Populaire pour le Progrès
SAARC	South Asian Association for Regional Cooperation
SACU	Southern Africa Customs Union
SADC	Southern African Development Community
SEPDF	Southern Ethiopian Peoples' Democratic Front
SNM	Somali National Movement
SPLA	Sudanese People's Liberation Army
TGE	Transitional Government of Ethiopia
TPLF	Tigrayan People's Liberation Front
UN	United Nations
UNCED	UN Conference on Environment and Development
UNDP	UN Development Programme
UNEP	UN Environment Programme
UNHCR	UN High Commission for Refugees
UNICEF	UN Children's Fund
UNITAF	Unified Task Force
UNOSOM	UN Operation in Somalia
UNSO	UN Sudano Sahelian Office
USAID	US Agency for International Development

Notes on the Contributors

Jon Abbink teaches at the Institute of Cultural and Social Anthropology at the University of Nijmegen in The Netherlands. He has written numerous articles on ethnicity and on relief activities in Ethiopia.

John Campbell teaches in the Department of Sociology and Anthropology, University College of Swansea, UK and has written various articles on development issues in the Horn.

Tseggai Isaac is Assistant Professor in the Political Science Department at the University of Missouri-Rolla, where he teaches international relations and Third World politics.

Assafa Jalata is Assistant Professor of Sociology and African and African-American Studies at the University of Tennessee in Knoxville. He is the author of *Oromia and Ethiopia* and has written several articles on ethnicity and politics in Ethiopia. He has been the President of the Oromo Studies Association and is an associate editor of the *Journal of Oromo Studies*.

Marion Kelly teaches at the Joint Centre for Public Health Studies, University of Wales College of Medicine. She has worked as a medical consultant for NGOs in Ethiopia, Sudan and Iraq and has published many articles on food and health issues in the Horn.

Helene Moussa is a private consultant in Toronto. She is the author of *Storm and Sanctuary*.

Roy Pateman teaches in the Department of Political Science, University of California, Los Angeles. He has published many articles on the history and politics of Eritrea and is the author of *Even the Stones are Burning*.

John Prendergast is Director of the Center of Concern in Washington, DC; he has written many articles on the Horn, available from the Center as *In the Horn of Africa*. He is the co-author (with Mark Duffield) of *Without Troops and Tanks*.

Timothy M. Shaw is Professor of Political Science at Dalhousie University. He has written and edited many articles and books on the political economy of Africa, including *Alternative Futures for Africa, The Political Economy of Foreign Policy in ECOWAS* and *Reformism* and *Revisionism in Africa's Political Economy in the 1990s.*

John Sorenson is the author of *Imagining Ethiopia* and co-editor (with Howard Adelman) of *African Refugees.* He has taught in the Department of Anthropology at the University of Manitoba, worked with the Eritrean Relief Association in Canada, and is a Research Associate of the Centre for Refugee Studies (York University) and the Disaster Research Unit (University of Manitoba). He is currently writing a book on nationalism, ethnic identity and the experience of exile among refugees from Eritrea and Ethiopia.

Jon D. Unruh teaches in the Department of Geography and Regional Development, University of Arizona. He has written extensively on ecological and social problems of the Horn.

Patrick Webb is Researcher at the International Food Policy Research Institute in Washington, DC, and the author of numerous articles and reports on the food situation in the Horn.

Okbazghi Yohannes teaches at the University of Louisville, Louisville, Kentucky. He has written several articles on Eritrean history and is the author of *Eritrea: A Pawn in World Politics.*

The Horn of Africa: Basic Data

	Ethiopia	*Sudan*	*Somalia*	*Djibouti*
Population	51.2 m	25.1 m	7.8 m	NA
Area (thousand sq. km)	1222	2506	638	23.2
Density (population per sq. km)	40	10	12	18
Population per physician	78 777	10 192	19 948	4 183
Access to health care (per cent of population)	44	70	20	NA
Access to safe water (per cent of population)				
Urban	69	NA	58	50
Rural	9	NA	22	20
GNP per capita (US $)	120	NA	170	NA
Share of agriculture in GDP				
1965	58	54	71	NA
1990	41	31	65	NA

Infant mortality per 1000 live births				
1965	165	160	165	NA
1990	132	102	126	115.3
Caloric supply per capita				
1965	1853	1938	1718	NA
1989	1667	1974	1906	NA
Primary school enrollment rate per cent				
1965	11	29	10	NA
1989	34	49	NA	47
Percentage illiterate (Aged 15 +)				
1990	NA	73	76	NA
Life expectancy at birth 1990	46	50	46	48
Rank, Human Development Index 1991	141	NA	149	153

Source: World Bank, (1992) *Social Indicators of Development 1991–92* (Baltimore: Johns Hopkins University Press).

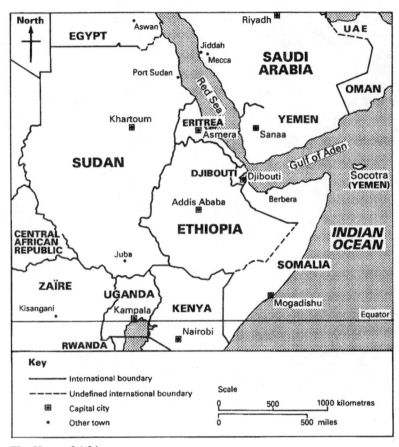

The Horn of Africa

1 The Horn of Africa: States of Crisis

John Sorenson

In a previous book, *Imagining Ethiopia*, I suggested that televised famines of the 1980s constructed Ethiopia as a quintessential symbol of disaster. Examining this symbol within the context of a discourse that presented the Third World not only as a zone of horrors but as a fundamental threat to the West, I suggested that with the end of the Cold War the Third World would function as the site of new images useful in hegemonic discourse. That prediction was borne out with Robert Kaplan's article 'The Coming Anarchy', written for *The Atlantic Monthly* (February 1994). Kaplan's survey of the Third World depicts a grim scenario: environmental catastrophe, overpopulation, poverty, disease, collapse of states, ethnic wars, increasing violence. These are real and urgent concerns. Yet Kaplan presents them as an assault launched by the poor against the privileged, alluding to liberalism and multiculturalism as part of the threat. Not unexpectedly, Africa plays a major role in his scenario but noticeably absent are historical and political-economic explanations of crisis and suggestions that efforts should be taken to alleviate poverty. Rather than subscribing to alarmist scenarios, we would do better to consider a more balanced view of disasters in impoverished areas, examining their history and suggesting possible solutions.

This volume of essays examines disasters in the Horn of Africa and considers prospects for development in the current decade. Contributors engage with various debates and issues which must be taken together to understand possibilities for development in the Horn, an area which serves as a key locus for disasters cited by Kaplan: poverty, population pressure, environmental collapse, recurrent famines, prolonged ethnic conflicts, huge refugee populations, large numbers of disabled people, vast areas strewn with land-mines, the spread of AIDS.

If the Horn is viewed as being in a state of crisis, it is evident that the crisis is also that of the state itself. The states comprising the Horn – Djibouti, Eritrea, Ethiopia, Somalia and Sudan – are in flux. In the 1990s, the end of the political system of global bipolarity that had provided economic and military support to regimes in the Horn resulted in significant changes. Several regimes were deposed, two new entities – Eritrea and

1

Somaliland – were created while the former Somali state disintegrated into a battle between feuding war–lords; southern Sudan poised on the brink of secession while the Khartoum government created a theocracy based on Islamic fundamentalism. Most regimes in the region had abdicated any moral claim to sovereignty through their oppression of domestic populations while battling or seeking to subvert neighbouring states; other dimensions to the undermining of state sovereignty included activities of non-governmental organizations (NGOs) running cross-border relief operations (into Eritrea, Tigray and southern Sudan) and the UN military intervention in Somalia (Duffield and Prendergast 1994). Ironically, these shifts in the nature of the state occurred in a context where the OAU dedicated itself to preserving entities inherited from European colonization. Most significantly, the OAU failed to address Ethiopia's 1962 annexation of Eritrea (after a brief federation) and its military attacks on the civilian population in order to crush an independence movement. Fearing that Eritrean success would set a precedent for other 'secessionist' movements, the OAU evaded the issue for decades. The OAU's dismal failure in regard to Eritrea was surpassed only by that of the UN, which bore responsibility for the disastrous and soon abrogated 1952 federation, but failed to take up the case, allowing prolonged conflict in Eritrea to contribute to regional disaster.

Political turmoil created by the formation of post-colonial states and economic decline associated with Africa's marginalization in the global economy combined with worsening environmental conditions to create disaster. For decades, the Horn endured not only terrible warfare but also recurrent drought. Drought has affected the region for centuries but its effects have become more severe. Despite obvious significance, environmental factors alone do not fully explain disasters such as mass starvation and famine must be seen in its social, political and historical context. In the Horn, environmental disruption was exacerbated by development policies, military conflict, population growth and the manner in which local economies with specific patterns of production, land tenure and trade were integrated into broader colonial relationships (Markakis 1987; McCann 1990).

International involvement intensified and prolonged local conflicts. All have roots in colonial history but were also encouraged by bipolar rivalries as the Soviet Union and US poured weapons into the Horn to support regional proxies. Among the most instructive lessons of the Cold War was the ease with which these relationships shifted. Until 1978, the US armed Ethiopia while the Soviet Union supported the Somali military; following Somalia's invasion of Ethiopia's Ogaden region, these alliances reversed. Eritrean nationalism, occasionally supported by various Middle Eastern states, was viewed as inimical to the interests of both superpowers and of Israel. Similarly, conflict in Sudan has been influenced by neighbouring African states, numerous Middle Eastern countries, the US and institutions such as the International Monetary Fund (IMF). By exacerbating internal political struggles and providing extensive arsenals, external interests influenced long-term development of the whole region. The end of the Cold War entailed a loss of Western (and East European) interest in the Horn. As is Africa generally, the Horn is now consigned to a peripheral role in the so-called new international division of labour, the process by which production has become internationalized and entire industries or aspects of them have been relocated to underdeveloped countries that provide cheap labour (Higgott 1986).

Overall, Africa's position in the global political economy is weak. Slavery and colonialism were followed by neocolonial relationships, integrating Africa into the world economy as a producer of primary products; failure to diversify production and reliance on imported technology ensured subjection to fluctuations of international markets. Poverty, lack of infrastructure, political upheaval, corruption, poor administration, and lack of education contributed to Africa's marginality. Population grew as production of subsistence food declined and reliance on imports increased. Africa's terms of trade worsened from the 1960s onwards, as prices for its commodities fell and costs of imports, especially oil, rose. After 1970 increased borrowing to import oil and manufactured products created insurmountable multi-billion dollar debts. For example, by the early 1980s, Sudan faced debt servicing payments of over one hundred per cent of its export earnings (Cheru 1989:24). Structural adjustment programmes imposed by the World Bank and IMF emphasized austerity measures, currency devaluation and termination of social services; these have not been effective in low-income African countries (Campbell and Loxley 1989; Loxley 1987). Effects included greater unemployment, inflation, deterioration of infrastructure, lower living standards, development of a 'parallel market', and food riots. Typically, the burden of these programmes falls on the poor, especially on poor women and children (Cornia, Jolly and Stewart 1987). Within this general picture, the situation of the Horn countries seems particularly bleak.

ETHIOPIA

Ethiopia is one of the world's poorest countries, with low life expectancy, high rates of infant and maternal mortality, poor health services and lack of food, safe water and shelter. Eighty-five per cent of the population (estimated at 32.7 million) lives in rural areas (Griffin 1992:275). Geographical variation and lack of communication systems encouraged social diversity. Like many other African countries, Ethiopia relies on one crop (in this case, coffee) for most of its exports.

In contrast to other 'artificial' African states created by European colonialism, Ethiopia is frequently depicted as an 'authentic' entity, one of the world's oldest states with national unity guaranteed by historical tradition. Yet the unity and authenticity of this state were challenged from within. In *Imagining Ethiopia*, I demonstrated how conflicting nationalist discourses clashed over the idea of Ethiopia: Amhara notions of an enduring entity deeply-rooted in the mystical past, the Eritrean narrative of an identity created from shared experience of Italian colonialism and the Oromo enterprise of creating a new state based on ethnic identity.

In the 1990s, the Ethiopian state was transformed. Three decades of war against Eritrean nationalists ended in 1991 with the defeat of government forces and Eritrean independence. Ethiopia's president, Mengistu Haile Mariam, fled to Zimbabwe and was replaced by Meles Zenawi who had led a coalition of Ethiopian opposition groups, the Ethiopian People's Revolutionary Democratic Front (EPRDF). Committed to a repressive version of Marxism, Mengistu's regime (the Derg, in the Amharic language) will be remembered for its brutality in Eritrea, violent suppression of domestic opposition and destructive impact on Ethiopia's economy. However, preconditions for disaster were established by the previous regime of Emperor Haile Selassie, which concentrated on developing a cash-crop economy while peasant agriculture declined and pastoralists were undermined by drought and restriction to marginal lands (Markakis 1987; Markakis and Ayele 1986; Robinson and Yamazaki 1986). Under this quasi-feudal system, a small elite monopolized land ownership and political power while an impoverished majority suffered from extraction of high rents, compulsory labour, and provision of tribute. In the 1970s, over 100,000 people starved to death during a famine that the regime not only ignored but actively sought to conceal.

In 1974, the Derg's deposition of this corrupt and senile monarchy and its subsequent land reform seemed to promise a new beginning. However, Mengistu's decision to pursue the Eritrean war rather than negotiate, and insistence on rapid collectivization, villagization, state farms and resettlement plunged Ethiopia into a downward spiral. Hundreds of thousands of lives were lost and the enormous cost of funding the war drained much-needed resources; industrial and commercial activity stagnated.

Involvement of external powers intensified local conflicts. In the post-Second World War period, Haile Selassie, seeking access to the sea through Eritrean ports, was armed by the US in return for access to a strategic communications base near Eritrea's capital, Asmara. The Derg, too, originally received Western arms but in 1978 turned to the Soviet Union. From 1978 to 1990, the Soviet Union supplied over twelve billion dollars worth of arms to Ethiopia, after dropping its former ally in Somalia. When the last arms agreement expired and the Soviet Union insisted on payment for oil supplies, Mengistu turned to Israel for weapons. Israel had consistently opposed Eritrean nationalism, regarding it as an Arab movement. During the 1970s, it trained Ethiopian troops and later supplied the cluster bombs used against Eritrean civilians in the final months of the war. As the Derg collapsed, Mengistu allowed Israel to airlift out Ethiopian Jews in exchange for weapons and a $35 million payment; Derg members also joined the flights to Israel.

Obsessed with territorial integrity and political power, the Derg ignored famine in the north and later attempted to block international aid from reaching areas controlled by opposition movements; it also continued the previous regime's strategy of directing military force at the civilian population. Poverty and repression encouraged resistance. Although the Derg slaughtered much of the civilian left-wing opposition in Addis Ababa, survivors fled to the countryside and took up arms. Opponents came from all points on the political spectrum, from monarchists to Marxists.

Most fighting took place in northern provinces such as Tigray, areas hard-hit by drought and famine. In 1975 the Tigrayan Peoples' Liberation Front (TPLF) formed; adopting Marxist-Leninist ideology, it originally sought autonomy or independence for Tigray but later asserted itself as a national Ethiopian movement and sought a broader base. In 1989, it became the main protagonist in the EPRDF coalition that eventually defeated the Derg.

In its 1990 national congress, the EPRDF announced an economic programme entailing state control over key sectors and continued nationalization of land. The US, realizing the Derg was finished, expressed support for the EPRDF takeover of Addis Ababa but exerted constant pressure on it to abandon Marxism. In July 1991, the EPRDF formed a Transitional Government (TGE), promising elections and a new constitution within a year and a policy of democracy, pluralism and a mixed economy. However, it inherited an ethnically divided country in economic ruins.

War intensified ethnic rivalries. Ethiopia is a multiethnic state created by military expansion of the Amhara people in the nineteenth century. Over eighty ethnic groups have been included within the borders of the state. Enthusiasts of Greater Ethiopia such as Levine (1974) and Clapham (1988) argue that Ethiopia's core identity is that of the Amhara, characterizing this as an open category providing national affiliation for all who adopt the Amharic language; Jordan (1989) critiques this perspective. Political opponents among the Oromo, Ethiopia's largest ethnic group, describe the Amhara as arrogant conquerors who denigrated and enslaved other cultures and argue that while Amhara and Tigrayan elites competed for state power, other peoples were subjugated. The Oromo formed an opposition movement, the Oromo Liberation Front (OLF), as did smaller groups such as the Afars and Gambela. Opposition also came from groups such as the Ethiopian Democratic Union, formed by Amharas who sought restoration of the monarchy, as well as Marxist groups with pan-ethnic Ethiopian identity. Complex political factionalism intensified after establishment of the TGE.

The TGE sought to overcome past ethnic imbalances by restructuring the state as a federation of largely-autonomous regions. It divided Ethiopia into ten administrative zones, each with a dominant ethnic population. Some saw this not as an effective resolution but as an intensification of the problem, a politicization of ethnicity rather than restoration of national identity. Opponents protested that regional governments were controlled by the EPRDF, that autonomy was illusory and that ethnic politics would shred the state. They saw groups such as the Ethiopian People's Democratic Movement and the Oromo People's Democratic Organization as EPRDF creations, intended to create legitimacy among Amharas and Oromos. In particular, Ethiopian nationalists criticized the TGE's position on Eritrea. The TPLF and the Eritrean Peoples Liberation Front (EPLF) had collaborated against the Derg and the TGE recognized Eritreans' rights to self-determination; it cooperated with a referendum on independence despite opposition from some factions of Ethiopian society and bitter criticism from Ethiopian exiles abroad. Following a virtually unanimous vote for independence, the TGE recognized Eritrea as an independent state. Meles Zenawi and Eritrean President Issayas Afeworki followed up with discussions on bilateral cooperation and both later encouraged peaceful negotiation of conflict in Somalia.

The end of conflict with Eritrea and negotiation of agreements on use of port facilities and regional cooperation promised a new beginning. However, the TGE found itself in charge of a state sapped by decades of conflict. Already poor, Ethiopia's economy was wrecked by the Derg's commitment to a military solution in Eritrea. When the EPRDF took power, Meles announced that Mengistu had driven Ethiopia into bankruptcy, with a debt of $8.6 billion, mainly for arms. The new government announced its top priority would be to restart relief programmes for 1.3 million people in immediate danger of starvation and 7 million facing famine. The EPRDF and EPLF reopened the Red Sea port of Assab to allow in relief supplies and relief agencies reported general satisfaction with the EPRDF's early initiatives to continue the flow of aid and to provide security for food convoys under attack from bandits.

The Ethiopian Relief and Rehabilitation Commission announced requirements for over a million tons of food aid in 1992, also indicating its intent to shift from relief to development activities in such areas as road construction, soil and water conservation and afforestation. Housing, water, sanitation and education were also noted as government priorities. The TGE introduced several early reforms. It substantially reduced the military budget, devalued the currency and lifted import and export restrictions. In October 1992, the IMF approved a three-year loan of $70 million related to a structural adjustment program to bring Ethiopia into a market-oriented economy. However, experience of other states demonstrates that the burden of such IMF programmes mainly falls upon the poor. While Ethiopia requires international assistance to rebuild a shattered economy, the international context in which the TGE came to power was rapidly changing. Collapse of the Soviet Union and the end of the Cold War immediately reduced Western interest in Ethiopia and international assistance programmes were quickly redeployed towards Eastern Europe. For example, in 1993 Canada slashed bilateral aid to Ethiopia, undermining support for subsistence agriculture, health care and housing precisely at the critical moment when such support could be most effective.

In addition to economic challenges, the TGE faced political problems. Decades of militarization meant large quantities of arms were present; unsurprisingly, in a context of extreme poverty and insecurity, where deadly weapons were readily available and ethnic tensions had been encouraged, violence erupted. Banditry made some regions unsafe. Food warehouses were looted and military deserters stole relief agency vehicles. In the south and east, bandits attacked UN relief convoys, blocking water supplies to 400,000 Somali refugees in the Ogaden. Over 100,000 Ethiopian soldiers and civilians fled into Sudan after the EPRDF took power; another 20,000 crossed into Kenya.

Following the Derg's downfall, numerous groups emerged with claims to power. Demonstrations against the EPRDF and the US role in its takeover were answered with violence. On 4 January, 1993, security forces in Addis Ababa fired on demonstrators protesting the Eritrean referendum; the TGE reported one person killed while anti-government groups abroad, such as the Coalition of Ethiopian Democratic Forces (COEDF) in

Washington DC stated seven people were killed and almost a hundred injured; the Ethiopian MEDHIN Party, also based in Washington DC, claimed twenty were killed and two hundred wounded. Both exile groups fiercely opposed Eritrean independence and the EPRDF. In September 1993, TGE forces attempted to arrest a priest in Gondar for anti-government statements; his supporters clashed with the troops and about fifty people were killed. In Addis Ababa, the Ethiopian Human Rights Council charged the TGE with numerous abuses.

Vowing to institute democracy by 1994, the TGE held regional elections in June 1992 but was charged with harassment and intimidation as opposition groups offices were closed and OLF and COEDF members were arrested. In January 1993, it dismissed forty-two academics from Addis Ababa University for anti-government activity. Both the government and the opposition movements were accused of assassinations and human rights violations.

Clearly, the transition to democracy was not a smooth one. However, it would be remarkable if no such violations occurred in the aftermath of Mengistu's rule, given Ethiopia's poverty, recent history of violence, intensification of ethnic hostility over the last decade, militarization of the region and competition for power. Abuses must not be overlooked but should be seen in the context of an overall improvement in human rights within an atmosphere of insecurity and tension; the early 1990s were a period of social upheaval resulting from the change from a centralized state-dominated economy to a more market-oriented system. As these changes took place, international aid dropped substantially and famine threatened much of the population.

The TGE also faced threats from various positions. Many groups were active mainly outside Ethiopia. The COEDF united the Ethiopian People's Union and the conservative Ethiopian Democratic Union (EDU) with the Ethiopian People's Revolutionary Party (EPRP) and the All Ethiopia Socialist Union (MEISON). The EPRP and MEISON shared Marxist ideologies but had nearly exterminated each other in the 1970s following the latter's decision to collaborate with the Derg. The EDU later dropped out of the COEDF and expressed support for the EPRDF. Goshu Wolde, foreign minister under the Derg, was a founding member of COEDF but left to create his own anti-EPRDF group, MEDHIN. Both COEDF and MEDHIN took strong centralist positions and bitterly opposed Eritrean nationalism. Claiming that MEDHIN was denied participation, Goshu vowed armed struggle but no action followed his declaration.

Opposition also had ethnic dimensions. Some Amharas, finding their previous elite status changed, charged discrimination and established the

All Amhara Peoples Association (AAPO) in 1992. The AAPO opposed the EPRDF's economic policies and called for full privatization of land. Organized among businessmen and intellectuals and led by Asrat Woldeyes, AAPO launched a propaganda war against the TGE and opposed the Eritrean referendum. The government charged AAPO with inciting ethnic violence; Asrat was arrested and later freed on bail but AAPO claimed that other members were harassed or killed. Ethnic violence did erupt in the aftermath of the Derg's collapse. Several Oromo groups (OLF, Islamic Front for the Liberation of Oromia [IFLO], Oromo Peoples' Unity Organization, Oromo Abo Liberation Movement) were charged with violence against Amharas in Arsi, Harar and Kufa Chole. Supported by Sudan as part of its effort to spread Islamic fundamentalism, the OLF clashed with the Sudan Peoples' Liberation Army near Gambela and attacked southern Sudanese refugees in camps in southwest Ethiopia, forcing 400,000 of them back across the border with no food or shelter into an area where they were bombed by the Sudanese air force.

Government troops clashed with opposition movements. Members of IFLO and the Sidamo Liberation Movement were shot at government checkpoints and OLF members were killed in eastern Ethiopia. The OLF withdrew from the TGE coalition in June 1992, charging that Amhara domination had been replaced with that of another northern group, the Tigrayans. Battles erupted between the OLF and government troops, causing undetermined casualties and the arrest of thousands of OLF troops. Abroad, OLF supporters charged the TGE with human rights abuses, prompting an Amnesty International appeal. However, a German parliamentary delegation concluded that OLF reports of ill-treatment of Oromo prisoners and of civil war in Ethiopia were false (*REST Bulletin*, April/May 1993). The OLF's status remains unclear. Many asserted that it was destroyed in this confrontation while supporters argued that the battles marked a decisive turning point in solidifying Oromo identity and resistance. An active Oromo nationalist organization exists in North America; supporters portray all Oromos as united in pursuit of a single goal, independent Oromia. Yet others, including many Oromos, question the extent of cultural unity, pointing to differences in regional dialect, religion and political commitments. While some do seek an independent state, others hope for equal participation in a democratic Ethiopia. Also, Oromia's borders have been variously imagined. The OLF presents the Oromo as a colonized people within the Ethiopian empire. While correctly noting that Oromo areas were conquered in the nineteenth century by Amhara troops from the north (sometimes with Oromo collaboration), Oromo nationalists overlook the fact that the Oromo had gained much of this territory through their own military expansion, conquering other groups. Regional history includes cycles of conquest and displacement, making claims to original possession of territory suspect. The OLF's proposed independent Oromia includes most of southern Ethiopia, where coffee, the key cash crop, is grown and the TGE is unlikely to give up this resource. Other opponents argue that Oromos are concentrated in two separate regions and members of other ethnic groups worry about their fate in an Oromo-dominated state.

Thus, the TGE faces several major challenges: providing basic needs to an impoverished population, reconstructing a ruined economy, negotiating ethnic demands and establishing a democratic system. The context – environmental collapse, economic marginalization, political opposition – is not promising.

ERITREA

After three decades of struggle, Eritrea emerged in 1993 as Africa's newest independent state. Its position on the Red Sea coast made it the target of various invaders over the centuries and was one factor that generated superpower interest in the Horn during the Cold War. Carved out as a distinct territory by Italian colonialism in the nineteenth century, Eritrea was federated with Ethiopia in 1951 by the UN after a decade of British administration. Nationalist aspirations were strengthened by Ethiopian violations of the federation and by outright annexation in 1962. Emergence of an armed independence movement was answered by violence directed against the civilian population. From 1967, vast numbers of Eritrean refugees poured into Sudan. Along with Tigrayans and other Ethiopians, these refugees eventually formed one of the world's largest concentrations of uprooted people.

Opponents depicted Eritrean nationalism as a Muslim separatist movement against Christian Ethiopia. Yet Eritrea itself is ethnically and religiously diverse with nine ethnic groups in a population almost equally divided into Christians and Muslims. Cultural and political differences within the independence movement flared into deadly civil war. This, along with a massive transfusion of Soviet weapons allowed Ethiopia to roll back Eritrean fighters who had nearly gained control of the country in 1978. The original nationalist organization, the Eritrean Liberation Front (ELF) drew support largely from the Muslim population and received some assistance from various Middle Eastern regimes. Internal conflict shattered the ELF; some fighters went into exile but most were absorbed into an off-shoot movement, the EPLF, which announced a socialist orientation and sought to overcome religious and ethnic differences. Establishing its base in the rugged northern mountains, in the context of a prolonged war, the EPLF undertook a social revolution. Working at night to avoid air attacks, the EPLF constructed an underground society; it made impressive progress in terms of primary health care and literacy, attempted to rebuild Eritrea's agricultural base, sought to modify exploitative relationships through land reform and encouraged emancipation of women.

While warfare provided the context for accelerated social transformation, it also exacerbated effects of drought through displacement of people, disruption of agricultural activities, interference with commercial activities and transportation routes, conscription, deliberate targeting of crop fields and livestock for destruction, withholding of food aid and imposition of a general reign of terror. Throughout the 1980s repeated droughts, crop failure and famine ravaged Eritrea.

While the Derg sought to block international aid to Eritrea and to Tigray in order to weaken the EPLF and TPLF, both groups established their own relief organizations to channel food to these areas. Given the context of a brutal war, rugged terrain, an ethnically diverse population and the recent history of political struggle within the nationalist movement, the Eritrean Relief Association coordinated an international network of volunteers in a remarkable aid operation (Sorenson 1994). The Relief Society of Tigray worked with fewer resources but was also quite effective in channelling food to Tigray.

With Ethiopia claiming sovereignty, no foreign government was willing to provide aid directly to Eritrea. Relief supplies to Eritrea and Tigray were channelled through NGOs and through the direct support of refugee communities abroad. The situation in the Horn during the 1980s constituted a turning point in international development. For many NGOs, famine in the Horn provided an opportunity to expand their operations and financial base; some continued to use images of mass starvation for fundraising even after the crisis had passed. This prompted many agencies to re-examine the images they employed and recognize the political nature of international aid. Famine in the Horn raised fundamental questions about relationships with Third World NGOs, the role of charity, and the matter of sovereignty in cases where governments use famine as a weapon against their populations. Cross-border operations constituted the first instance of the humanitarian interventions employed later in Kurdistan, Somalia and Bosnia and signalled a fundamental change in North-South relations (Duffield and Prendergast 1994).

In May 1991, the EPLF gained control over Eritrea. A provisional government administered the region for two years, until 99.8 percent of the population voted for independence in an internationally-supervised referendum. International recognition followed and the new government took its place in the UN and OAU, while establishing friendly relationships with states such as Israel and Saudi Arabia that had opposed Eritrean nationalism.

Although political independence was achieved, Eritrea faced daunting challenges. The country was in ruins; Ethiopian forces had neglected or destroyed much of the infrastructure. Although the World Bank's International Development Association approved a credit programme for $147 million, Eritreans faced enormous tasks of recovery. Destruction from the war was extensive. Over 150,000 people were killed; 70,000 EPLF fighters and civilians were injured, especially by land-mines. These devices will remain a deadly problem for years to come. The high cost of removing them (often paid to manufacturers of these weapons) will be a substantial drain on the economy. Rehabilitation facilities are rudimentary and insufficient, although an association of handicapped fighters formed in October 1993 to promote the rights and interests of the disabled. War also disrupted the traditional family unit, leaving thousands of orphans and elderly parents with no family support.

In terms of infrastructure, virtually all basic services were disrupted. Most towns were without services such as electricity, water and transportation for much of the war. Industrial sectors were wiped out and the ports were destroyed. Ethiopian forces bombed Massawa extensively during the last days of the war, killing many civilians, destroying most of the buildings and depopulating the area. Lack of funds delayed the task of rebuilding the town and the port facilities. Almost a third of Eritrea's population was displaced, either internally or externally across international borders. This constitutes not only a loss of educated and skilled workers needed for rehabilitation but also a problem for repatriation and resettlement. While the Provisional Government proposed plans for repatriation, international assistance was not forthcoming; the UNHCR, in particular, seemed unwilling to cooperate. Ignored by the UN for three decades, Eritreans now faced a UNHCR bureaucracy that refused to consider their own plans for repatriation or provide adequate support. Similarly, UNHCR was criticized in Ethiopia and Somalia for inefficiency and failure to recognize the urgency of the situation.

In 1993, the government announced plans to demobilize most of its armed forces. Out of 95,000 fighters, 56,000 were to be demobilized. Demobilization on such a scale requires effective means of reintegrating soldiers, including training programmes, projects for development in resettlement areas, and encouragement of business. While numerous foreign powers eagerly armed the Horn, similar levels of international support for demilitarization were not in evidence. Agricultural rehabilitation is central to development in Eritrea. Most of the population is rural, dependent on subsistence agriculture and concentrated in the highlands which suffer from consequent over-use of land. Deforestation, a major problem in the Horn, has contributed to land degradation. Land is available in the lowlands but utilizing these areas requires development of water conservation measures. Throughout the war, drought plagued Eritrea and the problem returned after independence. Erratic rainfall meant water shortages in some areas and floods elsewhere. Along with drought, locusts infested several provinces in 1993. Environmental concerns will persist as a constraint on reconstruction. Marine resources are an option for Eritrea's long Red Sea coastline but this requires resuscitation of a fishing economy wiped out during the war, as well as efforts to expand interest in this area. The port at Massawa offers potential but was heavily damaged by Ethiopian forces.

Government development programmes have focused on health care, including anti-malaria campaigns and construction of health facilities such as district clinics. Having suffered the spread of famine-related diseases and the wounds of war, the Horn now is affected by AIDS; in Eritrea, between 15,000 and 30,000 people were believed to be infected in 1991. Warfare contributed to the spread of AIDS through troop and refugee movements, impoverishment, prostitution and rape. Other concerns were education (including construction of new schools, recruitment of teachers), agricultural rehabilitation, water conservation (dams), and urban planning. Lack of housing remains a problem and presented an obstacle to repatriation.

War affected social relationships, especially in terms of gender. Traditionally, men dominated Eritrean society. Although women were regarded as inferior in most societies of the Horn, they performed essential labour necessary for survival. Both the EPLF and TPLF promoted women's emancipation; the OLF was less active. In Eritrea, women adopted new roles as fighters, doctors, drivers, technicians and mechanics and formed their own organizations; however, few women occupied leadership roles at the highest levels. The question remains as to whether or not women's advances in Eritrea will be rolled back, as has happened elsewhere in the aftermath of anti-colonial struggles. Typically, there is social pressure on women to return to traditional positions once a crisis has passed. However, the National Union of Eritrean Women was the first indigenous NGO recognized in Eritrea after independence.

Eritrea's new government also faces political opposition from several Eritrean groups (ELF-Central Command, ELF-Unified Organization,

ELF-Revolutionary Council, Eritrean Democratic Liberation Movement) who united in Saudi Arabia to form the Eritrean National Peace Alliance (ENPA). The ENPA supported independence but criticized the EPLF as a dictatorship that excluded other points of view. Sudan sponsored a fundamentalist group, Islamic Jihad, which launched attacks on Eritrea. Thus, independence does not preclude the threat of further conflict.

SOMALIA

Somalia became an independent state on 1 July, 1960 with the merging of British and Italian colonial territories. Often depicted as one of the world's poorest countries, it apparently had a comparatively healthy informal economy (De Waal and Rakiya 1993). In addition to undeclared remittances from Somalis working abroad, illicit trade, diversion of international development aid and cattle smuggling provided much of the country's wealth. A small elite controlled business licenses and agricultural inputs and was able to dispossess others from their land either through manipulation of the legal system or by force. Most of the population is involved with the pastoralist economy in some way and livestock accounted for almost all of Somalia's exports.

Somalia appears unique in Africa because Somalis share a common language, culture and religion. Somalis are divided into six main clan-families (Darood, Hawiye, Isaaq, Digil, Rahanweyn, Dir) and further divided into sub-clans and lineages. This structure provides a strong cultural identity but also allows clan hostilities to play the same divisive role that ethnic or 'tribal' tensions do elsewhere. Traditionally, Somali pastoralists paid allegiance first to immediate family, then to successively-wider lineage, sub-clan and clan levels; such connections dictated both loyalties and antagonisms but traditionally these were constrained by councils of elders, an ethos of self-reliance and respect based on one's productivity. Colonialism eroded these constraints through commercialization of livestock, urbanization and creation of a state which produced new roles and forms of social power unrelated to production (Abdi Ismail Samatar 1992).

Despite a proclaimed policy of ending clan divisions, Somalia's president (1969–1991) Mohamed Siad Barre institutionalized them as the basis of power, exacerbating hostilities by promoting the interests of his own Marehan clan at the expense of the Hawiye, Isaaq and Majeerteen clans that had dominated the previous government and which formed the main opposition to his regime.

Siad came to power through a coup after the assassination of President Abdirashid Ali Sharmarke in 1969, deposing a parliamentary democracy and instituting 'scientific socialism' in the form of a military dictatorship. The regime's repressive character and its human rights violations were widely reported. As in Ethiopia, the system of rule was largely personalized, with the president dictating state policies. Siad emphasized agricultural development through large state-owned farms and ignored smaller-scale agricultural and pastoralist strategies. The regime harassed independent community organizations, arresting and torturing members for alleged subversion.

In the nineteenth century, British, French and Italian colonialism divided the Horn. Since independence, Somalia sought to incorporate ethnic Somali groups in Djibouti, Ethiopia and Kenya into a Greater Somalia; this irredentist ideology propelled its 1978 invasion of Ethiopia's Ogaden region, which created a large refugee population and a realignment of superpower alliances. In 1974, Somalia had signed a friendship treaty with the Soviet Union which allowed Siad Barre to extend domestic control through a well-armed police and army. The Soviet Union built up the port of Berbera but abandoned Somalia after Ethiopia appealed for aid to oppose the Ogaden invasion. Somalia then turned to the US, becoming a major recipient of US arms in the 1980s. The US signed a $100 million access agreement for Berbera and began an aid programme for another $600 million; Germany, Italy, South Africa, Libya, Israel and China provided additional military aid. Siad's unreliability and the development of bases elsewhere on the East African coast and in Oman led to US disengagement by the late 1980s. By that time, however, superpower rivalry had militarized the entire Horn.

The Ogaden invasion was a turning point for the Siad Barre regime. The Greater Somalia ideology had provided a degree of unity but the Ogaden failure, political repression, human rights violations, discrimination against certain groups and general economic stress reinvigorated clan divisions and activated opposition in the form of the Somali Salvation Front, Somali Salvation Democratic Front, Somali Patriotic Movement (SPM), Somali National Movement (SNM), United Somali Congress (USC) and others. Discrimination and violence directed against Isaaq groups in northern Somalia encouraged the growth of the SNM. In 1988 Ethiopia and Somalia agreed to end support to each other's opposition movements and Ethiopia expelled the SNM from its territory; this prompted an SNM offensive in northern Somalia which the government answered by slaughtering thousands of Isaaq civilians, burning their villages and poisoning their wells because the SNM was mainly from this clan group. The SNM also murdered many civilians, especially those from clans that supported Siad Barre. Thousands were killed and hundreds of thousands fled to Ethiopia, Kenya and Djibouti; over a million people were internally displaced. Violence was also shaped by the presence of large numbers of Ethiopian refugees who had crossed into Somalia after the Ogaden war. Ethiopia regarded them as collaborators with invading Somali forces; the latter armed them and allowed them to loot Isaaq civilians in the north. As the SNM swept through the north, it attacked camps, driving out refugees and killing hundreds. The UN withdrew from Somalia as the central government collapsed and power fell to a number of heavily-armed clan-based groups. The SNM, controlling the north, declared the independence of what once had been British Somaliland as the Republic of Somaliland in May 1991. The SNM's leader Abd ar-Rahman Ahmad Ali became president until 1993, when former Prime Minister Mohamed Ibrahim Egal was elected. Some stability followed the declaration but the Republic received no international recognition and no support for reconstruction. Plagued by factional disputes, the SNM did not formulate effective policies for restoration of order or economic recovery. Stability depended on efforts of clan elders (Rakiya 1993).

Siad Barre's regime in Mogadishu fell in January 1991 but the president looted the treasury and national bank before leaving. Violence jeopardized much of the population. Over 300,000 Somalis died in the famine associated with the war; most of the population was internally displaced while hundreds of thousands fled as refugees to Ethiopia, Kenya and Yemen. In 1994, hundreds of Somali refugees who had sought shelter in Yemen were killed in civil war there.

Refugees in Somalia were also affected. Controversy had surrounded the number of refugees there. The government was accused of inflating their numbers to profit from international assistance and had been charged with abusing Amhara refugees in Shelembod camp and abducting Amharas from eastern Ethiopia because it identified them with the Ethiopian government. Some Ethiopian refugees were forcibly conscripted into the Somali army. At the end of the 1980s, over 800,000 refugees were estimated to be in camps in Somalia. With the collapse of the regime, hundreds of thousands of Ethiopian refugees were forced to leave UNHCR camps in southern Somalia; some returned to their original villages only to discover their relatives long gone and themselves with no means of support.

Fighting was concentrated in the south, around Mogadishu, Baidoa and Kismayu. Other areas were relatively calm and local leaders reestablished authority in some communities. Fighting continued in the capital from September 1991 to March 1992 but failed to bring a new government to power. The USC announced Ali Mahdi Mohamed as the president of a temporary government but the SNM and SPM opposed this. During fighting for Mogadishu 20,000 people were killed and most of the city was destroyed by artillery. Somalia's infrastructure was dismantled by looters who stripped the country; farm equipment, water pumps, wiring, piping, doors, window-frames and roofs were all removed and sold. Many people needed emergency food but armed raiders stole this as well. Basic health and education services were unavailable.

During 1991 Mohamed Farah Aideed and Ali Mahdi Mohamed, both of the USC but of different Hawiye subclans, fought for control of Mogadishu and of the state; thousands were killed as power struggles exacerbated clan rivalries. In 1992 Siad Barre's forces, the Somali National Front (SNF), also attempted to recapture Mogadishu but were repelled and Siad fled first to Kenya then to Nigeria as a refugee, where he died in early 1995. In this battle, Aideed gained more territory and established himself as the strongest of the various military leaders. At this point, over a million Somalis were estimated to be facing imminent starvation while millions more required food aid.

In February 1992, the UN organized a cease-fire and later recommended sending a peace–keeping force to Somalia. Ali Mahdi, who controlled less territory but was recognized as interim president, favoured UN intervention; Aideed opposed this, fearing it would erode his position. The UN intervention had the negative effect of weakening traditional leaders and community organizations while strengthening warlords who saw control over relief supplies as a means to guarantee their roles in the post-war hierarchy.

Conditions had worsened throughout 1991 but the UN took no effective actions until 1992. Just as the issue of sovereignty created imbalanced aid delivery in the Eritrean–Ethiopian conflict, such concerns delayed international intervention in Somalia despite the fact that the state had collapsed. Following a cease-fire agreement between warring factions in Mogadishu, in April 1992 the UN Security Council approved the United Nations Operation in Somalia (UNOSOM), involving armed peacekeepers to supervise food distribution but Somali factions delayed agreement until August. On 27 July, 1992, the UN Security Council adopted Resolution 767 calling for greater efforts to end starvation and hostilities; on 28 August, it passed Resolution 775 authorizing a UN security force. In October, a UN donor conference repeated calls for more effective efforts but by November it was clear that the UN security force was unable to meet its tasks and that UNOSOM required urgent review. The Security Council's Resolution 794, passed on 3 December, 1992, authorized the US-led Unified Task Force (UNITAF) to use military force to ensure food distribution. As an advance force of US Marines landed in Mogadishu, rival factions sought to expand their territory and fighting intensified outside the capital. The UNITAF forces took over the main towns in central and southern Somalia but clashed first with SNF forces now led by Siad Barre's son-in-law, Mohamed Siad Hersi 'Morgan', and then with Aideed's supporters in Mogadishu.

In March 1993, the UN Secretary General proposed UNOSOM II calling for deployment of 30,000 international troops to take over from the US-led UNITAF; the Security Council passed this as Resolution 814. This was the UN's largest peace-keeping operation; undertaken without consent of all Somali factions, it was to put the UN in charge of reconstructing Somalia. At the same time, a peace conference in Addis Ababa among Somali factions created a transitional council to govern Somalia for two years; despite this, battles between the factions continued.

The UN operation was plagued by embarrassing problems. The UN Secretary General's special envoy for Somalia, Ambassador Mohamed Sahnoun, was forced to resign for his criticisms of the operation. Many Somalis protested that the UN's humanitarian intervention was a cover for recolonization. In particular, Secretary General Boutros-Ghali was unwelcome due to past involvement in Somalia as Egypt's Minister for Foreign Relations and for support to Siad Barre. The human rights organization African Rights accused UN forces of numerous abuses. A white supremacist group was discovered among Canadian forces in Somalia and Canadian soldiers were found guilty of murdering a Somali civilian.

A year and a half after the post-Siad factional fighting began, the US announced an emergency aid programme to Somalia; the announcement that US troops would be sent was made by then-president George Bush just before the Republican Convention and seemed part of a cynical reelection campaign strategy. Claims by US officials that, prior to arrival of troops, eighty percent of food aid was being looted and that intervention stopped a full-scale civil war were criticized as exaggerations designed to present the mission as successful. Some NGOs opposed military intervention and were able to deliver twice as much food without military escorts.

Somali actions were no more admirable. In late 1992 armed UN troops landed in Somalia to ensure delivery of food aid through a territory divided between rival gangs of gunmen, mostly clan-based, who were profiting from looting of relief and extortion. The Hawiye clan, for example, controlled Mogadishu's airport and levied a 'tax' on all flights, including those bringing food aid. Aid workers were assassinated by Somali gangs who sought to control food distribution. A ship carrying food from the World Food Programme was shelled.

As elsewhere, emergency aid had negative effects. Relief came too late; Somalia's overall food supply had improved substantially before the intervention. Bad planning meant that food did not reach the most vulnerable groups; the military concentrated on towns and airports but more remote villages did not receive aid and security worsened in some areas. Availability of food aid kept prices low and provided no encouragement for farmers to grow crops. Thus, rehabilitation was delayed by emphasis on relief. Control over aid distribution benefitted warlords, whose power was strengthened as international representatives dealt with them rather than village councils, responsible elders, and womens' organizations. Through 1992, Mogadishu's population remained dependent on aid, provided by the largest such international mobilization since the previous decade. Some Somalis interpreted presence of UN troops as renewed colonization and Somali warlords protested arrival of UN forces. In June 1993, Mohamed Farah Aideed's faction killed twenty-three UN soldiers from Pakistan. The US responded with aerial bombardment and a warrant for Aideed's arrest. Warfare escalated between UN and Somali troops.

Controversy followed the decision to deploy US troops in Somalia. Many applauded it as a humanitarian gesture but some NGOs criticized intervention for its legitimization of factional leaders and its failure to address human rights abuses. Others saw it as a US-dominated manoeuvre designed to achieve strategic goals associated with Somalia's geographical location and to gain domestic support for maintaining the US military budget at high levels in the face of growing opposition and expectations of a post-Cold War 'peace dividend'. As well, US oil companies Conoco, Amoco, Chevron and Phillips acquired concessions to what are believed to be rich oil deposits in Somalia from Siad Barre. Conoco was directly involved with the US government's military intervention and the corporation's Mogadishu compound served as the US headquarters prior to arrival of troops. Citing lack of humanitarian concern for crises elsewhere and the history of military support that had provided such high levels of arms to Somalia, critics of Operation Restore Hope saw intervention as part of a global strategy. They also charged that the US plan to withdraw troops soon after deployment would only strengthen the warlords.

Islamic fundamentalist forces were also active in Somalia. The Islamic Union Party (*Ittihad*), with military bases in the Ogaden and northern Somalia, sought to establish a unified fundamentalist movement among Somalis in various states of the Horn. Saudi Arabia, Sudan, Iran and

Pakistan were believed to be the main supporters of Ittihad and other fundamentalist groups. In 1993, *Ittihad* assassinated a UNICEF doctor in Bosaso and later invaded the port city, declaring it an Islamic republic before being driven out by militias in a battle that left hundreds dead. In the Ogaden, *Ittihad* attacked relief convoys and attempted to capture towns. Other aspects of Middle East conflicts also affected Somalia; citing an Israeli threat to the Horn, Libya and Iraq provided weapons to Somalia in 1990.

In 1994, Somalia's future as one entity remained in doubt. In ironic contrast to the Greater Somalia policy promoted after independence and the population's alleged homogeneity, the state fragmented into warring factions. Although a new state appeared in the north it received no international recognition. As the Eritrean case demonstrates, many parties oppose any modifications to state structures. African governments have insisted on maintaining colonial borders; the US and other Western powers also opposed modifications to national boundaries. Whether a federal system could satisfy aspirations in the north remains to be seen.

SUDAN

Once considered to be among Africa's most promising nations, with the agricultural potential to serve as 'Africa's breadbasket', Sudan descended into disaster after decades of war, severe drought, badly-designed development strategies, corruption and mismanagement. Africa entered the 1990s in a state of economic crisis with twenty-seven million people in seventeen countries at risk of starvation. Over five million tons of food aid were needed – half of this by the Horn countries – in 1991, a period in which Eastern Europe and Middle East states affected by the Gulf war competed for international assistance. Sudan's famine was considered to be the worst on the continent and was presided over by a regime which deliberately sought to deprive food from those it considered enemies.

Ethnically diverse, Sudan is described as the meeting-place of Arab and African worlds. The meeting has been neither peaceful nor equitable. The north, mainly Muslim, has long exercised control over the south, inhabited by Christians and adherents of indigenous religions. These divisions extend back to the nineteenth century, when Ottoman Turks invaded southern Sudan and took non-Muslim peoples as slaves. British colonialism encouraged these divisions and attitudes of superiority have been characteristic among northerners. For much of Sudan's post-independence history, the regions have been at war. In 1955, just prior to independence, civil war erupted and lasted until Jaafar Nimeri's government negotiated an agreement giving regional autonomy to the south in 1972. However, this merely increased the south's isolation from a state controlled by the north. Khartoum's policies of diverting resources northward ended a short reconciliation period. Particularly significant were government plans to build a northern refinery and concentrate infrastructural development there to exploit Chevron Oil Company's discovery of oil in the south, a decision followed by armed rebellion. Repeated droughts in the 1980s led to grain riots elsewhere in Sudan.

In 1983, conflict intensified as the Sudan People's Liberation Army (SPLA) announced plans to overthrow the northern regime, now increasingly associated with Islamic ideology, and institute a democratic secular government. In that year, Nimeri's growing links with the fundamentalist Muslim Brotherhood led him to announce the 'September Laws' which made Islamic *shari'a* law the basis of the nation's legal code. This both offended the non-Muslim southern population and put them at a disadvantage.

Nimeri was ousted in a 1985 coup. Despite rhetoric of peaceful negotiation, Sadiq al-Mahdi's new government did not rescind the *shari'a*; conflict escalated as the government sought to manipulate ethnic tensions in the south by arming groups hostile to the Dinka, who provided much of the SPLA's support. With government encouragement, the Misseiririya and Rizeigat groups massacred and enslaved the Dinka (Fluehr-Lobban 1992).

On June 30, 1989, Sadiq al-Mahdi's government was deposed by the fundamentalist National Islamic Front (NIF), led by Hassan al-Turabi, which sought to create a theocracy. The NIF installed General Omar Hassam Ahmad al-Bashir as head of state, banned all other political parties and trade unions, purged the state bureaucracy, imposed strict control over the media and universities, and carried out widespread arrests, torture and executions of those it considered potential enemies. To existing security forces, the regime added new police forces and expanded the military through forced conscription. The NIF strengthened its ties with Iraq and Iran and received military assistance and training from the latter in its renewed war against the south; China and South Africa also provided weapons.

One of Africa's most repressive regimes, the NIF presented itself as a model for other Islamic movements and announced its aim to spread its ideology throughout the region. The Eritrean government sought good relations with Sudan, not only because of the debilitating experience of prolonged conflict but also because thousands of Eritrean refugees still remained there. Nevertheless, in December 1993, Eritrea's President Issayas Afeworki announced that government troops had battled an armed group known as Islamic Jihad sent into Eritrea by the NIF. Similar clashes had occurred in previous years on the border with Sudan. The NIF also sent agents into Ethiopia; the NIF favoured an independent state for the Oromo, many of whom are Muslim. The NIF also was suspected of operating training camps for terrorists. In August 1993, with the arrest of six Sudanese following the bombing of the World Trade Center in New York, the US condemned Sudan for supporting international terrorism.

The NIF refused to modify Islamic laws affecting the south. Fighting in the southern Darfur, Kordofan and Blue Nile provinces killed thousands of people. Along with other African countries, Sudan endured starvation in 1984; after a brief respite, there were clear indications in 1989 that famine would return. As elsewhere in the Horn, looting and deliberate targeting of livestock and food supplies exacerbated effects of drought and created famine. Hundreds of thousands of displaced people fled war and starvation in the south to squalid encampments in Khartoum and other cities. Drought struck hard in the south. Food shipments were deliberately withheld; disease and starvation spread. However, the NIF deliberately suppressed information on famine as a technique to defeat its enemies and al-Bashir dismissed reports of starvation as efforts to discredit the government. The NIF leader al-Turabi stated that mass starvation was a minor price to pay for establishment of an Islamic state. Only in late 1990 did Sudan request food aid from the UN Food and Agriculture Organization to assist with what it termed temporary shortfalls. By then, nearly eight million Sudanese were at risk of starvation. In Washington, US government officials criticized the regime's bombing attacks on food shipments to the south while it was requesting food aid. Aid intended for Sudan was withheld because of the regime's human rights record, which had been condemned by Africa Watch, Amnesty International and the UN.

The UN attempted to provide food to the area through Operation Lifeline, an umbrella organization. Throughout 1991, the NIF government sought to ban flights carrying emergency food aid to the south and to control truck convoys. Only Norwegian People's Aid and the Dutch *Médicins Sans Frontières* refused to abide by the NIF's obvious efforts to starve its enemies. The SPLA also inhibited international efforts to provide food to southern Sudan and stole food intended for civilians. In 1991 it shelled the main southern town, Juba, where government troops held 300,000 civilians captive in appalling conditions.

The NIF's attacks on civilians were not limited to the south. It launched genocidal strikes against mainly non-Muslim Nuba of more northern regions. Numerous human rights organizations protested the NIF's policy to drive the Nuba from their homelands, fertile areas attractive to the northern elite who sought to introduce mechanized farming methods for profit. The Nuba appealed to the UN, citing attacks on their villages by government troops, artillery and aircraft as a campaign to destroy their culture and seize their lands. Thousands of Nuba were transported to semi-desert areas further north or forced to work on commercial agricultural schemes.

Sudan's political turmoil is rooted in decades of flawed economic strategies and development policies that crippled the economy. Perceived as an attractive anti-communist ally under Nimeri, Sudan received preferential treatment from international financial institutions, receiving repeated reschedulings of its debt to the IMF and access to continued funding as the US intervened on its behalf. Despite an inflow of billions of dollars from Arab states, Sudan's agricultural sector suffered from environmental problems such as lack of water and fertile land. Commercial agriculture deprived subsistence farmers and pastoralists of land. Emphasis on large-scale, mechanized projects, generous concessions to foreign investors, dependence on foreign oil and machinery imports, a drop in world market prices for Sudan's products accompanied by rising oil prices, inflation, natural disasters, rampant corruption and huge military expenditures created a debt so large it surpassed the country's GNP.

In 1990, the IMF took the unusual step of issuing a Declaration of Non-Cooperation regarding Sudan, which had defaulted on repayments for several consecutive years. This made Sudan ineligible to receive loans from other international banks. In 1992, Sudan announced reforms but the IMF remained unsatisfied. In 1993 the World Bank terminated funding to projects in Sudan because the regime had not paid its debts. Apart from emergency aid, Western assistance to Sudan dried up in the post-Cold War atmosphere. Sudan's support for Iraq following the latter's invasion of Kuwait isolated it from other Arab regimes and from the flow of required capital from those sources, notably from the country's two dominant banking institutions, the Baraka Islamic Bank and the Faisal Islamic Bank, both Saudi-owned. Along with other Gulf states, Kuwait itself had been a significant source of foreign aid. This left Sudan dependent on Iraq, Iran and Libya for financial assistance, oil and weapons. As its economic and ideological links to the West became more tenuous, Sudan sought closer ties with these states. While thousands starved in the south, Sudan's government exported food to Iraq. Links to Libya have been erratic. Nimeri had accused Libya of supporting conspiracies against him, eyed Libya's invasion of Chad uneasily and sought closer relations with Egypt. After

Sudan's 1985 *coup*, relations with Libya improved while those with Egypt became more distant and, under the NIF regime, more hostile as Egypt accused Sudan of brewing fundamentalist revolution.

In addition to internal strife and economic failure, regional conflicts affected development. For decades, Sudan maintained a remarkably open refugee policy and, as a result, received over a million refugees from Ethiopia, Uganda and Chad. Most were settled in eastern Sudan where the government promoted an innovative policy of wage-earning settlements (Gaim 1990); Kuhlman (n.d.) examines the economic impact of Eritrean refugees on Sudan.

The south also suffered from warfare within the SPLA. In 1991, opposition to John Garang's leadership broke out. Under Riek Mashar, the SPLA–United faction made an agreement with the NIF allowing government troops to cross its territory to attack Garang's positions. The SPLA–United also was said to have received military supplies from the NIF. Ostensibly, conflict within the SPLA was based on opposition to Garang's dictatorial control but there was clearly an ethnic dimension, expressed in violence directed against civilians. The SPLA–United faction, controlling much of the Upper Nile region, was strongly Nuer while Garang's support was mainly among the Dinka. Divisions in the SPLA affected relief operations; Amnesty International and aid agencies charged both factions with human rights abuses, depicting them as waging war against the people of the south, obstructing relief aid and stealing food. In contrast to the EPLF and TPLF, the SPLA made no attempts to unify or provide assistance to the civilian population of areas it controlled; instead, it sought to exploit ethnic divisions to increase its own power. The UN suspended the Operation Lifeline network when the SPLA killed three UN aid workers and a journalist. In late 1993, SPLA factions announced reunification but power struggles continued. Internal SPLA splits allowed the NIF regime to recapture most of the towns held by the SPLA; the government launched a new offensive in February 1994, threatening the SPLA's supply lines and driving 100,000 refugees across the border into Kenya and Uganda. These actions intensified the risk of starvation for millions.

DJIBOUTI

Formerly known as French Somaliland, Djibouti became independent in 1977. It is the smallest of the Horn states; the population, estimated at between three and five hundred thousand, is concentrated in the capital city (also Djibouti) and is ethnically divided. Most are Issas; one quarter are Afars and another quarter consist of Somalis from northern subclans. Arab traders and French nationals, including a contingent of military troops, form the remainder of the population. Substantial numbers of refugees entered Djibouti from Ethiopia and Somalia. Complaining that this constituted an unsupportable burden on the country's limited resources, Djibouti's government forcibly repatriated large numbers of refugees in 1983. Although this was not a voluntary repatriation, the UNHCR cooperated.

Djibouti's main resources are its port and railway to Ethiopia. Much of the population is composed of pastoralist nomads. Although it exports vegetable products to France, Djibouti's agriculture is limited because of the harsh environment and most of its food (and fuel) is imported. It depends largely on foreign assistance, mainly from France and Saudi Arabia. Reduced French aid encouraged relations with Pakistan and China.

Djibouti's precarious economy means it is easily affected by regional events. The 1977 Ogaden war temporarily closed the railway to Addis Ababa while the 1991 Gulf War entailed considerable losses for Djibouti from Iraq, Kuwait and Saudi Arabia. During the Gulf War, Djibouti served as the regional base for French forces. This led to continued military assistance from France, although French troops have not intervened in the government's battle against the Afar-based *Front pour la restauration de l'unité et de la democratie* (FRUD). In 1992, Djibouti also served as a base for French troops that were part of the UN military operation in Somalia. In the early 1980s, Djibouti signed treaties of cooperation with other governments of the Horn; it remained neutral in regional conflicts, sought to act as a mediator and attempted to promote cooperation through the Inter-Governmental Authority on Drought and Development (IGADD).

Ethnicity has emerged as a political issue in Djibouti. The Afars had been privileged by the French and the move for independence was led mainly by the Issa. Hassan Gouled Aptidon, an Issa, became the country's first (and, by 1994, only) president; he created a single-party state under the *Rassemblement populaire pour le progrès* (RPP) but sought to demonstrate ethnic balance by ensuring that the prime minister would be an Afar and that various clans would be represented in the state bureaucracy.

Djibouti's ethnic diversity has political implications similar to those of neighbouring states. Afars are divided between Djibouti, Eritrea and Ethiopia; some sought an independent state to unite these groups. Somalia regarded Djibouti as one of its 'lost' territories and anticipated unification after the French relinquished colonial control, an outcome not favoured by Afars. In Djibouti, supporters of Somalia and Ethiopia battled each other in 1978 when the two states were at war in the Ogaden and fighting broke out between members of Somali clans who supported Siad Barre and those who backed opposition movements such as the SNM. Djibouti Afars resented Issa domination and formed armed opposition groups; conforming to a cross-border pattern common in the Horn, the *Front démocratique pour la libération de Djibouti* (FDLD) and the *Mouvement national Djiboutien pour l'instauration de la democratie* (MNDID) operated from a base in Ethiopia. The government responded with violence and was charged with human rights violations, including torture. In November 1991, FRUD began a military offensive to overthrow Gouled and was able to gain control of much of the north. While Gouled depicted FRUD as an externally-backed invading force seeking an independent state, FRUD presented its goal as political change within existing borders; Eritrea, Ethiopia and the Republic of Somaliland opposed separatism in Djibouti and did not encourage a FRUD victory because of apprehension about effects on their own Afar populations and a desire to maintain a relationship with the Gouled government (Schraeder 1993).

Some groups, such as the Afar Liberation Front sought an independent state but other organizations such as the Afar Revolutionary Democratic Union (ARDU) sought more autonomy for their ethnic groups through a federal arrangement in Ethiopia. The ARDU opposed Eritrean independence as a creation of European colonialism and proposed unity between Afars of Eritrea and Ethiopia. The ARDU had fought the EPLF and TPLF and its Djibouti-based leader, Mahmooda Gaas, called on Afars in that country to fight the Eritrean government. However, not all Afars opposed Eritrean independence and some had fought alongside the EPLF against the Derg. Economic prospects for an independent Afar state seem dim while continued fighting suggests a possible breakdown of Djibouti and degeneration into armed factionalism, as in Somalia.

DISASTER AND DEVELOPMENT IN THE HORN

In general, the Horn states have failed to provide peace, political rights or economic security. Most have appalling records of human rights abuses and have acted more as predators upon rather than protectors of their populations; often, opposition groups have been no less brutal or corrupt. Regimes that have controlled these states and their opponents imposed their rule through violence, failed to recognize democratic rights and have had little legitimacy. The state has served as a machine for profit, a means to exploit others. However, the Horn's problems are not purely internal; other states supported and influenced these regimes or their opponents in pursuit of their own objectives. Those who helped to create disasters in the Horn have a responsibility to assist with negotiating cessation of conflicts, assure basic human rights and provide aid for reconstruction and economic recovery. Establishing food security is a priority in the region. In Sudan and Somalia, the immediate concern is to end violence. In Eritrea and Ethiopia new opportunities exist for human rights, social justice and accountable government. The struggle to achieve these goals is not, of course, only an African concern.

This book examines several facets of the current situation. Asafa Jalata provides a vital historical description of how the Horn was incorporated into a European-dominated capitalist world system in the nineteenth century and how this transformed local economies and established conditions for modern disasters. Roy Pateman brings this discussion into the contemporary period by detailing hitherto unexamined links between external interests and intelligence agencies of the Horn states. Addressing one of the key political events of the early 1990s in the Horn, Eritrea's independence, Okbazghi Yohannes examines conditions for development in the new state and problems of economic transition, drawing comparisons with Asian cases. John Prendergast concentrates on Sudan, considering political roots of disaster and demonstrating that meaningful development activities depend on concentrated efforts to negotiate peace. Jon Unruh examines pastoralist-related development in Somalia in relation to the crisis of the state and addresses possibilities for recovery in this sector. Jon Abbink focuses on the Suri of south-western Ethiopia, depicting their self-rehabilitation during crisis through exploitation of new resources and considering changing ethnic relations related to crisis and development activities. Clearly, food security is a major concern. John Campbell examines this central issue in terms of the history of agricultural crisis in Ethiopia's highlands and conditions for recovery after the end of war. Patrick Webb argues that self-sufficiency in subsistence agriculture can no longer be viewed as a feasible goal and suggests different strategies. War and environmental crisis have also had a devastating impact on public health in the Horn. Marion Kelly's chapter provides a comprehensive discussion of this issue.

Gender analysis is a critical, but largely unexplored, dimension to understanding development. Throughout Africa, women play a key role in domestic work and other forms of production but their contribution has been overlooked; not only do women play a subordinate role in most

cultures of the Horn but their inferior position has been consolidated by
international development programmes that concentrate on men. Women
have suffered most from poverty; typically, they receive less food and,
therefore, are more subject to disease. Generally, they are cannot own
land, receive less education, are not allowed to hold political offices and
are legally subordinate to men. In urban areas, they receive lower wages
and have less chance to obtain skilled jobs; prostitution constitutes a last
resort for many Ethiopian women who cannot survive by other means
(Griffin 1992). Women also constitute a large proportion of the Horn's
massive displaced population. In this volume, Helene Moussa contributes
to greater understanding of this dimension by linking gender issues to the
problems of refugees.

Emphasis on conflict has overshadowed the possibilities for regional
cooperation. Tim Shaw takes us further in this direction in his chapter on
IGAAD. While the theme of regional cooperation forms the final chapter
of the book it should be taken as the starting place for further discussions
on development. There are several scenarios for the Horn's future. The
grimmest conforms to Kaplan's (1994) prediction: environmental collapse,
growing poverty, starvation, violence. This would seem the most likely
outcome as conflict continues in Djibouti, fundamentalist groups from
Sudan and Saudi Arabia threaten Eritrea and Somalia, Sudan's government continues genocidal attacks against the south, where the SPLA also
menaces civilians, and Somalia's warring factions squabble amidst the
cinders of the country.

Another scenario entails further fragmentation of existing states: secession of Southern Sudan, independent Oromia, Somalia's division into
enclaves, a breakaway Afar region. International recognition of any new
entities is another matter, however, as the case of Somaliland demonstrates. A third scenario involves proliferation of fundamentalist regimes.
Dedicated to exporting its repressive ideology, Khartoum's NIF regime
has encouraged violence in Eritrea, Ethiopia and Somalia. Fundamentalism has not gained much ground in these areas so far but poverty may
stimulate its appeal.

The final scenario is more positive. It calls for the Horn states to recognize a mutual interest in peace and security, cooperate in a loose regional
association, and concentrate on improving living standards of their populations. The end of bipolarity presents both problems and opportunities for
the Horn. With the toppling of externally-supported oppressive regimes
and the demonstrated willingness of new governments in Eritrea and
Ethiopia to cooperate, negotiate and mediate, regional integration becomes
more of a possibility. However, in terms of production and transportation,

much remains to be done to create the material basis for a complementary regional economy (Doornbos *et al.* 1992; Ravenhill 1986). Democratic change and popular participation are also necessary, as is an effective resolution of ethnic grievances. Sudan's prospects are not good; the NIF regime remains committed to a hostile ideology. Somalia does not present a promising picture but in some areas clan elders have reestablished order. Ethiopia's government faces enormous problems of poverty and ethnic tensions. If it can improve living standards and encourage popular participation it has some chance for success. Eritrea holds the best possibility for the future. As in the struggle for independence, success mainly depends on Eritrean self-reliance but that should not prevent activism in solidarity with them and with other peoples of the Horn.

References

Abdi Ismail Samatar, 1992. 'Destruction of State and Society in Somalia: Beyond the Tribal Convention', *Journal of Modern African Studies*, 30(4): 625–41.

Campbell, Bonnie and John Loxley (eds), 1989. *Structural Adjustment in Africa* (New York: St. Martins Press).

Cheru, Fantu, 1989. *Silent Revolution in Africa* (London: Zed).

Clapham, Christopher, 1988. *Transformation and Continuity in Revolutionary Ethiopia* (Cambridge: Cambridge University Press).

Cornia, Giovanni Andrea, Richard Jolly and Francis Stewart (eds), 1987. *Adjustment with a Human Face* (Oxford: Oxford University Press).

De Waal, Alex and Rakiya Omaar, 1993. 'Somalia: Adding 'Humanitarian Intervention' to the U.S. Arsenal', *Covert Action Quarterly*, 44: 4–11, 53–4.

Doornbos, Martin, Lionel Cliffe, Abdel Ghaffar M. Ahmed and John Markakis (eds), 1992. *Beyond Conflict in the Horn* (Trenton: Red Sea Press).

Duffield, Mark and John Prendergast, 1994. 'Sovereignty and Intervention after the Cold War', *Middle East Report*, 24(2–3): 9–15.

Fluehr-Lobban, Carolyn, 1992. 'Protracted Civil War in the Sudan Its Future as a Multi-Religious, Multi-Ethnic State', *The Fletcher Forum of World Affairs*, 16(2): 67–79.

Gaim Kibreab, 1990. *The Sudan From Subsistence to Wage Labour* (Trenton, NJ: Red Sea Press).

Griffin, Keith, 1992. *The Economy of Ethiopia* (New York: St. Martin's Press).

Higgott, Richard, 1986. 'Africa and the New International Division of Labour', *Africa in Economic Crisis*, John Ravenhill (ed.) (New York: Columbia University Press) pp. 286–306.

Jordan Gebre-Medhin, 1989. *Peasants and Nationalism in Eritrea* (Trenton: Red Sea Press).

Kaplan, Robert D., 1994. 'The Coming Anarchy', *The Atlantic Monthly*, 273(2): 44–76.

Kuhlman, Tom, n.d. (1990?) *Burden or Boon?* (Amsterdam: Vu University Press).

Levine, Donald, 1974. *Greater Ethiopia* (Chicago: University of Chicago Press).

Loxley, John, 1987. 'The IMF, the World Bank, and Sub-Saharan Africa: Policies and Politics', *The IMF and the World Bank in Africa*, Kjell J. Havnevik (ed.) (Uppsala: Scandinavian Institute of African Studies).

Markakis, John, 1987. *National and Class Conflict in the Horn of Africa* (Cambridge: Cambridge University Press).

Markakis, John and Nega Ayele, 1986. *Class and Revolution in Ethiopia* (Trenton, NJ: Red Sea Press).

McCann, James, 1990. 'The Myth and Reality of Agricultural Crises in Ethiopia: Empirical Lessons from History, 1900–87', Marina Ottaway, (ed.), *The Political Economy of Ethiopia* (New York: Praeger) pp. 177–96.

Rakiya Omaar, 1993. 'The Best Chance for Peace', *Africa Report*, 38(3):44–8.

Ravenhill, John (ed.), 1986, *Africa in Economic Crisis* (New York: Columbia University Press).

Relief Society of Tigray, 1993. *Bulletin* (April–May)

Robinson, Warren C. and Fumiko Yamazaki, 1986. 'Agriculture, Population and Economic Planning in Ethiopia 1953–1980', *Journal of Developing Areas*, 20:327–338.

Schraeder, Peter J., 1993. 'Ethnic Politics in Djibouti: From 'Eye of the Hurricane' to 'Boiling Cauldron', *African Affairs*, 92(367):203–21.

Sorenson, John, 1993. *Imagining Ethiopia* (New Brunswick: Rutgers University Press).

Sorenson, John, 1994. 'Refugees, Relief and Rehabilitation in the Horn of Africa: The Eritrean Relief Association', Howard Adelman and John Sorenson (eds), *African Refugees* (Boulder: Westview Press). pp. 69–93.

2 Poverty, Powerlessness and the Imperial Interstate System in the Horn of Africa

Asafa Jalata

This chapter examines historical and contemporary factors that have contributed to underdevelopment, poverty, powerlessness and disaster in the Horn. Since the region's incorporation into the European-dominated capitalist world economy in the second half of the last century, except for successive ruling classes, its peoples have lost control of their lives and resources. Alliances that emerged through incorporation of successive ruling classes and their states with the imperial interstate system undermined autonomous development initiatives and perpetuated powerlessness, poverty, conflict, war and disaster by excluding dominated classes, groups and ethnonations from decision making processes. Successive dictatorial Horn regimes and the imperial interstate system have failed to advance meaningful development measures to eliminate war, poverty and disaster. Expropriation of productive resources by elites and expenditure of substantial resources on social control agencies to enforce politics of order denied necessary resources for developing the local initiatives, participatory development strategies and multicultural democracy that are prerequisites for sustainable social and economic development.

COLONIZATION AND INCORPORATION

The Horn, via the Red Sea and Indian Ocean coasts, has attracted external interests for centuries; Arabs, Greeks, Romans and Portuguese influenced the region. The Greco-Romans introduced Orthodox Christianity to the Habashas[1] in the fourth century[2] and in the seventh century the Arabs spread Islam to areas now called Sudan, Ethiopia, Djibouti, Somalia, Eritrea and Oromia through commerce, intermarriage and colonial expansion.[3]

Various ethnonational groups struggled over religion, land, trade routes and power; for the last five centuries, conflicts and wars are well recorded.

31

Religious and economic connections gave these conflicts international dimensions. For instance, when war began between Christians and Muslims in sixteenth century Abyssinia, the Portuguese supported the Christians and the Arabs supported the Muslims.[4] With Portuguese assistance, the Habasha Christians regained power.[5] The Portuguese assisted them to block trade to the Muslim world; both the Arabs and the Ottoman Empire dominated commerical activities in the Horn until European capitalism expanded there in the nineteenth century.[6]

Lewis argues that Islam has been 'the unifying force which played so significant a part in the sixteenth-century conquest of Abyssinia, and which remains the living faith of the Somali and many of the peoples of present Ethiopia.'[7] The Oromo were caught in the wars of Christian and Muslim empire-builders. Bates asserts that the Oromo 'of the southern and western highlands watched this struggle with interest. They had suffered in their time from both parties, and were waiting in the wings for opportunities ... to recover lands which had been taken from them.'[8] Struggles between Oromos and Habashas continued from the sixteenth to late nineteenth century when the latter colonized the former, assisted by European imperialism.[9] Observing the Oromo during this period, Almeida commented:

> What makes the Gallas [Oromo] much feared is that they go to war and battle determined and firmly resolved to conquer or die. The Emperor Seltan Cagued [*sic*] recognized this quality in them and in most of the Abyssinians the exact opposite. To this he used to ascribe the victories of the Gallas and the defeats and routs of the Abyssinians, though the latter are usually much more numerous and have better horses, muskets and coats of mail in plenty.[10]

Oromo and Habashas infiltrated each other's territories for economic and political reasons for centuries, with neither establishing permanent colonial control.[11]

Similarly, various peoples of the region fought over economic resources and power. Capitalist penetration in the late nineteenth century changed the balance of power between the Habashas and others (Oromo, Sidama, Afar, Somali, Walayita, etc.). Britain occupied Aden between 1839 and 1840 on the Arabian side of the Red Sea for 'the strategic necessity of assuring imperial communication to India'.[12] France sent two scientific expeditions to the Amhara Kingdom of Manz in 1839 and 1842–43; in 1857 it started trade with this kingdom and in 1862 colonized Obock, an important commercial center on the Red Sea. France began its colonization by establishing businesses and creating an intermediate class to collaborate in colonizing practices.[13] Opening of the Suez Canal in 1869 directly linked the Mediterranean and Red Seas, intensifying commercial and political activities and colonization.

Italy took an important role after 1879 both on Africa's Red Sea and Indian Ocean coasts. In this period, Turko-Egyptian power was weakened by the Mahdist revolt in Sudan; Turko-Egyptian forces abandoned garrison towns on the Somali coast, Harar and eastern Oromia. With the Turko-Egyptian withdrawal, 'European imperialism became more active, and the three western powers already involved in the Horn of Africa strove to fill the vacuum. The British occupied the ports of Zeila and Berbera, the French made treaties with the sultans of Tadjoura and Gobaad for cessions of their territory, and Italians asserted claims to the Assab area.'[14]

Most Ethiopian and Ethiopianist scholars do not see occupation of Oromia, Ogaden-Somalia, Afar, Sidama, Walayita and others by the expanding Ethiopian state as colonization. While Oromia was partitioned between Britain and Ethiopia, Somaliland was divided among Britain, France, Italy and Ethiopia. France, Italy and Ethiopia partitioned Afarland. The French occupied the Ambado and Djibouti areas between 1885 and 1892; Djibouti became the capital of French Somaliland in 1896. On 20 March, 1897, the French commandant Lagarde signed treaties with Menelik, defining the boundary between the French colony and the Ethiopian colony of Somaliland. France allowed Ethiopia to use Djibouti as its port for commerce; later a railway was constructed between Finfine (Addis Ababa) and Djibouti. Commerce 'between Djibouti and Ethiopia grew with the progress of the railroad, while camel caravans continued to carry merchandise between the port and Harar and Shoa.'[15]

When Britain, Germany and Italy blocked arms sales in East Africa in the late nineteenth century, Djibouti became an active centre of the underground arms trade.[16] When other Africans were prohibited from buying firearms on suspicion that they would use them against Europeans, Habasha rulers, because of their collaboration with European imperialists, were allowed to buy weapons and participate in the 'scramble for Africa'.[17] According to Beachey, 'This port, the terminus of the Jibuti-Addis Ababa Railway commenced in 1896, was the entry-point for thousands of guns for Menelik, Emperor of Abyssinia, and the French were arming him against their colonial competitior, Italy.'[18] Italy occupied the Red Sea coast in 1869, gradually carving out Eritrea and Italian Somaliland. Britain's occupation of Somaliland was not limited to the coast but extended to the hinterland later called British Somaliland. El Mahdi asserts that 'different European states were pressing their colonial claims in eastern and western Africa and had encircled the Mahdist state from the south, the east and the south west.'[19] Britain occupied the area now called Kenya in 1896; after colonizing Egypt in 1882, it occupied Sudan in 1899. Ethiopia also colonized various independent ethnonations, assisted by European imperialist powers. A critical look at the evolution of this empire is essential to understanding disasters, such as war and famine, that have struck the region.

ETHIOPIAN COLONIALISM AND EUROPEAN IMPERIALISM

Emergence of the Ethiopian Empire and creation of the modern Ethiopian state occurred in conjunction with expansion of the European-dominated capitalist world economy. In the second half of the last century, Habasha monarchs allied with France, Italy and Britain founded the modern Ethiopian state and the Ethiopian Empire.[20] Holcomb and Ibssa note: "Ethiopia' is the name that was eventually given to the geographic unit created when Abyssinia, a cluster of small kingdoms in northeast Africa, expanded in the mid-1800s by conquering independent nations in the region using firearms provided by European power.'[21] The main reason for colonial expansion was to obtain commodities such as gold, ivory, coffee, musk, hides and skins, slaves, and other agricultural products valued in international markets.[22] Since the empire's creation, the Ethiopian state has been the domain of Amhara-Tigrayan ruling classes who collaborated with Euro-American allies, excluding colonized peoples and the Ethiopian masses from decision-making.[23]

The Ethiopian state controlled colonized peoples by establishing local colonial administration in strategic garrison towns; it also created local intermediaries who served between colonialists and the local population.[24] Settlers and the collaborative class protected Abyssinian power and played an important role in acquiring resources of colonized peoples. The garrisons gradually developed into urban areas where the Habashas used labour and resources of the Oromo, Sidama, Afar, Somali and others to build offices, prisons, churches, and schools. These institutions were established to assure continuation of Ethiopian colonial dominance and extraction of produce.

The colonialists created the *naftanya-gabbar*[25] system, the collaborative class, the colonial landholding sytem, and intensified slavery. Colonized farmers who lost control of their lives, children and resources were forced to work for their colonial masters, intermediaries, and the state for a certain number of days each week.[26] Some were enslaved to be sold or to work for the colonialists; for instance, Menelik and his wife had 70,000 slaves at one time.[27] The Ethiopian state claimed absolute rights over three-quarters of the land of colonized populations and provided portions for its officials, collaborators and mercenaries in lieu of salary.[28] Until colonial capitalism emerged in the 1930s, the *naftanya-gabbar* system and slavery were the main coercive labour recruitment systems.[29]

Marriage of Ethiopian colonialism and global hegemony later facilitated the development of agrocapitalism, sharecropping, and tenancy that gradually replaced slavery and the *naftanya-gabbar*. system.[30] Holcomb and Ibssa depict the true nature of the Ethiopian state when they assert: 'By officially recognizing the initial infrastructure of the Abyssinia/Ethiopian state, the imperial powers of Europe [and later North America] were able to legitimize it as a dependent colonial state, a test case for the kind of model for the control by finance capital (usually termed neocolonialism) that flourished later throughout Africa.'[31]

EVOLUTION OF THE OTHER MODERN STATES

The modern states of Sudan, Somalia and Djibouti emerged through colonization and expansion of the European-dominated capitalist world economy. However, Turko-Egyptian conquest initially laid the foundation of a central state in Sudan on the wreckage of regional governments.[32] Turko-Egyptians introduced modern innovations such as schools, the telegraph and a railway; they hunted slaves, using their labour on cotton plantations and irrigation schemes. Opposing foreign domination and resource-exploitation, a Sudanese movement known as the Mahdia dismantled Turko-Egyptian rule. Mahdism 'was both a religious and a political movement which aimed at a return to the Orthodox Islamic constitution in government, culture, and religion, it was bound to conflict with the existing government.'[33] The Mahdist state ruled until 1898, when Britain colonized Sudan.

The British colonial government established administrative, economic and social services in Sudan, encouraging capitalist development in agriculture, commerce and transportation. Explaining how the colonial state intensified capital accumulation, El Madhi notes: 'The increase in the national income resulted in an increase in government revenue from its share in agricultural schemes, its income from communications and customs dues, public works and other sources and from taxes on rain cultivation and Nile lands, from water-wheels, palm-trees and cattle and camel herds.'[34] The colonial government also developed service and regulatory institutions, such as schools, police, army and legal machinery. Analysing colonial capitalism, Mahmoud comments:

> British imperialism through the colonial state, subjected the country to both an economic and socio-economic transformation. Colonial rule established the colonial state apparatus and introduced an education and administrative system geared to serving the objectives of the state. Transport and communications were established to link areas where export commodities were produced for foreign markets. Import commodities were introduced including various levels of integration in the money economy.[35]

The colonial state intensified capital accumulation by organizing capitalist enterprises and linking subsistence and pastoral economies into the world economy. While some capital was siphoned off to a foreign country, what remained was invested in large capitalist businesses with little relevance to the condition of the majority. Mahmoud notes that the 1924 Gezira Scheme, the largest capitalist business, 'was mainly established to supply British industrial capital with cotton. The state emerged as a large capitalist entrepreneur, investing in production and infrastructure, and henceforth hiring wage labour.'[36] This created economic disarticulation that negatively affected the Sudanese masses.[37]

Before colonization of Somaliland by Ethiopia, Britain, Italy and France, there was no centalized Somali state; government emerged only on the coast.[38] The Sultans of Mijerteyn and Obbia maintained autonomous governments to the mid-1920s by signing treaties with Britain and Italy.[39] Breaking these treaties, Britain established direct rule in Northern Somaliland in 1920 (renaming it British Somaliland) while Italy established direct rule over the Sultanates of Obbia (1925) and Mijerteyn (1927). Italy encouraged colonial agricultural capitalism, subsidizing Italians to start modern farms along the Shebelle River.[40] Italians developed sugar and banana plantations but could only secure an adequate supply of workers through forced labour.[41] Castagno mentions that 'Somali agriculturalists preferred to work their own farms only, and pastoralists regarded agricultural work as demeaning.'[42] After the 1930s, banana plantations became the main area of concession agriculture and chief export product. Italy, Britain, and France did not encourage industrial development but intensified commercial activities that linked products of agriculturalists and pastoralists with the capitalist world economy to siphon off surplus produce without fundamental changes in productive forces.

Surrounded by Italian, French and British colonies, the Ethiopian Empire remained landlocked. Without commercial routes from the interior, these colonies were economically useless. To maintain commercial interests and avoid war among themselves, European imperialist powers preferred that the Ethiopian Empire stay under a technologically backward and dependent Ethiopian ruling class. When Menelik was sick in the first decade of the twentieth century, Italy, France and Britain suspected the empire might disintegrate with his death or that one of them might directly colonize Ethiopia; they signed a tripartite treaty in 1906 agreeing to maintain their respective spheres of influence should the empire collapse.[43] Creation of a centralized state dependent on European weapons, trade, expertise, and investments tied Ethiopia's economic resources to European interests.[44] The practice of supporting neocolonial states in the Horn in accordance with the interests of the imperial interstate system began with the creation of the modern Ethiopian state.

Foundations of the modern Horn states were laid by European imperialism and the imperial interstate system. Because of Christian ideology and willingness to collaborate with European imperialist powers, successive Ethiopian rulers had access to European technology, weapons, administrative and military expertise and other skills needed to construct the modern state. Although the other Horn states evolved by different routes, after decolonization they achieved similar neocolonial status. To provide cheap skilled labour and create a collaborative class, European colonial states opened a few technical and vocational schools, and sent some Africans to Europe for education.

These educated elements gradually organized themselves and African workers and farmers in their respective countries to challege European colonial states; they eventually emerged as political forces that could manipulate the existing crisis to their advantage.[45] The post-Second World War situation did not favour direct colonialism in the capitalist world economy; the US, as the emerging hegemonic world power, preferred indirect control or neocolonialism and supported decolonization that would allow it to expand its influence.[46] This global political situation, emergence of educated leaders and dissatisfaction of colonized peoples with colonial domination and exploitation created conditions which allowed local forces to take over state power. However, peoples who had been incorporated into the Ethiopian Empire did not get this opportunity, although some began their ethnonational struggles during this period.[47]

When various Sudanese political forces demanded national self-determination, the British colonial government announced its intention to decolonize Sudan and relinquished power on 1 January 1956 to a

Sudanese nationalist government. Similarly, educated Somalis who acquired modern organizational and technical skills organized political forces to demand independence. As a result, British and Italian Somaliland obtained independence and joined to form the Somali national state in 1960. Similarly, Djibouti obtained independence by the referendum of 8 May 1977. Eritrea became independent through armed struggle in 1991, followed by a 1993 referendum. As indicated by ongoing ethnonational liberation struggles of the Oromo, Afar, Sidama, and Southern Sudanese peoples,[48] the decolonization process is not yet complete.

DICTATORSHIP, POWERLESSNESS AND POVERTY

Since the colonial era, African peoples have been under dictatorial regimes of one form or another. Sucessive regimes – colonial, civil or military African regimes – imposed authority through repression to gain absolute control over the means of compulsion (the state) and the means of consumption (productive resources) (see Tssegai, this volume, Chapter 4). Most Africans have been denied representation in governments that rule them; they have become powerless. Classes and ethnonations that collaborated with the imperial interstate system gained from incorporation into the capitalist world economy and continued to benefit from it. But classes, groups and ethnonations that were denied access to state power within this system became poor and powerless:

> Structurally the nature of the distribution of the social product is critical because it exerts a fundamental influence upon the process of social and political change. A process of cumulative causation can be shown to operate in these matters, those classes which are able to appropriate the bulk of the surplus will, by so doing, increase their ability to influence the future structure of production and the institutions of social and political control; those who cannot will find their influence progressively reduced.[49]

Lack of accountablity by successive governments ensured that Africa's produce is not properly channeled toward development but goes to conspicuous consumption and consolidation of the ruling class. In Africa's backward economies, surplus is limited; hence there is a life-and-death struggle for its appropriation. Access to state power is the major channel through which surplus is siphoned off from actual producers. That is why the struggle for political power is violent. As organs of local and international capital,[50] African states are supported by foreign powers including international and regional organizations.

Why have Ethiopia, Somalia, Djibouti and Sudan failed to solve human disasters, such as war, famine and poverty? The processes of decolonization and state formation are not yet completed; and the imperialist state-building strategy has completely failed.[51] The Horn is probably the first region where ideologies of both the West and East failed so drastically and resulted in such extensive human tragedies. Capitalist incorporation and state formation were means to an end; successive ruling classes and their international counterparts sought wealth and capital accumulation through control of the state. This required the hierarchical organization of peoples both socially and ethnonationally in order to intensify looting, enslavement, coercive labour recruitment systems, tenancy, sharecropping, etc.

Imperialist state-building strategy promoted establishment and stability of 'nation-states' that can control various peoples and maintain them under capitalist manipulation. This allowed building of ruling classes of certain ethnonational groups or clans that used their power bases to dominate and exploit other peoples. Explaining how an ethnonational power base is used, Shaw notes: 'whilst officially denying and decrying "ethnicity", ruling classes use it in practice to maintain personal networks: the construction of power. The articulation of 'factionalism' has in fact been ubiquitous on the continent as ethnic connections have become the hard-core of any support nexus.'[52]

Ethnicization or 'clanization' of state power prevented construction of legitimate states that reflect multicultural societies. Evolution and practices of Amhara-Tigrayan, northern Sudanese, and Marehan and Issa ruling classes and their respective states in Ethiopia, Sudan, Somalia and Djibouti reflect this. Further, radicalization of these states through imported ideologies, such as Islam and 'Marxism' intensified existing contradictions. In Ethiopia both Christianity and 'Marxism' were used to maintain the empire. Currently the new Tigrayan colonial regime, assisted by regional and international allies, attempts to suppress or destroy the Oromo national movement led by the Oromo Liberation Front. In addition to his clan power base, Siad Barre tried to use Islam to expand territory and incorporate Oromia into Somalia. Sudan has intensified Islamization of the state to exclude non-Muslims from power.

Modernization theorists believed that ethnonational groups would disappear with the transition of 'backward' peoples to 'modernity'. They assume that modernization eliminates social problems by providing opportunities for all groups. Exposing the major weaknesses of this theory, Markakis argues:

[it] assumes that development generally has a positive effect upon all population groups and social classes. This assumption is called into question by the concept of uneven development.... From this perspective, development is seen as a discontinuous and uneven process which differentiates between regions and economic sectors, depriving some for the benefit of others, and also discriminates among population groups and social classes, conferring power and privilege on some at the expense of others.[53]

Similarly, mainstream Marxists assumed that capitalism universalizes culture, politics and language, and divides the world into capitalist and working classes. Marxist theorists assumed capitalist development would produce revolutionary forces to dismantle social and ethnic hierarchies and establish egalitarianism, social justice and socialist democracy.

Influenced by such utopian assumptions, some Marxists accepted modernization theory's notion that assimilation and cultural universalization are inevitable. Global experiences demonstrate that assimilation and cultural universalism have very limited success; wherever these processes have taken place, as in North America, even basic and social contradictions remain unsolved. In the Horn, since dominant ethnic groups are numerically insignificant, they could not and cannot assimilate dominated groups. Failing to understand this, Marxist groups in Ethiopia, Sudan, and Somalia could not provide alternative solutions to ethnonational and development problems and became tools of dictatorial regimes that attempted to solve everything through military power.

Considering the scarcity of economic resources, uneven development and ethnicization of the labour force, it is clear that interests of working classes of different ethnonational group coincide. Social classes and ethnonations that dominate in political economy also use cultural resources to maintain their advantages.

Cultural elements themselves may have a material dimension if, as often the case, they mediate access to power and privilege. Language, the basic cultural attribute of nationalism, often plays this role in multiethnic states with a single official language. Groups whose languages are ignored by the state may find themselves at a distinct disadvantage in competing for access to education and state office. This is the case in Ethiopia and the Sudan, for example. Similarly, religion may be endowed with a material dimension.[54]

Disasters in the Horn are mainly caused by government policies and political contradictions. The Horn states, chiefly interested in maintaining the status quo, play zero-sum politics. They invest their meagre economic surplus on destructive weapons and unproductive civilian and military bureaucracies to protect themselves from political opposition and ethnonational liberation fronts. Henze writes: 'Military priorities in ... Horn countries had an increasingly negative impact on economic development. During the mid-1980s it became dramatically apparent that diversion of resources to military purposes and continual involvement in military operations directed against internal discontent had undermined the capacity of these countries to feed their populations, and large-scale famine occurred.'[55] The priorities of these states and the imperial interstate system make peaceful redefinitions of social and ethnonational relations impossible. Under such conditions, the state is an instrument of the ruling class because it denies the masses and subordinated ethnonations political representation in a decision-making process. Under such conditions, subordinated classes, groups and ethnonations are denied political and economic rights. The results are wars, economic crises and under-development.

Powerlessness results in underdevelopment, characterized by inadequate production of food, lack of heavy industry, low economic growth, low productivity, lack of forward and backward linkages between agriculture and industry, and expropriation of meagre surplus by intermediary classes and foreigners who do not invest in African productive forces.[56] Ethiopia, Somalia and Sudan even 'fell below the African average in absolute and *per capita* GNP growth during the 1970s;' the average per capita GNPs for this decade for all Africa, Ethiopia, Somalia and Sudan were 712, 121, 344 and 425 US dollars respectively.[57] Recently this condition has deteriorated. In 1987, the per capita GNP for all Africa, Ethiopia, Somalia and Sudan were 611, 112, 199 and 369 respectively.[58]

Social classes and ethnonations that dominate the means of compulsion and the means of consumption are engaged in accumulation of wealth and capital with the help of the imperial interstate system at the cost of the masses and dominated ethnonations. According to Mamdani, 'state connection is a necessary precondition for membership in the African ... [ruling class and] gives a life-and-death character to the political struggle within it. A political position does not simply reinforce a pre-existing economic position or open up new opportunities where old ones already existed, it is in fact the very foundation of wealth.'[59] The governments' failure to invest available surplus in development of productive forces has left the peoples of this region culturally, technically, economically, and politically backward.

Economically speaking, 'imports rose much more rapidly than exports and exports showed a tendency to stagnate or decline' during the 1970s.[60]

Rural populations have failed to cope with changing social, political and natural environments. Failure to invest in development of productive forces, internal and external wars, farmers' discouragement due to expropriation of their grains and animals, and conspicuous consumption of ruling classes have slowed the introduction of technical innovation in the agricultural production system. The Horn's regimes have failed to establish authority because their policies cause political destabilization. 'The strain is economic and social and, in political terms, has become increasingly serious because the exertions of Horn armies have not advanced regimes' objectives of maintaining territorial integrity or domestic peace.'[61]

These governments have exacerbated crises and food shortages through their policies. 'While it has been customary to see drought and famine as "natural" phenomena,' Lawrence and Livingstone argue, 'recent analyses have put forward the view that these have socio-economic causes which lie in the policies pursued by colonial and post-colonial governments in Africa.'[62] While farmers and pastoralists produce for consumption and exchange, governments encouraged cash crops at the cost of food production, because cash crop markets increase their revenues. Furthermore, as Lappe and Collins note, 'Governments beholden to urban classes demanding cheap food have paid peasants so poorly for their crops that they have often had little incentive to produce for the market.'[63] Such policies have caused food deficits. Lawrence and Livingstone assert: 'Much of the failure to remain self-sufficient in food production can be traced to government policies of encouraging export cash crop production, principally by setting relatively lower producer prices for domestic food crops.'[64]

Recognizing the serious effect of relationships in the imperial interstate system, Lofchie and Commins blame collaboration of governments from developed countries with corrupt African regimes: 'Government-to-government assistance runs a very great risk of supporting corrupt and venal regimes and, to this degree, can be held partly accountable for the growing mood of cynicism and disillusionment with African leaders.'[65] Since the Horn states and the imperial interstate system, spearheaded by the US, refused to recognize and provide alternative solutions to the complex processes of decolonization and state formation, today we witness conflicts, wars, social dislocation and crises. War between the Issa and Afar in Djibouti, between the Oromo and Tigrayan occupying forces in the Ethiopian Empire, between Somali clans, and between northern and southern Sudan demonstrate both historical and contemporary contradictions that facilitate disaster.

CONCLUSIONS

Old policies of building states based on hegemony of one ethnic group in multinational regions, promotion of cultural universalism at the cost of cultural particularism, blind acceptance of state sovereignty without recognizing rights of dominated peoples, promotion of politics of order at the cost of democracy and lack of vision to build a multicultural democracy based on ethnocultures and universal values of humanism, equality, social justice, and progress have intensified social problems and disaster. Policies of Horn regimes and the imperial interstate system have been dominated by an ideology of cultural universalism and a top-down paradigm that ignored the peoples of this region and their cultural traditions.

Cultural universalism is an ideology that created and socialized an intermediate class in the modern world system through subordinating or destroying multicultures in the name of science and technology.[66] Wallerstein notes that cultural universalism that rejects local traditions and cultures 'did not make its way as a free-floating ideology but as one propagated by those who held economic and political power in the world system of historical capitalism.'[67] While some intermediate classes and their states in Asia and Latin America are making progress in development because of their relative strength, ruling classes and their states in the Horn in particular and Africa in general are weak and have failed to promote meaningful development strategies. According to Logli, 'In 1981 Africa was responsible for only 1 per cent of the world's Manufacturing Value Added (MVA) as compared to with 5.9 per cent and 4.2 per cent for Latin America and Asia respectively.'[68]

Peoples of the Horn, except for dominant classes and groups, are powerless and exposed to disaster. Describing the causes of powerlessness as 'a scarcity of democracy', Lappe and Collins argue, 'Wherever people have been made hungry, power is in the hands of those unaccountable to their people. These antidemocratic governments answer only to elites, lavishing them with credit, subsidies, and other assistance. To protect the privileges of the wealthy minority, they increasingly funnel public resources toward the military.'[69] Without a new democratic paradigm that will allow dominated classes, social groups and ethnonations genuine representation within state power, existing states, regional, continental and international political structures are inadequate to provide solutions for the Horn's complex problems.

The Horn's peoples are at a crossroads: Social and cultural systems that traditionally provided social and material needs have broken up, and they have not yet established states responsive to their social and economic needs. Rural populations are dislocated because of modern development projects, wars, marginalization of pastoralism and subsistence agriculture, poverty, and government policies.[70] The imperial interstate system, regional and nongovernmental organizations (NGOs), apart from providing emergency relief during famine, have not helped the peoples of the region. Many do not take preventive actions and only respond when the media report famine. In fact, they have supported dictatorial regimes and strengthened their positions against the peoples of this region.

Governments that have relations with the Horn regimes have a moral resposibility to deal with the problems of these peoples since they have supported these dictatorial regimes both financially and politically. Modernization strategies, military assistance and trade relations have had serious consequences for African producers. As Lappe and Collins explain: 'Colonizers, subsequently, national and international agencies, have discredited peasant producers' often sophisticated knowledge of ecologically appropriate farming systems. Promoting "modern" often imported, and ecologically destructive technologies, they have cut Africa's food producers out from economic decisions most affecting their very survival.'[71] Western governments must stop financing antidemocratic forces that cannot promote meaningful development.

In particular NGOs have a social and moral responsibility not to help antidemocratic governments. By mixing the work of innocent and humanist volunteers with that of spies, profiteers, and callous career bureaucrats, 'aidgame' politics subordinates humanism to state interest both locally and internationally and intensifies social problems.[72] According to Clay, 'During the Ethiopian famine of 1984–1986, Western humanitarian agencies collaborated with the government, both actively and passively, in programs [resettlement, collectivization, etc.] that both intensified the famine where it existed and extended it to new areas.'[73] Because of their state-to-state relations many humanitarian organizations 'attempted to block researchers' efforts to uncover the intent of Ethiopia's programs, as well as their long-term impacts.'[74] Since the old policies of these organizations failed to address causes of disasters, their efforts could not go beyond feeding hungry people.

Humanitarian organizations must build people-to-people relations to promote better development strategies through identifying causes of disasters and providing solutions. They have a moral responsibility to feed the hungry; practice the philosophy of democratization of economic and political life; work to empower the poor, women, and dominated ethnonations; promote research that can provide alternative sources of information[75] and resist being tools of dictatorial regimes and their international counterparts. All humanist and religious organizations and individuals should support implementation of such strategies and assist dominated groups and peoples to empower themselves culturally, politically and economically in order to prevent greater disaster.

Notes

1. Habashas or Abyssinians descended from the mixture of Arabs and Africans; they later called themselves Ethiopians to legitimize domination of peoples brought under their control during expansion of the European-dominated capitalist world economy in the late nineteenth century. Classical European historians gave the name Ethiopians to all black people. Realizing the political significance of this name, the Habashas called themselves Ethiopians. Historically speaking, Ethiopians and Habashas were not one and the same people, although the Habashas were among the Ethiopians. Currently Amharas and Tigrayans call themselves Ethiopians while others brought into Ethiopia through colonization prefer to call themselves by their ethnonational names. Most Eritreans are Habashas.

2. A. H. M. Jones and Elizabeth Monroe, *A History of Ethiopia* (Oxford: Clarendon Press, 1935), p. 6.

3. Ibid., pp. 6–7; R. Pankhurst, *An Introduction to the Economic History of Ethiopia from Early Times to 1800* (Woodford Green: Lalibela House, 1961), pp. 56–7.

4. E. W. Luther, *Ethiopia Today* (London: Oxford University Press, 1958), pp. 13.

5. Jones and Monroe, *A History of Ethiopia*, p. 85.

6. A. Jalata, *Oromia and Ethiopia: State Formation and Ethnonational Conflict, 1868–1992* (Boulder: Lynne Rienner, 1993), pp. 34–6; J. S. Trimingham, *Islam in Ethiopia* (New York: Barnes & Noble, 1965), pp. 107–121.

7. I. M. Lewis, *The Modern History of Somaliland: From Nation to State* (London: Weidenfeld & Nicolson, 1965), p. 20.

8. D. Bates, *The Abyssinian Difficulty: The Emperor Theodorus and the Magdala Campaign. 1867–1868* (Oxford, 1979), p. 7.

9. Jalata, *Oromia and Ethiopia*, pp. 19–25; 36–7; 47–62.

10. M. De Almeida, 'The Travels of the Jesuits', *Travellers in Ethiopia*, Richard Pankhurst (ed.), (London: Oxford University Press, 1965), pp. 36–47.

11. Jalata, *Oromia and Ethiopia*.

12. V. Thompson and R. Adloff, *Djibouti and the Horn of Africa* (Stanford: Stanford University Press, 1968), p. 5.

13. Afar chiefs collaborated in colonization of Obock and received 10,000 thalers (1 thaler = 71.4 US cents). From 1881 France established companies there (Compagnie Franco-Ethiopienne, Société Francaise d'Obock, Compagnie Mesnier, etc.). Darkwah states: 'France would help Shewa to develop in such a way that she would spearhead the regeneration of the empire of Ethiopia; a regular commercial route would be opened between

Shewa and Obock; a colony of French artisans would be established in Shewa ...the Shewan army would be trained on European lines; order and efficiency would be introduced into the Shewan governmental system.' R. H. K. Darkwah, *Shewa, Menelik and the Ethiopian Empire 1813–1889* (London: Heinemann Educational Books, 1975), p. 623.

14. V. Thompson and R. Adloff, *Djibouti and the Horn of Africa* p. 7.
15. Ibid., p. 9.
16. R. W. Beachey, 'The Arms Trade in East Africa in the Late Nineteenth Century', *Journal of African History*, III, 3 (1962) pp. 451–67.
17. Ibid.; Jalata, *Oromia and Ethiopia*.
18. Beachey, 'The Arms Trade in East Africa', p. 462.
19. M. El Mahdi, *A Short History of the Sudan* (London: Oxford University Press, 1965), p. 116.
20. See Jalata, *Oromia and Ethiopia*; B. K. Holcomb and S. Ibssa, *The Invention of Ethiopia: The Making of a Dependent Colonial State in Northeast Africa* (Trenton, NJ: Red Sea Press, 1990).
21. Ibid., p. 1.
22. M. Stahl, *Ethiopia: Political Contradictions in Agricultural Development* (Stockholm: Raben & Sjogren, 1974), p. 378.
23. Jalata, *Oromia and Ethiopia*, pp. 83–146.
24. Ibid., pp. 62–73.
25. Under the *naftanya-gabbar* system, colonized peoples (Oromo, Sidama, etc.) were divided among Ethiopian colonial settlers to produce commodities freely for local consumption and international markets. It was a semi-slavery system. See Charles McClellan, 'Perspective on the Neftenya-Gabbar System: The Darassa of Ethiopia', *Africa*, 33 (1978), pp. 426–40.
26. Ibid.
27. R. Pankhurst, *Economic History of Ethiopia 1800–1935* (Addis Ababa, 1968), p. 75.
28. Jalata, *Oromia and Ethiopia*, p. 70.
29. Ibid., pp. 83–5.
30. Ibid., pp. 83–108.
31. B. K. Holcomb and S. Ibssa, *The Invention of Ethiopia*, p. 140.
32. P. M. Holt and W. Daly, *The History of the Sudan: From the Coming of Islam to the Present Day* (Boulder: Westview Press, 1987); El Mahdi, *A Short History of the Sudan*, p. 70.
33. Ibid., p. 19.
34. Ibid., p. 127.
35. F. B. Mahmoud, *The Sudanese Bourgeoisie: Vanguard of Development?* (London: Zed Press, 1984), p. 14.
36. Ibid.
37. See Jay O'Brien and Ellen Gruenbaum, 'A Social History of Food, Famine, and Gender in Twentieth Century Sudan', *The Political Economy of African Famine*, R. E. Downs, D. O. Kerner, S. P. Reyna (eds) (Durham: University of New Hampshire, 1991), pp. 177–202.
38. Lewis, *The Modern History of Somaliland*, p. 33.
39. M. Castagno, *Historical Dictionary of Somalia* (Metuchen: Scarecrow Press, 1975), p. xx.
40. Ibid., p. 35.

41. Ibid.
42. Ibid., p. 57.
43. H. G. Marcus, *The Life and Times of Menelik II, Ethiopia 1844–1913* (Oxford: Clarendon, 1975), pp. 204–258.
44. Jalata, *Oromia and Ethiopia*. pp. 47–74.
45. See P. M. Holt and W. Daly, *The History of Sudan*, p. 145; M. Castagno, *Historical Dictionary of Somalia*, p. 47.
46. A. Y. So, *Social Change and Development: Modernization, Dependency and World-System Theories* (Newbury: Sage Publications, 1990), p. 17.
47. Oromo, Ogaden-Somali and Eritrean ethnonational liberation struggles began in the 1960s.
48. See *New African*, 'Ethiopia: Struggle Continues', June 1993, p. 18; various 1993 OLF military communiques, particularly 20 September 1993; *BBC: Focus on Africa*, 'Djibouti: What is FRUD?,' July–September 1993, vol. 4, no. 4, pp. 13–15; Helen C. Metz (ed.), *Sudan: A Country Study* (Washington, DC, Department of the Army, 1992); Mark Huband, 'While People Starve', *Africa Report*; May/June 1993, pp. 36–9.
49. E. A. Brett, 'Problems in Analysing Colonial Change', *African Social Studies: A Radical Reader* (New York: Monthly Review Press, 1977), pp. 52–3.
50. B. Beckman, 'Imperialism and the "National Bourgeoisie", *Review of African Political Economy*, no. 22, 1982; pp. 5–19; B. Beckman, 'State and Capitalist Development in Nigeria', *Review of African Political Economy*, no. 23, 1982, pp. 37–51.
51. Conditions of Somalia, Sudan and Ethiopia aptly demonstrate failure of the neocolonial state; but the US and other Western powers attempt to salvage these states by recruiting new elites without addressing fundamental contradictions. As far as democratic principles are rejected, collaboration of new elites and the imperial interstate system only intensifies existing contradictions and social problems.
52. T. M. Shaw, 'Ethnicity as the Resilient Paradigm for Africa: From 1960s to 1980s', *Development and Change*, vol. 17, no. 4, p. 589.
53. J. Markakis, 'Material and Social Aspects of National Conflict in the Horn of Africa', *Civilizations*, vol. XXXIII, no. 1 (1983), p. 276.
54. Ibid., p. 279.
55. P. B. Henze, *The Horn of Africa: From War to Peace* (New York: St. Martin's Press, 1991), p. 130.
56. See for example, W. Rodney, *How Europe Underdeveloped Africa* (Washington, DC: Howard University Press, 1982).
57. Henze, *The Horn of Africa*, pp. 102–3.
58. Ibid., p. 115.
59. M. Mamdani, 'Peasants and Democracy in Africa', *New Left Review*, March/April, 1986, p. 47.
60. Henze, *The Horn of Africa*, pp. 109–10.
61. Ibid., p. 114.
62. P. Lawrence and I. Livingstone, *Africa South of the Sahara* (Europa Publications, sixteenth edition, 1987), p. 70.
63. F. M. Lappe and J. Collins, *World Hunger: Twelve Myths* (New York, Grove Weidenfeld, 1986), p. 13.

64.   Lawrence and Livingstone, *Africa South of the Sahara*, pp. 74–5.
65.   M. Lofchie and S. K. Commins, 'Food Deficits and Agricultural Policies in Tropical Africa', *The Journal of African Studies*, 20 (1982), p. 23.
66.   I. Wallerstein, *Historical Capitalism* (London: Verso, 1983), p. 83.
67.   Ibid., p. 85.
68.   P.'Logli, 'Industry in Africa', *Africa South of the Sahara* (Europa Publications, sixteenth edition, 1987).
69.   Lappe and Collins, *World Hunger*, pp. 4 and 6.
70.   See for example, S. Kontos, 'Farmers and the Failure of Agribusiness in Sudan', *Sudan: State and Society*, J. O. Voll (ed.), (Bloomington: Indiana University Press, 1991), pp. 137–61; O'Brien and Gruenbaum, 'A Social History'; James McCann, *From Poverty to Famine in Northeast Ethiopia: A Rural History 1900–1935*, (Philadelphia, University of Pennsylvania, 1987); John Markakis (ed.), *Conflict and the Decline of Pastoralism in the Horn of Africa* (London: Macmillan Press, 1993). This book explains how commercialization and capitalism undermined Southern Sudan, Beja, Afar, Boran Oromo, and Somali pastoralists without providing alternative means of livelihood.
71.   Lappe and Collins, *World Hunger*, p. 13.
72.   Myles F. Harris, *Breakfast in Hell: A Doctor's Eyewitness Account of the Politics of Hunger in Ethiopia* (New York: Poseidon, 1987).
73.   J. W. Clay, 'Western Assistance and the Ethiopian Famine: Implications for Humanitarian Assistance', *The Political Economy of African Famine*, R. E. Downs, D. O. Kerner, S. P. Reyna (eds), (Durham: New Hampshire, 1991), p. 168.
74.   Ibid., p. 169.
75.   Ibid., pp. 137–49.

3 Intelligence Operations in the Horn of Africa

Roy Pateman

The ostensible purpose of intelligence collection and activity is preservation of national security. In the developing world, intelligence agencies have played a major role in nation building and have developed potent forms of coercion to such a degree that, at times, it is appropriate to talk of agencies occupying their own countries. Agencies have frequently worked to the considerable disadvantage of Africans, and have contributed mightily toward the disasters that have been visited upon the Horn. In this chapter, I will deal with each of the five countries that constitute the Horn, discussing the organization of indigenous intelligence services and the role played by foreign powers in some of the most crucial political events in recent history.

DJIBOUTI

The major security service – modelled on that of other former French Dependencies – is the *Service de documentation et de sécurité* – Documentation and Security Service (SDS). There is also a Military Intelligence Security Service, whilst the *Brigade spéciale de recherche de la gendamerie* is also active in interrogation (Amnesty International 1984:110). Until 1980, Lieutenant. Amir Adaweh was head of Military Intelligence; an Afar, he fled to Ethiopia to escape intimidation from the Issa Government (*Indian Ocean Newsletter* 1985:177; 1986:256).

A Presidential Security Unit was established in 1978 under the command of Captain Medhi Sheik, whilst a special counter-intelligence unit was formed in 1987 under Major Ahmed Yunis (*Africa Confidential* 1987:7). The Head of Security (and Chief of Staff of the Armed Forces) was Ismael Omar Guelle – nephew of President Hassan Gouled Aptidon – until he became even more powerful as Cabinet Director (*Indian Ocean Newsletter* 1986:259; 1992:541). As elsewhere, we notice that the head of intelligence in a country is often a close relative of the Head of State. Hassan Said Khaireh became Director of SDS after Ismael.

During Mengistu Haile Mariam's rule in Addis Ababa, all Djiboutian units cooperated with the Ethiopian army in rounding up and repatriating refugees to Ethiopia (Quarrie 1986:90; Amnesty International 1988:37). The Djibouti government has also cooperated with Iraq, and terrorist attacks in September 1990 were traced back to SDS, whose leader had developed close contacts with Iraq after a security treaty signed in 1989 (*Indian Ocean Newsletter* 1990:448).

During French colonial rule, Israel had a presence in Djibouti in the form of Asher Ben-Natan (Arthur the handsome), formerly Israeli intelligence chief in Europe. He was general manager of an Israeli government owned meat processing company, Red Sea Incoda (Raviv and Melman 1990:63). Djibouti proved an ideal spot for this Israeli listening post from 1955 to 1964 (Beit-Hallahmi 1987:52).

France maintains an active and large intelligence network in this small, quasi-independent, country situated so strategically on the shores of the Red Sea facing Arabia. Djibouti is a main military security base for DPSD, the main French anti-terrorist outfit and a vital base for French units operating in Kuwait and Somalia (*Indian Ocean Newsletter* 1991:464.) In 1991, all French intelligence heads in Djibouti (i.e. of *La Direction générale de la sécuritié extérieure*, which deals in foreign operations and counter-espionage, *Deuxième Bureaux* in charge of military security, as well as the Military Attaché) were transferred, after Jacques Fournet, head of *La Direction de la surveillance du territoire*, which is concerned with domestic intelligence in France and its overseas departments and territories, decided that they were too close to the Djiboutian President to function in France's best interests (*Indian Ocean Newsletter* 1991:493.) It will be only a matter of time before French intelligence resumes its intimate involvement in political and military life in Djibouti.

ETHIOPIA

Friends and Allies

US interest in Ethiopia dates from World War II (although some African-Americans displayed considerable interest in Ethiopian history and strongly supported the Emperor against the 1935 Italian invasion). In 1942, the US signed an agreement with the United Kingdom, then in occupation of Eritrea, to lease Kagnew base in Eritrea, which became one of their most important communications facilities. Kagnew was of immense importance during the Korean war, relaying messages from Washington to US troops in Korea. During the 1950s, Ethiopia received the bulk of US military assistance to Africa. By 1960, the US had 6000 military personnel in Military Assistance Advisory Groups (MAAG) in Ethiopia; such formations provided 'cover' for CIA officers stationed abroad (Wolpin 1972:120). Americans were present in Ethiopian military formations down to battalion level, and were heavily involved in training (Marcus 1983:126). The US Army and Airforce were based at Kagnew, whilst the Navy were in Massawa. The US had two bases on the Sudan border (Mt. Hamid and Mt. Khorahabad) until 1965, when they were stood down after supply convoys were ambushed by the Eritrean Liberation Front (ELF) (*Eritrean Review* 1973:July 15).

There are indications that US personnel were actively engaged in intelligence and combat missions against Eritrean guerrillas. In 1973, the US Consul General in Asmara was Thomas Mulvihill, who had previously worked in military intelligence. In 1974, the State Department expressed concern over the increasing involvement of Americans in covert counter-insurgency operations and Edward Korry, US Ambassador in Addis Ababa, transferred at least one Colonel attached to the Army Security Agency because of involvement in such operations (Powers 1980:224–5). The presence of large numbers of US personnel also facilitated intelligence cooperation with the Israelis.

The Central Intelligence Agency (CIA) was also active within the embassy in Addis Ababa even if its effectiveness was possibly slight ('there were persistent errors in their reports' (Spencer 1984:314)). However, during an attempted military *coup* in December 1960 while the Emperor was visiting Brazil, the CIA was active and effective. The most active diplomats apart from the Ambassador were: William McGhee (who doubled as First Secretary and CIA Chief of Station (COS)) and the army attaché, Colonel. William H. Crosson. Crosson later became Head of two counter-intelligence branches in Vietnam from February 1965 until April 1966, and Head of the Peace Corps in Zaire in 1976 (*Africa Contemporary Record* 1976/1977:B.536).

At the start of the attempted coup, the Head of the American MAAG, General de Grave, told his men to stay away from their assigned units and not interfere. However, some personnel intervened on the Emperor's side; for example, American airmen flew a reconnaissance mission over the palace in an attempt to intimidate the rebels (Marcus 1983:140–41). But on December 15, when it became known that the Emperor was back in Africa and in contact with a loyal garrison in Eritrea under General Abiye, de Grave stated that the US should assist the Emperor. The Ambassador agreed. The Emperor was able to use the powerful US Air Force radio in Liberia (at that time the headquarters of communications in Africa) to direct operations against the rebels.

The Emperor was restored to his throne but with reduced prestige; clearly, in the future power would lie with a united military, and cultivation of friends among these men appeared fruitful. Seeing the US potential for training his rivals, the Emperor elicited support from a source which seemed more loyal – Israel.

Although Beta Israel (Falasha) Jews lived in Ethiopia for centuries, it was not until 1975 that Israel's Chief Rabbis acknowledged them as Jews – the lost tribe of Dan thought to have disappeared 2700 years ago. The Falashas were once 1 million strong, ruling a kingdom in the Semien mountains, but over the past 350 years their numbers fell through disease, persecution and conversion, to an estimated 1975 population of 15,000 people at the bottom of the social ladder in one of the world's poorest countries.

Since the nineteenth century, a few prominent Jews concerned themselves with the Falashas, but until the severe 1984 famine, most Falashas were not encouraged to return to Israel. They are black, poor and mostly illiterate – reasons which no doubt led South African-born Abba Eban to dismiss them as marginal (Rapoport 1980:6). Until the 1960s, Israeli interest in the other thirty million Ethiopians was also marginal, apart from a brief period during World War II when Irgun and Stern gang terrorists, including former Premier of Israel Yitzhak Shamir, were interned in Eritrea. Israeli and Italian Jewish businessmen were involved in Eritrea; for example, they owned the Yonah Darom fish processing plant in Massawa. Ethiotextile, a large company employing over 2000 workers, was controlled by Israeli capital. Two meat packing plants, INCODA and SOPRAL were owned by Israelis and a third, Red Sea Development Corporation, had substantial Israeli equity (Amdemichael Kahsai 1977:20). To serve the Jewish community in Asmara there was a synagogue (*Vanguard* 1976:13).

Israel opened diplomatic links with Haile Selassie in 1961 but never pressed him on return of the Falashas. Israel acquiesced with the Emperor's view that the Falashas were as much his subjects as were the Muslims, for the same reasons as it maintained close contact with the later military dictatorship of Colonel Mengistu. Israel felt it had to support a centralist Ethiopian empire if it hoped to regain a strong diplomatic presence in Africa, prevent a united Afro-Asian stand on recognition of Palestinian claims and relieve pressure caused by its close ties with racist South Africa.

Much credit for Israel's successful policy of cooperation with its non-Arab neighbours lies with Reuven Shiloah. He developed the peripheral strategy: cementing clandestine ties with non-Arab minorities throughout the Middle East. Among such friends were Turkish and Iranian governments, the Kurds of Iraq, Maronite Christians in Lebanon, Royalists in Yemen and, from time to time, the southern non-Muslim, Sudanese, as well as Ethiopia (Raviv and Melman 1990:21, 153).

Close ties with Ethiopia were also intended to facilitate exchange of students and professional workers and create a favourable impression of Israel. Israelis hoped that this would be reflected in Ethiopia's voting record in the UN; although this hope was not realized, Israel persisted in its overt and clandestine diplomacy. Although Israel had abstained in UN vote 390 A (v) of 1950 which federated Eritrea with Ethiopia, it had built up credit with the Emperor during the attempted *coup* when it helped him talk with supporters in Eritrea (Erlich 1983:57). Israelis claim to have saved the Emperor from two other *coup* attempts (Beit-Hallahmi 1987:52).

Israelis trained Eritrean police officers in commando units as well as the Emperor's secret police. The commando units were used in counter-insurgency actions against the ELF that had begun the armed struggle for independence from Ethiopia in 1961. Both Israel and the US saw the Eritrean liberation struggle as an Arab-backed, Muslim-separatist, secession movement which might block the Bab el Mandeb straits at the southern end of the Red Sea (Erlich 1983:38; Lauffer 1967:171).

Ethiopia was also a vital conduit for Israeli communication with the Anya Nya rebels in Southern Sudan (Beshir 1975:91). Israelis recruited Southern Sudanese rebels from the field and Uganda and flew them to Asmara, from where Ethiopian Army officers drove them to Wukro in Tigray for training by Ethiopian and Israeli officers (Dawit Wolde Giorgis 1989).

By 1966, Israel had a military mission of 100 men in Ethiopia, the second largest foreign military contingent in the country. Colonel Ben Nathaw was in charge of training in Decamare, whilst Colonel Don was responsible for training Ethiopian Marine Commando Forces in Massawa (Lobban 1972:16). They trained on average, 500 men every six months (Silverberg 1968:50–75). An Israeli also served as Military Attaché to Asrate Kassa, Governor General of Eritrea from 1964–1970 (Sherman 1980:75). By 1970, Eritrean forces trained by Israel reached battalion size. Israel's intelligence services were also active (Jacob 1971:178). The main Israeli intelligence center was in Asmara (*Eritrean Review* 1975:21). There was considerable cooperation between Israel, the US and Ethiopia in establishing an air base at Jebel Hamid and there were reports of Israeli presence in the Dahlak islands (*Ethiopian Herald* 1974:October 17). Israelis established complex radar stations on the islands of Fatima off Assab and Maleb in the Dahlak archipelago by 1977 (*Eritrean Revolution* 1977:October–November). (See pp. 260–1 below.)

As the Soviet Union gained influence among Ethiopian military rulers, the CIA continued to monitor events. In 1977, US diplomats Richard Hammond and Colonel Edwin Hamilton were expelled from Ethiopia, allegedly because of intelligence activities. More likely this formed part of the TORCH disinformation operation, a probable fabrication by the Soviet bloc which claimed that the CIA were plannng to kill Chairman Mengistu (Dawit Wolde Giorgis 1989:35–6). In 1980, the US Ambassador to Ethiopia, Frederic L. Chapin, was declared *persona non grata* – presumably not because of spying but because he was behind the invocation of the Hickenloper amendment (US Congress legislation banning aid to countries that had nationalized US assets) against Ethiopia, for nationalizing American assets without compensation (*Africa News* 1980:6).

Intervention in Ethiopia became part of Reagan's crusade against communism in the 1980s. The CIA channelled half a million US dollars annually to the London-based, conservative opposition, Ethiopian People's Democratic Alliance (EPDA) (Kaplan 1988:157). A CIA agent, with diplomatic cover, was caught by Ethiopian security forces and gaoled for three years for liaising with the EPDA; only personal intervention by General Vernon Walters, Deputy Director of the CIA, secured his release. On another occasion, it is thought that Mossad found out where two captured CIA agents were being held and informed Washington. Yonas Deressa represented EPDA at a World Anti-Communist League conference in Dallas in 1985 (*Indian Ocean Newsletter* 1986:230). It seems EPDA lost their CIA subsidy in 1990 (*Africa Confidential* 1990:14). Some US funds may have found their way to new bodies like KITET, led by Kifle Wodajo, and Goshu Wolde's Ethiopian Movement for Democracy, Peace and Unity. The First National Bank of Maryland and Associated Trades Corporation of Balitimore (a CIA front) diverted 60,000 rifles from India to 'rebels' in the north of Ethiopia (*Indian Ocean Newsletter* 1989:367).

There was for a time a disinformation campaign on alleged CIA backing of the TPLF. Such support seems unlikely as the US President was advised in strong terms by the National Security Council adviser on the Horn (1977–78), Paul Henze, that it was comprised of Marxists with no hope of achieving power. Henze, later consultant to the Rand Corporation, was formerly CIA COS in Addis Ababa and Ankara.

The US continued to hope for an ideological turnaround by Mengistu. Its allies also continued to support Ethiopia; the British company, Plessey Communications installed a monitoring base for Ethiopian use on the North East Sahel coast (Dines 1988:161).

Although the Emperor – to maintain solidarity with his African and Arab brothers – had broken off diplomatic relations with Israel on 13 October, 1973, and the Derg had paid lip-service to this position, Israel's ostracism did not last long. Economic and trade links survived the October war and the Ethiopian revolution, and the new military regime invited the Israelis back in early 1975. The Israelis trained the *Nebalbal* ('Flame') battalion at Arba base in Ethiopia. It was involved in the Anseba river battle of 1976 when Ethiopia tried unsuccessfully to break the Eritrean People's Liberation Front (EPLF) siege of Nacfa (Pool 1982:42). Israelis had little impact on the fighting in Eritrea (Erlich 1983:75). They did, however, teach Ethiopians to operate Soviet tanks captured from the Somalian invasion force in 1977. Support from the Flame battalion was vital to Mengistu in his power struggle with General Teferi Bante, which led to Teferi's murder and Mengistu's bloody dictatorship.

The last Israeli parachute instructors left Ethiopia in 1976, but Israeli technicians continued to service jets supplied by the US and arms, including cluster bombs, were sent to the Derg at least until 6 February 1978. The Derg was then extremely embarrased by Israeli Foreign Minister Moshe Dayan's claim that, as Israel was arming the Derg, he was surprised at its fulminations at the 'racist, zionist state of Israel' (Halliday and Molyneux 1981:233). The Derg justified purchase of arms from Israel as 'a simple business deal made on a commercial basis' (*Ethiopian Herald* 10 February 1978).

After February 1978, Israeli military advisers were expelled and migration of Falashas to Israel was suspended. However, trade and Jewish-backed development programmes continued. Some forty per cent of Ethiopia's export/import shipping trade was handled by the Israeli company, ZIMA (*Eritrea in Struggle*:1977).

A key role in maintaining relations between Ethiopia and Israel was played by Kassa Kebede, educated in Israel, fluent in Hebrew, a former Ambassador – and at the same time, a 'notorious confidante' of Mengistu, a 'pathological liar' and a long serving Mossad agent (Dawit Wolde Giorgis 1989:321–2; 331). Kassa Kebede was by some accounts Mengistu's half-brother, by others, his uncle (Teshome Wagshaw 1992).

In 1982, Israel was still selling large quantities of military spare parts to Ethiopia and, moreover, had resumed arms supplies to Southern Sudanese rebels (*Africa Confidential* 1982:25). In 1985, Israel's arms sales to

Ethiopia were via Amsterdam through Amrian, a company based in Addis Ababa; it was thought that these were on a commercial basis but also on the understanding that Ethiopia would facilitate Falasha emigration (*The Australian*, 8 January 1985).

Israel and prominent Jews provided needed assistance to Ethiopia during the 1985 famine. Israeli teams, including reserve intelligence officers, built famine shelters. Ethiopian Foreign Minister Goshu Wolde, and the Director of the Relief and Rehabilitation Commission, Dawit Wolde Giorgis, held secret talks with David Kimche, Director of Israeli Foreign Affairs, a great believer in the peripheral strategy (and an intelligence operative) on the possibility of normalizing relations (Raviv and Melman 1990:330–1; Dawit Wolde Giorgis 1989).

Israeli military advisers were again observed in Ethiopia from late 1988 (Adulis 1989:January). Arms sales, including howitzers and cluster bombs, were resumed, as was military and security training. A battalion of surplus T-55 tanks and some Kfir planes were supplied, and Israelis began to establish a plant in Debre Zeit to manufacture Galilee rifles (*Africa Research Bulletin* 1990:9661).

There were still discreet intelligence links: secret arrangements under which Israel provided assistance to Ethiopia in sensitive areas (Curtis and Gitelson 1976:337; *Jerusalem Post* 11 April 1980). One such area was in informing the Derg of activities of the EPLF in its overseas missions; when the Israelis occupied West Beirut in July 1982 they seized EPLF documents which they turned over to the Derg. Along with most other countries and liberation movements, the EPLF supported the claims of the PLO to statehood.

Ironically when the leader of Eritrea's Provisional Government, Issayas Afeworki, was taken gravely ill in early 1993, it was Israeli doctors who cured him and the Israeli Foreign Minister, Shimon Peres, visited Issayas in hospital (FBIS 1992:January 13). It seems at last that Israel realized it could befriend both Ethiopia and Eritrea.

Domestic Intelligence Agencies

Under the Emperor, an elaborate security apparatus was established, consisting of several bodies who spied on each other as well as the Ethiopian population (Bereket Habte Selassie 1993; Kapuscinski 1983:7).

Under the Derg, Ethiopia expanded its intelligence agencies at an even faster rate than it expanded its armed forces. Its major security body was the Central Revolutionary Investigation Department (CRID) *Maekalawe Abyotaw Mirmera* of the Ministry of State and Public Security; its headquarters in Addis Ababa was conveniently near the University (*Africa Contemporary Record* 1979/1980:B.208).

Its Asmara centre was the Mariam Gimbi prison (Amnesty International 1987a:February). Arrests were carried out by a special squad called *Tewarwari Budin* (*Eritrea Information* 1980:1). Prisoners were held in the basement of the Emperor's palace in Asmara and in the Expo 1967 trade fair complex (Abeba Tesfagiorgis 1992:102–3; Dawit Wolde Giorgis 1989:100).

The Derg had its own security unit – *Liyu Mirmera* – in Addis Ababa situated close to the UN Economic Commission for Africa. Thousands of political prisoners were held in the Central prison – *Wehini Beit* – opposite the OAU Headquarters and in Sembel men's prison and Haz-Haz women's prison in Asmara. The Public Security Organization's Office for Internal Security – *Hizb Dehninet* (security 9) – also played a role when economic 'crimes' were investigated. *Dehninet* agents also attempted to exploit tensions within opposition movements (Adulis 1989:2–3).

The head of all external and internal security services was Colonel Moges, a man trained in Israel during the time of the Emperor (*Indian Ocean Newsletter* 1985:205). For many years, Brigadier. Getachew Shibeshi was head of Menigistu's palace security (*Africa Confidential* 1989:11).

The Role of the Soviet Bloc

Until 1979, Soviet Military Intelligence, *Glavnoye Razvedyvatelnoye Upravleniye* (GRU) played a larger intelligence role in Ethiopia than the *Komitet Gosudarstvenno i Bezopasnosti* (KGB); then the KGB sent an intelligence liaison officer to Addis Ababa, and Ethiopian intelligence officers were trained in Moscow (Andrew and Gordievsky 1990:558). The Soviet Ambassador, Rutinov doubled as KGB Resident in Addis Ababa (Amare Tekle:1991).

East Germans played an important role in security services until the Ethiopian military débâcle in Eritrea in 1983; then, according to one report, Israelis took over many of their functions (Albright 1983:66). East German engineers constructed a dry dock in Massawa which could accommodate Soviet cruisers (Valenta and Butler 1981:162). In 1988, fifty East German officers returned to Eritrea, set up an office in Asmara, and took over the Army communications network (*Adulis* 1989:1). Their stay was short; one of the first consequences of the disintegration of communist rule in East Germany was the hurried departure of State Security Service, *Staatssicherheitsdienst* (SSD) or 'Stasi' security men from Ethiopia (*Indian Ocean Newsletter* 1989:410).

The Soviets proved a little more durable, as Ethiopia was a useful ally. In 1984, the Soviet Military Attaché, Colonel Igor Alexendrovich Bardeev, a GRU operative expelled from Canada in 1978, visited the Dahlak Islands Soviet military base; the islands and the surrounding twenty-mile exclusion zone, were closed to most Ethiopian visitors (*Africa Confidential* 1984:25). From 1979 until 1983, the Soviet Union's Indian Ocean Squadron averaged about seventy visits a year to the floating dry dock at Dahlak; they were joined from 1983, by ships from the Soviet Mediterranean fleet (Whelan and Dixon 1986:207).

The Soviet agencies did not have a totally trouble-free ride in Ethiopia. In 1986, Ivan Pavlovski, First Secretary in charge of KGB operations, and another diplomat were expelled. Later in the year, a telex (no 417342) – supposedly from the KGB – surfaced, purportedly saying that Comrade Brutents' Department (International Department of the Central Committee of the Communist Party of the Soviet Union) planned to get rid of Mengistu and replace him by Legesse Afaw (*Indian Ocean Newsletter* 1984:123; 1986:228). The Soviets played a vital (if ultimately ineffective) role in the war against Eritrea. They dominated communications intelligence, supplying Ethiopia with satellite pictures of Eritrean troop concentrations and records of intercepted phone calls and battlefield traffic. The Eritreans proved even more adept at intelligence. Ethiopian troops could hardly move without this being conveyed to the EPLF by Eritreans and sympathizers in the highest ranks of the Ethiopian military, public service and security establishment. In 1989, the Eritreans captured three high ranking Soviet intelligence officers when they overran Ethiopia's main strategic base in Afabet.

After the Derg

In the tense atmosphere of May 1991, as the Ethiopian People's Revolutionary Democratic Front (EPRDF) moved in on Addis Ababa, Israel seized the chance to lift out as many Falashas as it could. With the connivance of the US and the EPRDF – possibly involving substantial retainers to Mengistu and President Mugabe of Zimbabwe, to ease the former's flight to his estate near Harare, the delaying of the start of the London conference, and through bribes to Ethiopian security – Israeli forces took virtual control of roads leading from the centre of Addis Ababa to the airport. Israel's Deputy Commander in Chief, Ammon Shahatt supervised the operation which involved over 500 Israeli troops. Along with the hundreds of Falashas flown to Israel, were Kassa Kebede and Einemo Almenech, Director of Mengistu's Secret Service (*Indian Ocean Newsletter* 1991:482, 482.)

Although some of the big security fish escaped before the new government could try them for their crimes, a surprising number of security police were captured by the EPRDF and EPLF. This was made easier by the fact that the Derg kept meticulous records of their networks, and had not shredded this damning evidence. Askalu Menkerios, Chair of the Eritrean Women's Association, told me in September 1991, how after her organization moved into offices vacated by the Ethiopian Women's Association in Asmara, they found detailed records of payments to some women for informing on their neighbours.

It is unlikely that the Transitional Government (the ERDF dominated body that has ruled Ethiopia since 1991) has managed to exist without a security service. However, little is known about its operations. There are few political prisoners, and a new atmosphere of calm and tolerance will help maintain this happy state of affairs. However, a surprising number of opponents of the EPRDF have recently met with violent and untimely deaths both in Ethiopia and abroad.

ERITREA

The only liberation movement active militarily inside Eritrea after 1982 was the EPLF. Until March 1987, security was the province of its Political Committee. Ali Said Abdella was Security Chief until August 1986, when he became Chairman of the Military Committee following the death of Ibrahim Afa, the former Chairman (*Indian Ocean Newsletter* 1987:277). After the EPLF Congress in 1987, Security and Intelligence became a separate administrative department (Leonard 1988:117). Petros Solomon was chief of security forces at that time (*Indian Ocean Newsletter*, 1991, 483.) There are some unsubstantiated allegations, by writers consistently hostile to Eritrean independence, of human rights violations by EPLF and ELF intelligence operatives (Erlich:1983).

After Eritrea's liberation in May 1991, the EPLF's immediate intelligence and security concerns lessened, and there now seems to be only a minimal oppressive security and intelligence surveillance in Eritrea. However, in May 1993, several hundred Eritrean and Ethiopian members of the Ethiopian Worker's Party were either undertaking forced community work or were in prison.

During the thirty-one year liberation struggle there were some defections from the Eritrean ranks. Teklai Gebre Mariam, an EPLF Central Committee member with security responsibilities went over to the Derg in 1980. There was considerable speculation whether Teklai acted as a double agent after his defection – this rumour is fictionalized in the novel *Oromay* (Baalu Girmay 1984). A former associate of the EPLF (alas I can only name him, 'Mr X', as he is still alive) was active as a CIA agent in the Emperor's time and left Ethiopia one day before a plane hijacking which ended in the death of all participants at the hands of forewarned Ethiopian security personnel.

Haile Wolde Selassie, who was in charge of the ELF central security department, also defected (*Ethiopian Herald* 6 October 1979; 24 December 1980). Another significant defection from the ELF was that of a senior field commander, Solomon Ghiorghis, who was later given a position by the Derg; he was gunned down in the streets of Addis Ababa by an unnamed assailant in 1992.

The Ethiopians ran disinformation campaigns about the Eritrean rebels; the main effect was to sustain morale among the Derg's dwindling band of supporters. Indeed, a 'morale boosting organization' (MOGED), was established for this purpose. Its only tangible success seems to have been the expulsion of two Libyan and two Sudanese diplomats from Addis Ababa during the Gulf War; in turn, two Ethiopians were expelled from Khartoum (*Indian Ocean Newsletter* 1991:472). This did not encourage Western powers to look more kindly on the disintegrating regime.

Often, rumors surfaced at conferences of intellectuals. A typical one was circulated at a conference on the Horn held in East Lansing, Michigan in April 1989, to the effect that there had been a revolt among the EPLF and a number of senior officers had been executed. Other untrue reports were circulated and grasped eagerly by some exiles. In August 1990, one report claimed that 30,000 EPLF troops had been killed in Asmara and that Ethiopia had reoccupied Massawa. A fictitious story was also put out that two Ethiopian Generals, Tilahun Kifle and Ali Hadji captured by the EPLF at Massawa in February 1990, had given up the port after being bribed (*Indian Ocean Newsletter* 1991:468.) Another story was spread that Issayas Afwarki, EPLF General Secretary was dying of cancer. Also in 1990, the Ethiopian Embassy in Stockholm circulated a forged statement endorsing Iraq's occupation of Kuwait, purportedly published by the EPLF's Washington Office (EPLF 1990:3 September).

After the fall of the Derg, the disinformation centre moved to the US. Many stories were manufactured to prevent Eritreans from holding their Sovereignty Referendum in April 1993. Unsubstantiated rumours about executions and the death of Issayas flowed freely from the pens of Amharan intellectuals. Electronic mail provided a preferred and speedy way of distributing propaganda.

It is unlikely that an independent Eritrean government will dismantle its security and intelligence apparatus. One can only hope that it will be possible for democratically elected legislative, executive and judiciary institutions to oversee the intelligence operations more effectively than in countries such as the US, the United Kingdom and Israel – to name three cases with which I am familiar.

SOMALIA

Although the US lost some credibility in the Arab world over its prolonged inabililty to dispose of Libyan leader Muammar Gadafi, policy successes were achieved elsewhere in North Africa. For example, in Somalia CIA funds were made available to a pro-Western party, the Somali Youth League, in the 1967 elections; this resulted in the election of their candidate for Premier, Mohammed Ibrahim Egal (Morris and Mauzy 1970:38). This successful covert operation laid the foundations for a continuing intelligence involvement in Somalia, an intervention it now seems will continue indefinitely.

A 1969 *coup* brought to power a group of radical army officers, 500 of whom had trained in the USSR under a 1962 defence pact signed in 1962 after the US – closely locked into a defence arrangement with Ethiopia, Somalia's foe – had refused to grant Somalia any weapons of more than domestic utility. Siad Barre (a former Special Branch Sergeant under the British) led the *coup* (Said Samatar 1990:92). It is claimed that the USSR pressed the deposed democratic government for early repayment of the mounting debts incurred by the Somalis; this destablized the parliamentary system, led to a perception that the system lacked legitimacy and laid the groundwork for the *coup*. Moreover, the USSR may have promised the *coup* makers full economic and military assistance should they seize control (Payton 1980:504). Ample evidence shows that the army and police under Siad Barre misused public office and funds and preempted any official enquiry (Ali K. Galaydh 1990:7). Rumours circulated recently by the anti-Barre leadership in Mogadishu that Barre was also in the pay of the KGB are less convincing.

Israel's brief period of influence in this almost completely Muslim country saw the Israeli construction company Histradut build the airport; this had only a limited intelligence payoff (Lodge 1962:49). France had some influence in Somalia, both through its presence in neighbouring Djibouti and via its membership of the Safari club, that played a key role in persuading Siad Barre to expel the Soviets in 1978 in exchange for arms (Faligot and Krop 1989:257).

For a while, after the Soviet ouster, the US developed Somalia as a regional base. According to the former US Chargé d'affaires in Mogadishu, in ten years the US spent $50m on Somalia; $17m was devoted to construction of a massive communications centre at the embassy, and much of the rest in retooling a Soviet-built radar complex (Rawson:1992).

The major intelligence institutions, the National Security Service (NSS) and the National Security Court (NSC) expanded greatly under President Siad Barre. In the 1970s the President's son-in-law, General Ahmed S. Abdulle was head of NSS (Africa Watch 1990:17). In 1971, Brigadier Mahmoud Ghelle Yusuf was appointed President of the NSC (which observed no right of appeal) (Amnesty International 1987:98). Under the 1970 National Security Law, 'subverting or weakening state authority' carried a mandatory death sentence. Mogadishu's NSS prison known as *Godka* (the Hole) was a particularly unsavoury place (*Africa News* 1988:6).

East Germans designed and constructed the major detention centres of Laanta Bur and Labaatan Jirow (Ali K. Galaydh 1990:13). In 1982, a mobile military court, *Maxkamada Wareegta*, was established to deal out summary justice to soldiers and civilians alike. Regional Security Councils, *Gudida Nabadgelyada Gobolka*, were set up, superior to all other security services, to determine sentences and to decide curfews etc. (Africa Watch 1990:44–6). In 1988, four men were executed for the murder of a NSS regional commander, Colonel Ahmed Aden Abdi (Amnesty International 1988:70).

In 1988, with clan wars reaching murderous levels in the north, twelve senior officers including the Regional Director of the NSS were removed for their personal safety (*Indian Ocean Newsletter* 1988:328). In 1989, Major General Mohamed Jibril was Commander of the NSS (*New African* 1989:November 12). East Germany trained the security service, whilst North Korea, with which Somalia opened diplomatic relations in 1972, also played a role (Kanet 1981:46). Military Intelligence, *Hayada Nabadgelyada Gaashaandhiga* (HANGASH) was created in 1978.

Another branch of the military police was known as *Dabar Jabinta* – the backbreakers. Other security bodies included: *Koofiyad-Casta*, the red berets; *Barista Hisbiga*, the security force of the ruling Somali Revolutionary Socialist Party (Africa Watch 1990:September 12). A large paramilitary force, *Gulwadayaal*, Victory Pioneers, modelled on Cuba's Defence of the Revolution Committees, operated (and terrorized) at the neighbourhood level under the President's direct supervision and was led by Abdirahman 'Gulwade', yet another son-in-law of the President (Africa Watch 1990:iii, 17; Arayeh Neier 1990:72).

There was a large and growing, if fragmented, opposition movement. Colonel Miskino – the Ethiopian coordinator of an important Somali exile group, the Somali Democratic Front for the Liberation of Somalia – was an intelligence agent (*Africa Confidential* 1985:23). Another rebel group, the Somali Salvation Democratic Front was neutralized through the actions of Ethiopian security, attempting to secure a peace accord with the Somali government (Compagnon 1990:36).

Siad Barre signed a secret agreement with South Africa which allowed civilian and military planes to refuel in Mogadishu on flights to the Persian Gulf (*Africa Contemporary Record* 1984/1985:A.125). Secret contacts began in 1979 via Winterfreight Ltd and Hassan Jahi Ahmed, a director of the firm in Johannesburg. Two South African defence teams visited Somalia in late 1982. General Samatar (Somalia's Defence Minister) visited South Africa on 16 May, 1984 and agreed to place a South African Military Adviser in NSS. In 1983, Abu Dhabi sold Somalia some Hawker Hunter fighter-bombers and South African pilots lent their experience of these aircraft to the Somalis (Greenfield 1989:32–5). A European mercenary, François de Villiers, acted as a go-between with South Africa arranging arms transfers; Somalia (along with the Comoros) was a vital link in the arms trade between the Middle East, South Africa and the Mozambique resistance group, MNR (*Indian Ocean Newsletter* 1984:159; 1985:180).

Somalia assisted West Germany in freeing hostages on a Lufthansa plane held at Mogadishu airport in October 1977. In return the Germans trained a special force for Barre, which was disbanded later (Ali K. Galaydh 1990:25). This vast security apparatus did not prevent Barre losing office in 1991. As Mogadishu collapsed into chaos in late 1990, the US mounted a successful intelligence mission. Scores of other foreign personnel poured into the US embassy compound and were lifted off by Marines and Navy SEALS (Gellman 1992: 7 January). Once all US personnel were in safety, there was no further reason for the US to help Siad, or anyone else, stay in power.

Ever since the Soviets were ousted in 1978, the US has devoted some attention to gathering security information in and around Somalia. So the US intelligence community was not unprepared when George Bush decided to intervene in Somalia following his election defeat in November 1992. Indeed, it appears that as early as August 1992, US intelligence operatives were preparing for 'Operation Restore Hope' (*Indian Ocean Newsletter* 1993:558).

The Defense Intelligence Agency (DIA) had some knowledge of the various factions' military capabilities and political prospects and unfortunately lost one of its most knowledgeable men as the first US casualty in the operation. But the crisis indicated several severe gaps in US knowledge of the region; for instance, only four Somali speakers could be found to accompany the intervention force. Few academics had more than a superficial and dated knowledge of Somali politics, history and culture.

But even augmented DIA expertise is not enough to deal with the enormous problems that will accompany the introduction of a large UN military contingent to pacify the country for the foreseeable future. There is no UN agency to coordinate the vast intelligence activity that will be needed in the years ahead if Somalia is ever to exist again as a unified and democratic country. Somalia will be a fruitful area for intelligence operations for years to come. It may be relevant that President Clinton's appointee as Assistant Secretary for Africa, George E. Moose, served time as an analyst in the African Affairs Bureau of the Intelligence and Research Service of the State Department, from 1974–1976 (*Indian Ocean Newsletter* 1993:559).

After the Somali National Movement consolidated its hold on what was once British Somaliland, they declared independence as the Republic of Somaliland in June 1991. Not only did no other country recognize them but most NGOs deserted them. The President, Abdurahmane Ahmed Ali 'Tur', was a former member of Somalia's intelligence service, NSS (Greenfield 1992:private communication).

SUDAN: ISRAEL, ANYA NYA AND IDI AMIN

Israel's interest in the non-Muslim Southern Sudan predates the Anya Nya I rebellion of 1965–1972. Sadiq el-Mahdi, later Prime Minister, and members of Umma and other nationalist parties who were apprehensive over the expansionist aims of Nasser's Egypt, met with Israelis and Britain's MI-6 in London in 1954 (Raviv and Melman 1990:84). A senior member of the National Party of the Sudan visited Israel secretly in 1955 (Derogy and Carmel 1979:164). In 1957, Israeli Foreign Minister, Golda Meir met with Abdallah Khalil, the Sudanese Prime Minister, in Paris. Contacts ended when Abdallah Khalil was overthrown in a *coup* in 1958 (Raviv and Melman 1990:84).

The US also took close interest in Nasser's southern neighbour, particularly after a communist was elected to Sudan's parliament. Another legacy of British trusteeship in Sudan was free trade union activity, and by 1958 the US was concerned over growing leftist influence in the 20,000 strong transportation and communications union (Lodge 1962:35). It may be no coincidence that one of the first acts of the newly independent Sudanese government was to outlaw trade union activity.

But although the Sudanese had shown that they were a compliant ally, the US was still not satisfied with their leadership. The CIA may have been involved in the military *coup* of 1958 (Agee 1975:82). The CIA's Africa Intelligence Division had been set up in 1958, so this was an early test of its ability (Africa Research Group 1970:24). The new Sudanese government by no means prevented the CIA from pursuing an activist policy in the region; in 1961 the CIA COS in Khartoum prevented a consignment of Soviet arms from being transhipped to Gizenga's rebel group in the Congo (Copeland 1974:275).

By 1963, however, Sudan's military regime had become less oriented towards the West and the Israelis listened sympathetically to advocates pleading the cause of the non-Muslim southerners (six million out of a total population of fifteen million). Approaches were made in a number of African capitals (Beshir 1975:91). Joseph Lagu, a southern officer, was trained in Israel in 1968 and returned to Sudan to spearhead the Anya Nya resistance. According to a World Council of Churches Report, he was the first of twenty-six rebels to be trained by Israel (Scherf 1971).

Above, I described joint Israeli/Ethiopian training of Anya Nya recruits. There was also an Israel military advisory and training team at Torit close to the Ugandan border. Israel made parachute drops of Soviet equipment to rebels stationed at Owing-ki-bu (Eprile 1974:140). Israel also furnished advisers to the separate southern rebel group of Colonel Abu John (*Africa Contemporary Record* 1970/1971:B.48).

In 1968, Idi Amin, head of the Ugandan army, visited Anya Nya units in Sudan accompanied by Israeli officers and Colonel Lagu. However, even though Israel had helped Amin assume power in a miltary *coup* in 1971, diplomatic links were broken by Uganda in April 1972. By then the border issue with Sudan had been settled.

Israeli arms supplies to the rebels were funded by the CIA and channelled from an Israeli air base in Uganda only eight miles from the Sudanese border (O'Ballance 1977:26–8). Israel's Ambassador in Kamapla, Uri Lubrani, was in charge of the operation (Beit-Hallahmi 1987:48). Reportedly, American Peace Corps officials supported Anya Nya activities. From 1970 to 1971 there were twelve CIA agents in the country providing supplies and training to Anya Nya (*Africa Contemporary Record* 1977/1978:A.77–8).

Rolf Steiner, a mercenary employed by a small splinter group of the southern rebels, also revealed that Lagu spent eight months in Tel Aviv in

1967; following his visit, groups of four Israeli advisers would come into southern Sudan from Kampala and spend from five to six weeks at a time with Anya Nya troops (Steiner 1976:203). The Soviets were also busy; an agent called Andrei blackmailed an archivist at the British embassy to hand over the cypher key and a number of documents (Dobson and Payne 1986:143).

However, the Sudanese military government, badly shaken by an unsuccessful communist *coup* in 1971, opened peace talks with the southerners; these talks resulted in the 1972 Addis Ababa agreement, a cease-fire, 'autonomy' of the South and incorporation of rebel leaders into provincial and national governments. Israel's support, never openly acknowledged, became an embarrassment to the southerners and Israeli overt influence ceased (*Grass Curtain* 1970–72:inter alia). However, such is the resilience of the Israelis, that from 1972, Mossad merely transferred its operations to Khartoum and developed close relations with President Jaafar al-Nimeri and the Sudanese Security Organization, with the CIA's blessing.

Israeli involvement in Muslim Sudan lapsed after a *coup* against Nimeri on 6 April 1985; they revived their commitment to the South following reemergence of the Southern movement and Sudan's realignment towards Libya and against the US (Beit-Hallahmi 1987: 48–9). Nimeri had reneged on the 1972 Addis agreement by dividing the South into three provinces. He became a born-again Muslim fundamentalist, and attempted to introduce *Sharia* into the non-Muslim South. Many Southern troops deserted to form the Sudan People's Liberation Army (SPLA) which soon occupied much of the South. The SPLA leader, Colonel Garang received weapons from Israel – concerned over Nimeri's increasing reliance on the Muslim Brothers and his overtures to Gadafi. After Israel reestablished diplomatic relations with Kenya in late 1988, arms deliveries to Garang via northern Kenya became more important (*Indian Ocean Newsletter* 1989:390). In 1989, Israel supplied the SPLA with heavy artillery and technical advisers (*Indian Ocean Newsletter* 1989:398).

Nimeri received considerable CIA support and had a lucrative alliance with Youssef Magarieff, leader of the Libyan opposition, which then came under direct control of the Sudanese Security Organization (SSO) – *Al Amen al Goumi* (Woodward 1987a:339–40). Nimeri also met the Head of Rhodesia's Central Intelligence Organization (Flower 1987:206). To reinforce the view that he was prepared to sup with the Devil, he also met with South Africa's Bureau of State Security chief, Van den Bergh in 1976, to discuss payment by South African Airways for overflying rights (Rhoodie 1983:148).

Nimeri managed to alienate his backers, the major ones being Egypt, Saudi Arabia, the IMF and the US. He was particularly inept in economic matters; squandering much on large-scale but unworkable projects. When he attempted to increase prices of basic foodstuffs, civilian opposition reached levels not seen in Khartoum for twenty years. While visiting President Reagan in 1985, Nimeri was replaced by a military junta.

During Nimeri's rule, numerous political prisoners were held in Dabak detention centre near Khartoum; most were released after the April 1985 *coup* (Amnesty International:1982). In 1986, State Security Courts were abolished along with the State Security Act, which allowed for detention without trial for indefinitely renewable three month terms. (Amnesty International 1987:106).

The new regime was considerably more open than Nimeri's. One of its revelations was the involvement of Nimeri's government in the airlift of Ethiopian Jews from Sudan to Israel. The first mass operation took place as early as February 1982, facilitated by the appointment of a special CIA coordinator in Khartoum (Ahmed Karadawi 1991:41.) Jewish agencies donated $2 million to assist their co-religionists during the 1984–1985 famine. As noted, thousands of Falashas were assisted to escape to Sudan. They were then transported to Israel in 'Operations Moses and Sheba', supervised by the US embassy in Khartoum. Vice-President Bush made the arrangements with Nimeri on his 1985 visit to Sudan (Indian Ocean Newsletter 1985:175). In addition to an airlift, Israeli frogmen also facilitated removal of Falashas by sea from a resort run by a dummy corporation, Navco, on the coast near Port Sudan (Raviv and Melman 1990:240; personal observations). The CIA paid Nimeri and Vice-President Omar Mohamad el-Tayeb, head of SSO, $2m to ensure support for the operation (*Africa News* 1986:xxvii, 21).

Under Nimeri, the main security body was the SSO. Its budget was as large as the Army's; at the height of its power, it possessed 6000 vehicles and 400 safe houses (Kaplan 1988:133). It was disbanded after the 1985 revolution. One of its main functions was to counter Libya's activities; after all, Libya trained those who attempted to overthrow Nimeri in 1977 (*Africa Contemporary Record* 1976/1977:B.107). One of the first acts of the new military junta of General Bashir, which seized power from the civilian regime in July 1989, was to reinstate the SSO as a 'revolutionary' security service, and enourage it, under the leadership of Lt. Colonel Bakri Hassan Salih, to arrest and torture security suspects (*Indian Ocean Newsletter* 1989:391; 1990:428). Nafei Ali Nafei was the number two man (*Africa Confidential* 1992:15.)

Styling themselves 'the human rights association', Islamic security forces established their base in the club of the former Sudanese Bar Association (*Africa Research Bulletin* 1990:9635). Many assume that the army seized power as it feared the government would conclude a cease-fire with the SPLA, diminishing the power of northern officers. Bashir's junta was rent with conflict between those, like Bashir, who were determined to introduce both Islamic rule and military dictatorship, and others who wanted secular military rule.

During the 1990 Gulf crisis Sudan sided with Iraq, incurring the displeasure of the Saudis, who withdrew their considerable deposits in Sudanese banks, thus plunging the country into a severe economic depression. The SPLA announced support for Saudi Arabia and pledged 500 troops to the UN forces (*Indian Ocean Newsletter* 1990:447). There is considerable concern in neighbouring countries that Sudanese fundamentalists, with Iranian support, may attempt to subvert their governments. Intelligence services in Ethiopia, Eritrea, Uganda, Kenya and Egypt, are devoting efforts to counter this threat.

As usual with authoritarian regimes, both the number and power of security services in Sudan have increased. A General Security Service, successor to SSO, is led by Assem Kiachi. The National Islamic Front (NIF) has its own security service and is led by Nafeh Osman Nafeh, Governor of Darfur province, and the person in charge of cooperation with Iranian military and intelligence training squads (*Pasdarans*) in the region. General Al Zubeir Mohamed Salah oversees military intelligence, while Mohammed Ahmed Al-fateh Orawa, the junta's second most powerful man, is in charge of a Special Security Service. Its function is to spy on all other services (*Indian Ocean Newsletter* 1992:553, 555). As long as the military and NIF rule Sudan the prospects for improvement in human rights seem extremely remote.

References

North-east Africans are listed under their first names.

Abeba Tesfagiorgis, 1992. *A Painful Season and a Stubborn Hope* (Trenton, NJ: Red Sea Press).

Adulis, 1989. VI, 1, January; February–March.

Africa Confidential, 1982: 25; 1984:24; 1985:23; 1987:7; 1989:11; 1990:14; 1992:15.

Africa Contemporary Record, 1970/1971. C. Legum and Rex Collings (eds). London, p. B.48; 1976/1977: p. B.10; p. B.536; 1977/1978: pp. A.77–8; 1979/1980: p. B.208; 1982/1983: p. B.166; 1984/1985: p. A.125.

Africa News, 1980. xv(6); 1986. xxvii(21); 1988: 29, 6.

Africa Research Bulletin: Political Series, 1990. p. 9635; p. 9661.

Africa Research Group, 1970. *Africa Report* (Cambridge, MA).

Africa Watch, 1990. *Somalia: a Government at War with its own People* (New York) p. iii; p. 17.

Africa Watch, *News from Somalia*, 12 September.

Agee, Philip, 1975. *Inside the Company: CIA Diary* (New York: Stonehill).

Ahmed Karadawi, 1991. 'The Smuggling of the Ethiopian Falasha to Israel through Sudan', *African Affairs*, 90(358):23–49.

Albright, David E., 1983. *The USSR and Sub-Saharan Africa in the 1980s* (New York: Praeger).

Ali K. Galaydh, 1990. 'Notes on the State of the Somali State', *Horn of Africa*, XII(1&2):1–28.

Amdemichael Kahsai, 1977. 'Interview', *MERIP Reports*, 62:19–23.

Amnesty International, 1982. *Report* (London).

Amnesty International, 1984. *Torture in the Eighties* (Oxford: Martin Robertson).

Amnesty International, 1987. *Report 1987* (London: Amnesty International Publications).

Amnesty International, 1987a. *File on Torture*. Ethiopia (February).

Amnesty International, 1988. *Report 1988* (London: Amnesty International Publications).

Andrew, Christopher and Oleg Gordievsky, 1990. *KGB: the Inside Story of its Foreign Operations from Lenin to Gorbachev* (New York: Harper-Collins).

Arayeh Neier, 1990. 'Somalia: Human Rights and the Law', *Horn of Africa*, XII (1 & 2):69–77.

The Australian, 1985. 8 January.

Baalu Girmay, 1984. *Oromay*, Addis Ababa (in Amharic).

Beit-Hallahmi, Benjamin, 1987. *The Israeli Connection: Who Israel Arms and Why* (New York: Pantheon).

Bereket Habte Selassie, 1993. *Riding the Whirlwind* (Trenton, NJ: Red Sea Press).

Beshir Mohamed Omer, 1975. *The Southern Sudan: from Conflict to Peace* (New York: Barnes & Noble).

Compagnon, Daniel, 1990. 'The Somali Opposition Fronts', *Horn of Africa*, XII(1 & 2):29–54.

Copeland, Miles, 1974. *Without Cloak or Dagger: the Truth about the New Espionage* (New York: Simon & Schuster).

Curtis, M. and S. A. Gitelson (eds), 1976. *Israel in the Third World* (New Jersey: Transaction Books).

Dawit Wolde Giorgis, 1989. *Red Tears* (Trenton NJ: Red Sea Press).

Derogy, Jacques and H. Carmel, 1979. *The Untold History of Israel* (New York: Grove Press).

Dines, Mary, 1988. 'Ethiopian Violations of Human Rights in Eritrea', B. Davidson and L. Cliffe (eds), *The Long Struggle of Eritrea for Independence and Constructive Peace* (Nottingham: Spokesman) pp. 139–61.

Dobson, Christopher and Ronald Payne, 1986. *The Dictionary of Espionage* (London: Grafton Books).

Eprile, Cecil, 1974. *War and Peace in the Sudan 1955–1972* (Newton Abbot: David & Charles).

Eritrea Information (1980) 1.

Eritrea in Struggle (1977) 11, 3 December.

Eritrean People's Liberation Front (1990) *Press Release*, 3 September.

Eritrean Review 1973: 2, 15 July; 1975: 21.

Eritrean Revolution (1977) 2,3, October–November.

Erlich, Haggai, 1983. *The Struggle over Eritrea 1962–1978* (Stanford: Hoover Institution Press).

Ethiopian Herald 1974: 17 October; 1978: 10 February; 1979: 6 October; 1980: 24 December.

Faligot, Roger and Pascal Krop, 1989. *La Piscine: the French Secret Service since 1944* (trans.W. D. Halls) (Oxford: Basil Blackwell).

Flower, Ken, 1987. *Serving Secretly An Intelligence Chief on Record Rhodesia into Zimbabwe 1964 to 1981* (London: John Murray).

Foreign Broadcasting Information Service, 1992. 'Israel', 13 January.

Gellman, Barton, 1992. 'Daring US Rescue from Mogadishu Got Little Notice', *Guardian Weekly*, 7 January.

Grass Curtain (1970– 72) *inter alia*.

Greenfield, Richard, 1989. 'Somalia/South Africa', *Africa Events*, 5 April, 4, pp. 32–5.

Halliday, Fred and Maxine Molyneux, 1981. *The Ethiopian Revolution*, (London: Verso).

Indian Ocean Newsletter 1984: 123, 159; 1985: 175, 180, 205; 1986: 228, 230, 259; 1987: 277; 1988: 328; 1989: 367, 390, 391, 394, 398, 410; 1990: 428; 447, 448; 1991: 464, 468, 472, 481, 482, 483, 493; 1992: 541, 544, 553, 555; 1993: 558. 559

Jacob, Abel, 1971. 'Israel's Military Aid to Africa', *Journal of Modern African Studies*, 9(2):165–87.

Jerusalem Post, 1980. 11 April.

Kanet, Roger E., 1981. 'East European States', T. H. Henriksen (ed.), *Communist Powers and Sub-Saharan Africa* (Stanford: Hoover Institution). pp. 23–56.

Kaplan, Robert D., 1988. *Surrender or Starve: the Wars behind the Famine* (Boulder: Westview).

Kapuscinski, Ryszard, 1983. *The Emperor* (trans. W. R. Brand and K. Mroczkowska-Brand) (New York: Vintage Books).

Lauffer, Leopold, 1967. *Israel and the Developing Countries: New Approaches to Cooperation* (New York: The Twentieth Century Fund).

Leonard, Richard, 1988. 'Popular Participation in Liberation and Revolution', B. Davidson and L. Cliffe (eds),*The Long Struggle of Eritrea for Independence and Constructive Peace*, (Nottingham: Spokesman). pp.105–35.

Lobban, Richard, 1972. *Eritrean Liberation Front: A Close-Up View* (Munger Africana Library Notes) 13.

Lodge, George C., 1962. *Spearheads of Democracy: Labor in the Developing Countries* (New York: Harper & Row).

Marcus, Harold D., 1983. *Ethiopia, Great Britain and the USA 1941–74* (Berkeley: University of California Press).

Morris, Roger and Richard Mauzy, 1970. 'Following the Scenario: Reflections on Five Case Histories in the Mode and Aftermath of CIA Intervention', R. L. Borosage and J. Marks (eds), *The CIA File* (New York: Grosman) pp. 28–45.

New African 1989: 12 November.

O'Ballance, Edgar, 1977. *The Secret War in the Sudan, 1955–1962* (London: Faber & Faber).

Payton, Gary D., 1980. 'The Somali Coup of 1969: the Case for Soviet Complicity', *Journal of Modern African Studies*, 18(3):493–508.

Pool, David, 1982. *Eritrea: Africa's Longest War* (London: Anti-Slavery Society).

Powers, Thomas, 1980. *The Man who Kept the Secrets: Richard Helms and the CIA* (London: Weidenfeld & Nicolson).

Quarrie, Bruce, 1986. *The World's Secret Police* (London: Octopus).

Rapoport, Louis, 1980. *The Lost Jews: Last of the Ethiopian Falashas* (New York: Stein and Day).

Raviv, Dan and Yossi Melman, 1990. *Every Spy a Prince: the Complete History of Israel's Intelligence Community* (Boston: Houghton Mifflin).

Rawson, David 1992. 'Dealing with Disintegration: Donors and the Somali State, 1980–1990', Sixth Northeast African Studies Conference, Holiday Inn, East Lansing, MI, 25 April.

Rhoodie, Eschel M., 1983. *The Real Information Scandal* (Pretoria: Orbis).

Said S. Samatar, 1990. 'An Open Letter to Somalist Scholars', *Horn of Africa*, xii(1 & 2):88–95.

Scherf, 1971. *Report on Sudan* (World Council of Churches).

Sherman, Richard, 1980. *Eritrea: the Unfinished Revolution* (New York: Praeger).

Silverberg, Sanford, 1968. 'Israeli Military and Paramilitary Assistance to Sub-Saharan Africa: a Harbinger for the Role of the Military in Developing States', unpublished Masters Thesis. American University, Washington, DC.

Spencer, John H., 1984. *Ethiopia at Bay: a Personal Account of the Haile Sellassie Years* (Algonac, MI: Reference Publications).

Steiner, Rolf, 1976. *The Last Adventurer* (Boston: Little, Brown).

Teshome Wagaw, 1992. 'The Love-Hate Relations of Ethiopia, Israel and the United States during the Mengistu Era', Sixth Northeast African Studies Conference, Holiday Inn, East Lansing, MI, 25 April

Valenta, Jiri and Shannon Butler, 1981. 'East German Security Policies in Africa', *Eastern Europe and the Third World: East vs. South*. M. Radu (ed.) (New York: Praeger) pp. 142–68.

Vanguard, 1976. 1,13, January, New York.

Whelan, Joseph G. and Michael J. Dixon, 1986. *The Soviet Union in the Third World: Threat to World Peace?* (Washington, DC: Pergamon-Brassey's).

Wolpin, Miles D., 1972. *Military Aid and Counterrevolution in the Third World* (Lexington, MA: D.C. Heath).

Woodward, Bob, 1987. *Veil: the Secret Wars of the CIA* (New York: Simon & Schuster).

4 Carrying Each Other's Burden: Political Challenge in the Horn of Africa

Tseggai Isaac

The Horn has endured recurrent hardships in the last half century. Ethiopia, Eritrea, Somalia and Sudan have suffered combined effects of domestic neglect and natural calamities. Devastated by war, famine, and pestilence, each is extremely vulnerable and faces an uncertain future. By all measures of the development scale, they are at the bottom.[1] The post-colonial decades have been squandered on conflicts, because disagreements that could have been solved by reason and mutual understanding were allowed to grow into emotional hostilities, irrational policies, and destructive wars. The landscape is strewn with the corpses of humans and animals and the wreckage of war machines. Scars of war are visible in the unprecedented level of handicapped and disabled citizens languishing in overcrowded towns and desolate villages, deprived of minimum rehabilitation facilities. Why did regimes in the region fail to resolve national crises before they became catastrophes? Why did institutions established after decolonization fail? Are civil wars the only vehicle for achieving national unity and building civil societies? Why did international and regional political organizations refuse or hesitate to offer assistance, or engage constructively to preempt or contain conflicts?

These questions require sustained analysis of causes of regional turmoil. Here I analyse colonial and post-colonial political legacies that are determinants of the current crisis. First, general political challenges are outlined, followed by analysis of colonial and traditional foundations of the state, using two designations to explain patterns of government: the constitutional state and the garrison state. Prospects of regional and domestic peace depend on how new post-garrison regimes follow their stated objectives of peace and prosperity through cooperation.

THE CHALLENGE AND THE BURDEN

Sudan has embarked on a path of self-destruction mainly due to the ruling regime's emphasis on religious commitment rather than welfare of the population. The realization that governments ought to govern by observing a balance between individual choices, accountable authority, community and group norms, has escaped the regime. Political agendas are cast as complements to religious convictions, devotion and demonstration of puritanical living. In its ideological rigidity, the regime overlooks forces that may rend it apart. It believes it can solve the southern problem by depopulation and forced conversion. Such an undertaking will require enormous political, economic and military investment.

In post-independence Somalia, political issues amenable to bargaining, consensus and conciliation degenerated into tests of wills among groups and clans. Politics of disorder triggered the 1969 military *coup*; when he assumed power, Siad Barre invoked 'scientific socialism' but at every major policy decision, his government committed errors of judgement, transgressing political rights of the Somali people. These manipulative politics climaxed in utter chaos and complete destruction of Somali institutions. The well-being of Somalia and its people were sacrificed to create an authoritarian cult figure around whom swarmed congeries of profligate elites who drained the country's resources and the Somali people of their human dignity.

The level of prostration to which Somalia fell under its own elites was so low that it required the US to orchestrate a global response to attempt to reverse the scourge of famine. In addition to help from humanitarian organizations, *mainly from the West*, the international community responded. Pakistanis, Americans, Nigerians, Canadians, Italians and others did what Somali elites were neither able nor willing to do for their people and undertook mercy missions in the midst of resistance and thuggery from those who saw themselves benefiting from further destruction of the country.

Ethiopia, too, had its share of catastrophes. The regime which replaced Emperor Haile Selassie became one of the continent's most abusive. The Derg justified its 1974 *coup* by pointing out that the Emperor allowed thousands to starve as his regime squandered resources. Yet, a worse famine claiming more lives took place under the Derg. It waged war against Ethiopians of all backgrounds and its methods of ruling became intolerant, irrational and barbaric. In the process not only did Ethiopia lose most of its educated and talented citizens, but its policies on Eritrea and the north compromised the goodwill that prevailed in the pre-Derg years.[2] Possibilities now exist for regional peace and good relations. Yet, the destruction of material and human resources wrought by the Derg will tax whatever goodwill and dedication to progress Eritreans and Ethiopians may exhibit.

INTERNATIONAL PRETEXTS

The post-Second World War international order encouraged conflict and instability among nations. Two philosophies that shaped the post-war environment were the revitalization of the nation-state and the doctrine of realism in global affairs. The nation-state was viewed as an entity to be accorded limitless independence. Yet, despite its autonomy, it was expected to observe certain norms, including adoption of a constitution to define the role, rights and responsibilities of citizens to organize and direct the state. Another expectation was the state's ability to protect its territory and borders. A third crucial international norm was the self-discipline the territorial state was expected to show by disavowing involvement in internal affairs of other states.

Nation-states operate under doctrines of realism, a pessimistic world view in which states envision their environment as filled with hostile other states. To ensure security the state must be prepared for violent eventualities, as when other states attack its sovereignty. The world of realist politics is one of suspicion, secrecy, and paranoia on the part of statesmen and diplomats. The politics of the Horn fell into the trap of global realism as regional regimes worsened local tensions by involving themselves in the worst manifestations of realist politics within the East–West conflict.[3] The type of regime that assumes state authority determines the type of policies and the prospects for success in introducing changes. In the Horn two generalized types of states are significant: the constitutional state and the garrison state.[4]

CONSTITUTIONAL STATES

The term constitutional state refers to the original intentions of post-colonial regimes and brief efforts at democratization when the regimes genuinely attempted to forge constitutional governments. As regimes appear in the political arena, it is expected that they are motivated to introduce positive changes to improve the lives of citizens. At first they come in humility, with 'nation-regarding' spirit and zeal. However, angry groups who come to power condemning incumbent regimes and vowing to bring about fast changes often find themselves embattled by their own follies, blunders and unwillingness to correct errors.[5] At the stage where regimes are conciliatory, responsive, inclusive, and willing to subject themselves to constitutional accountability, they are constitutional regimes. The constitutional regime has two characteristics identifying it as one struggling to achieve genuine democratization. They are capacity enhancement and authority.

A regime's capacity is enhanced when it creates a conducive political climate for citizen–state interaction. As it attempts to make its writs accepted and observed, it adheres to democratic principles and practices to promote common welfare and resolve national problems. At the national level, multiparty elections, universal suffrage, organized participation, separation of powers, gestures of instituting credibility and efficiency in the public service are attempted. At the institutional level it becomes essential for regimes to possess enabling constitutions to structure, regulate and monitor choices of citizens and organized groups.

Capacity enhancement relates to organization of government, explicating institutional functions and allocation of authority. The constitution is a description of political power and spatial relations among centres of power. It delineates the rules by which political power is constitutionally allocated, keeping in mind needs for order, stability, freedom and equality. Ideally, it should clearly describe roles and functions of component parts of the state. It is a general affirmation declaring the state as the ultimate repository of power wholly autonomous from manipulation and contrivances of other elements in society.

Exercise of political power is the clearest indicator of state autonomy. Vigorous states are those which gauge the scope of their power and exercise it constructively. Political power is an abstract resource reserved for the populous state – the state which considers itself a proxy of the citizens from whom it derives constitutional authority. Undue influence by organized groups at the expense of individual citizens creates dysfunctional trends and threatens the state's viability. States and constitutions atrophy when their power and autonomy are undermined. Strong states acquire strength by deepening their roots in the thinking of elites and citizens.[6]

A prevailing expectation regarding the constitutional state is that it will ensure universal equality, protect citizens' liberties and maintain community order. The ultimate goal of the constitutional state is genuine democratization. However, soon it becomes obvious that democratic undertakings do not lend themselves to expediency, because time is essential in developing capable institutions. States succeed or fail in trying to balance between capacity building and wielding power. In the Horn, constitutional democratization was preempted by failure to maintain that balance. Dictatorial regimes crushed constitutional states and replaced them with garrison states.

Regimes in the Horn came to power to preside over the constitutional state but all exercised power as though it were the personal prerogative of elite groups. Domestic issues lending themselves to constitutional arbitration escalated into power struggles and the spirit of constitutional government was abandoned. Intense global competition within the realist framework involving the US and the Soviet Union encouraged this. Horn regimes linked themselves to that conflict, because it nurtured extra-constitutional wielding of state power.

In the past thirty years, the Horn countries were heavily burdened with security needs. To enhance their power, they relied on militarization, seeking weapons to carry out extra-constitutional means to control resistance. Seeking to advance their own interests, the superpowers found ready recruits from the contestants and armed them, allowing them to suppress constitutional political culture. Arms expenditures far outweighed their domestic obligations. Such skewed policy priorities resulted from a failure to observe the writs of the constitutional state. At a time when constitutional states needed to consolidate legitimacy by exercising their mandates within the framework of a constitutional government, global interests of the two superpowers intruded in the Horn. The constitutional state was thus converted into an embattled garrison state ready and willing to serve as an obliging superpower client.

GARRISON REGIMES

The garrison regime is one determined to resolve domestic political objectives by military means. It is anti-constitutional in its exercise of power, myopic and rigidly predisposed to military buildup. Several reasons exist for the garrison regime's shortsightedness in handling domestic and regional challenges.

First, it is intolerant of domestic opposition and suppresses dissenting views violently. Such impulsive reaction to domestic crisis and discord is based on a belief that eliminating them violently clears the landscape of confrontational politics. Garrison regimes forget that politics at every level involves conflicts that must be resolved by honest governmental attitudes. Aversion to constitutional precepts is rationalized by assertions that the regime is the only one capable of providing a peaceful society and stable government. Garrison regimes perpetrate conflicts because their unwillingness to allow any form of participation opens the door for growing resistance and violence.

Secondly, national interests are prioritized by military considerations. Dogmatism forces garrison regimes to concentrate power in the hands of military minded elites. Maximum centralization of power does not allow conflicting views to be considered in policy decisions. The 'military mind' develops a culture with a view of military solutions even to national affairs amenable to non-military approaches.[7] No effort is made to include alternatives and opinions from outside the circle on which the regime depends for support. The constitutional state is viewed as inexpedient. Negotiating, bargaining, and heeding majority opinions are unacceptable to the garrison regime.[8]

Although the garrison regime depends on force and centralized power, it often needs the support of other groups to implement its policies. It is sustained by support from external and internal sources. External support comes from states willing to accept it as a client. Garrison regimes are meek and compliant in dealing with superior states.[9] They are clever at self-promotion and at manipulating the international environment, using world fora to present themselves as embattled by ideological adversaries. Relying on the doctrine of noninterference in domestic affairs, they can appear to be legitimate and to have uncontested authority.

Cold War tensions provided an opportune setting for proliferation of client garrison states. In Latin America, Asia and Africa dictatorial regimes with little regard for constitutional law ruled arbitrarily. As the superpowers manoeuvred against each other, they recruited client garrison regimes to serve as sentinels in return for military support.

Diplomatically, garrison states were sustained at the world forum and defended in abuses against their domestic adversaries. Their voice at the UN General Assembly was traded for such support. Such issues as regional intervention, disarmament, foreign aid, and even international sports became diplomatic commodities and were used to cement client–patron relationships.[10] The end of the Cold War proved that garrison states were expendable; they were abandoned to deal with domestic unrest without the military and diplomatic support they had relied upon to perpetuate their violent rule.

As its violent tendencies spark further violence from opponents who have given up hope of democratic resolutions of their grievances, the garrison regime is confronted with the burden of justifying its effectiveness. Often, garrison regimes are found to be less than competent in their performance. One scholar describing African regimes stated: 'The African state is weak by any conventional measure of institutional capacity; yet it remains the most prominent landmark on the African institutional landscape'.[11] Its 'prominent' status, however, is based on the 'international legitimacy' that many garrison regimes were able to secure in the postcolonial decades.

CHARACTERISTICS OF POST-COLONIAL STATES

Efforts to explain Third World retardation by colonial experience have been revived recently to highlight the value of indigenous political systems.[12] Whereas conventional scholarship noted the economic devastation caused by colonialism, the new outlook focuses on distribution of political power and the extent to which indigenous power was used to nurture community well-being.[13] Following is a brief outline of the indigenous political culture that contributed to formation of post-colonial states in the Horn.

Countries in the Horn declared independence by pledging to allow their citizens to construct the tools by which they wanted to be governed. Regimes in Ethiopia, Sudan and Somalia saw they could not rule legitimately unless they presented their respective peoples with constitutions. There are ample indications that they were willing to submit themselves to provisions of constitutions they created.[14] However, the regimes which replaced them subverted these constitutions. Constitutional states degenerated into garrison regimes unable to govern but sufficiently armed to inflict widespread destruction.

Ethiopia exemplifies an indigenous political system that could have provided a foundation for modern democracy. Sudan and Somalia had similar backgrounds. However, their colonial experience retarded and compromised the effectiveness of their respective political cultures. Their political culture also rendered the state vulnerable to dictates of the Quran. The standard of political effectiveness defined by the Quran, exacting scriptural formulas for individual and community conduct, renders the state rigid, ineffective, ideological and unrealistic in that it seeks heavenly laws for earthly governance.

EMERGENCE OF THE CONSTITUTIONAL STATE

Constitutional states in Ethiopia, Sudan, Somalia and Eritrea appeared after World War II. In Ethiopia the state was overshadowed by Emperor Haile Selassie's massive ego; in Sudan and Somalia, political groups and parties weakened the states' effectiveness.

ETHIOPIA

Ethiopia prided itself as a continuously-organized nation-state until its claims were challenged by the combined assault of regional and colonial adversaries. Although most scholars depict Ethiopia as a traditional feudal state, its administrative structures and legal codes testify to a nation that had institutions committed to governance by the consent of the masses.

Ethiopia, as a monarchy, had prospects of developing institutions similar to those of England, Japan or Spain. However, as it was in the process of modernizing its institutions and consolidating state power, European colonization and Islamic zeal thwarted its efforts. The stand of Ethiopians in confronting foreign aggression and the religious and political system forged in the process created a highly developed sense of political culture.[15]

Haile Selassie's determination to modernize Ethiopia created pressures for further institutional change. The state emerged in its modern constitutional form with the 1931 constitution. The aim was to consolidate state power while establishing a pseudo-republican form of government under the strict watch of the throne.[16] Haile Selassie wanted to modernize government institutions and the educational sector. He did so by resorting to drastic centralization of provincial authority, considering absolute power necessary for modernization. Subsequent actions reflected his determination to further expand modernization under a relaxed constitution promulgated in 1955.[17]

Another motive for revising the constitution was Haile Selassie's plan to annex Eritrea. To do so, he required help from Eritrean elites. To ease their fears of despotism, he issued a national constitution as progressive as that of Eritrea. Even though he nurtured modernization and constitutional government, his status as supreme ruler was reconfirmed by the 1955 constitution.

The new constitution also reflected the Emperor's determination to continue modernization by gradually relaxing authority and transferring it to the Cabinet. This was an important step toward creating modern government. A bicameral legislative body was created with limited legislative mandates. The upper house constituted of appointed dignitaries attached to the various regions which had competed for authority ever since the *Zemene Mesafint* (Era of the Princes/Judges) in the eighteenth century. Although Haile Selassie was authoritarian, he may have envisioned a 'constitutional monarchy' rooted in Ethiopian values.[18]

The 1955 constitutional revision came at an opportune time for Ethiopia and Eritrea. It provided opportunities for seeking democratic avenues for uniting the two countries. Most elements of Eritrean society were amenable to unity. Democratic practices which flourished in Eritrea from the 1950s offered opportunities for expanding such practices in Ethiopia. Furthermore, Eritrean skill and experience gained from exposure to Italian

and British colonialism were valuable resources for vigorous modernization in all regions. The regime's discrimination and shortsightedness, its
refusal to see Ethiopia as including non-Amhara peoples, and Haile
Selassie's refusal to relax despotic rule undermined his objectives and his
power.

The state was upstaged by the Emperor's absolute powers in all areas.
Haile Selassie retained all political authority, rendering subordinates weak
and fearful of making significant decisions. For instance, while his modernization programmes were effective, producing an educated class and,
with US aid, consolidating a modernized bureaucracy and army, he considered himself the patron of the civil servants and the armed forces,
expecting full allegiance and loyalty as prescribed in the constitution.

As modernization continued under centralized authority, a smouldering
conflict that started with a 1961 *coup* attempt exploded in full revolutionary fury in 1974. The constitutional state faced the first of a series of challenges which deprived it of the time and consistency it needed to mature
and flourish. Haile Selassie's own 'modernized elites', posing as propo-
nents of democracy, pushed aside the constitutional state. Ethiopia
retreated from modernization and democratization and degenerated into
garrison socialism.

SUDAN AND SOMALIA

The constitutional state in Sudan and Somalia evolved in a similar pattern.
However, a significant difference is the fact that both countries were under
colonial domination in the nineteenth century while Ethiopia resisted colonization. Thus the political residue of colonialism, significant in the evolution of the constitutional state, manifested itself in the rush to
multi-party representation. Sudan and Somalia embarked on a frenzy of
political party organization in the immediate pre-independence years.
They were encouraged to accept liberalism by colonial administrations in
both countries but in contrast to Ethiopia (where numerous historical and
political legacies served as means for universal political acculturation,
conditioning citizens' expectations, aspirations and values), colonialism
retarded indigenous political practices.

In pre-colonial Sudan and Somalia, regional sultanates administered
autonomous and uncoordinated communities.[19] Until the late nineteenth
century when the Mahdi in Sudan and Sayyid Mohammed Abdullah Ibn
Hassan in Somalia made their brief and eventful resistance to colonialism,
there were no mechanisms that could sustain coordinated, united and insti-

tutionalized political values at the national level. The community organizations that existed in pre-colonial days were designed to enhance Islamic teachings. When colonialism intruded, Islam was forced to compete with liberal institutions.

Colonialism imposed severe limitations on efforts to create and administer national governments. Such methods as 'indirect rule' provided limited political socialization in modern governance. Political aspirations with a genuinely national outlook were circumvented by colonialists who dominated macro-politics. This led to proliferation of parochial politics mainly at village and regional levels. The enlightened political dynamics which manifested themselves in Ethiopia involving resolution of religious and political discords were absent in Sudan and Somalia. Also absent were mechanisms of transferring government power from one legitimate royal or ruling house to another.[20] In Ethiopia the constitutional state emerged from a tradition of political travails. In Sudan and Somalia, the post-colonial state was superimposed on colonial structures designed to implement and facilitate colonial exploitation.

Colonial administrative offices in both countries were authorized to establish legislative and judicial institutions to meet colonial objectives and policies. Nationals were recruited to serve in legislative and judicial colonial branches mainly on an apprenticeship basis. Administrative offices, with broad powers of executive authority, wielded disproportionate influence and exercised a discretionary veto to manipulate African communities designated as administrative regions, 'protectorates' and 'condominiums'.

Economic and political priorities of colonial powers were the determinants of colonial administrations in Sudan and Somalia. However, those interests were advanced by sacrificing the economic and political future of African communities.[21] Colonial administrators saw any expenditure for local welfare as disinvestment and deviation unless it was directly linked to colonial objectives.[22] The sterility of the colonial heritage is reflected in the political and socio-economic challenges that 'liberated' nations experienced in their post-colonial life.

In the late 1940s, the British were in colonial retreat. Establishment of local institutions replicating colonial administrative systems and structures made sense to them, even though these systems may not have been suited to local peoples. Notwithstanding the frailty of their foundations, constitutional states were born with the independence of the two countries.

Between 1952 and 1973 successive Sudanese governments were deadlocked, never able to garner authoritative capacity to ordain a permanent constitution. The manner in which they wielded power reflected state fragility and institutional disorientation. Sudan was governed by *ad hoc* constitutions intermittently written in 1952, 1971 and 1973. The fact that the regimes did not abandon hope of creating a national constitution to legitimate their rule indicates their dilemma. They recognized constitutions as legitimating tools. However, yearning for a constitutional state was thwarted by inability of various groups and political parties to balance religious and secular idiosyncracies and adopt a national constitution that would enfranchise all Sudanese citizens. Sectional interests severely weakened the state as common expression of the will of all citizens. In the absence of a credible constitution explicating state capacity and empowering it to exercise a national will, murderous and corrupt regimes presided over Sudan. Southern Sudanese, loathed by their fellow citizens, became permanent victims of the state. Despite a felt need, successive regimes failed to design an impartial constitution guaranteeing universal rights for all Sudanese.

In 1969 Jaafar Nimeri ushered in the garrison regime; this was replaced by another pluralist constitutional regime in 1985. A sense of political pluralism seemed to exist when Sadiq al Mahdi's government was about to announce the Addis Ababa agreement which would have suspended Islamic law and pledged a national reconciliation. This was preempted by a 1989 military *coup* led by Colonel Umar Hassan Ahmad al Bashir. Bashir's government is a classic garrison regime, dependent on foreign political and military support in its effort to win an unending guerrilla war. Such wars, by virtue of their flexibility, have deluded many a garrison regime into claiming victory only to find themselves slowly decaying under resilient guerrilla assault.

In Somalia the constitutional state was inaugurated with the 1961 constitution. This established the framework of government, allowed multiparty representation, established a legal system and recognized Somali citizenship. However, inter-ethnic divisions fostered and nurtured by the Italians and British became major burdens for the state. In sharp contrast to Ethiopia where Haile Selassie's modernization programmes allowed the state to slowly make its appearance as a legitimate uniting force,[23] the Somali state was stillborn from the outset, superseded by parochial centres of power.

Post-independence political parties, particularly the Somali Youth League, the Somaliland National League, the United Somali Party, and the Greater Somali League endeavoured to erase the lines of ethnic and clan divisions. These parties, however, like those in Sudan, were side-tracked by inter-ethnic and clan squabbles. Excessive levels of pluralist participation without commensurate levels of economic and welfare participation generated further party fights.[24] Between 1960 and 1969, Somalia experienced dynamic but confused political life. Political organization and participation flourished as vehicles for participation by political entrepreneurs who practised politics as a vehicle for clan- and self-promotion.[25]

In Somalia those who appeared sensitive to the politics of order and clan-based participation were too hasty in anticipating the withering of ethnic/clan conflicts.[26] Corruption and factionalism paralysed the government. The constitutional state expired in 1964 and the country was without a government from February to the end of September. In 1967 President Aden Abdallah Osman chose Abderazak Haji Hussein as Prime Minister and presented him for parliamentary approval. Parliament was divided because the incumbent Prime Minister, Abdirashid Ali Sharmarke, initially chosen to balance top leadership posts among the important clans, was bypassed by younger and educated members of the major parties. Although the President's intention was worthy in that he attempted to rely on merit and talent in appointing cabinet posts, his actions backfired because he failed to realize that the parties were not prepared for such a drastic transition.

The Horn countries needed a slow transition to democratization by allowing the state to play its representative role. There was awareness among various parties and groups that factionalism was weakening the state but they remained unwilling to allow the state to flourish and enhance its democratic capacities, leading to further disorder. Simultaneous military *coups* in 1969 led by Siad Barre in Somalia and Nimeri in Sudan can only be seen as symptoms of deep frustration on the part of egotistic elites unwilling to observe the line of demarcation between state power and group interests.

THE STATE AND THE PROSPECTS FOR REGIONAL DEVELOPMENT

Prospects for development in the Horn can be realized only under regimes conscious enough to balance demands for meagre resources with necessities for change. Of the two types of states discussed, the garrison state is not equipped to implement development due to its emphasis on militarization, unwillingness to modify inappropriate policy actions, and propensity to exploit border frictions as means to prolong its political life.

Throughout the previous decades, garrison states proved wasteful because their militaristic tendencies imposed heavy burdens on society. Their inability to resolve domestic conflicts, adherence to dogmatic and dictatorial methods, and rigidity in managing policy choices and seeking alternatives predisposed them to ongoing domestic conflict. Garrison states governed the Horn through coercion and force and rejected any input from other social forces or institutions. They refused to acknowledge that they had strayed from rational policy choices and continued further in the same direction, aggravating policy actions that had already gone drastically wrong. Their legacy will be a long-lasting burden.

In contrast, the constitutional state is conducive to social development. The flexibility of its institutions and the willingness of elites to tolerate measured change enable the state to maintain orderly progress. One development method that fits the capacities of the constitutional state is functional integration. Scholars of international cooperation hypothesize that frequent contact among nations and citizens enhances peace and development. The theory of international integration was advanced on this basis.[27] Its main assumptions are:

1. Transborder movements of people and economic goods generate familiarity among citizens of two or more nation-states.
2. Functional organizations can be created to promote, facilitate, and monitor transborder movements.
3. Functional organizations work better if they limit themselves to technical or non-political missions although, eventually, they can be upgraded to handle political problems.
4. Functional organizations contribute more toward creation of goodwill among peoples when they start by specializing in economic and social issues. Eventually, however, they expand their mandate to include political issues of regional importance.
5. The process is a piecemeal developmental goal requiring years of experimentation and patience.

The importance of integration theory is that it is relatively easy to apply in industrialized as well as non-industrialized societies. Some argue that it may even be more possible to implement in less developed economies.[28] Industrialized economies are extensively entangled with standard routines of domestic politics. Steering them to non-political routines requires considerable change in focus. Such traditional habits of political exchanges between domestic agencies and the clients they were designed to serve can be impaired by shifting attention to integrating agencies. The state is then faced with having to ration attention between its domestic obligations and external interests.

In less complex economies, the process can begin on a small scale involving plans that the state can afford to delegate to integrating agencies. Such tasks as monitoring and administering border markets, cultural exchanges, humanitarian programs, health-care provisions, literacy programs, technical education, agricultural cooperation, border patrols and other programmes can be administered jointly. The East African Community exemplifies a functional organization which achieved a wide-scale union including monetary integration. Although the Community had problems, it was able to gradually institutionalize itself until Idi Amin's ascendance to political leadership in Uganda sealed its demise.

PROSPECTS FOR THE HORN

It is too early to entertain prospects of integration in the Horn. Essential conditions need to be met to carry out full scale integration. One of the most essential conditions is regional peace. As has been the case in the Horn for the last half century, regional conflicts erupted as a result of domestic politics. Regimes relying on sectional politics and neglecting inclusive politics alienated large segments of their citizens. Elites who saw themselves as representing sectional groups refused to accommodate such issues as ethnic and religious differences. Those who were alienated sought redress by taking up arms and waging protracted struggles. For integration to occur, establishment of conciliatory regimes with deep commitment to democratic principles such as universal equality and justice is crucial. Although cooperation and integration are technical programmes with political neutrality, a conducive political environment is the surest guarantee for their success. Areas which exhibit democratic norms can guarantee peace and stability.

Based on these assumptions, a campaign for regional cooperation is underway to deal with common problems. Some promising endeavours have been pursued since the Derg's fall in Ethiopia. One such endeavour concerns bilateral agreements. Ethiopia and Eritrea are benefiting from past economic and social relations and building a promising framework for further development of integrating networks. They have endorsed a common currency, common administration of ports and waterways, free movement of goods, drastic reductions in tariffs and duty on essential products, (with some exceptions on coffee and tea), uniform immigration laws and professional licensing.[29] Most important from an integration perspective is that the two countries have formally agreed to cooperate on border provinces. Although it is not clear yet as to what the linkage issues are, obviously the main goal is promotion of technical projects such as environment, agriculture, transportation and commerce.

Prospects for rehabilitation would seem hopeless were it not for some recognition of common regional interests. One positive step that has been taken is the pledge by Ethiopia, Eritrea, Kenya, Sudan, Somalia and Djibouti to build multilateral cooperation. All have agreed to strengthen the Intergovernmental Authority on Drought and Development (IGAAD) (see Shaw, this volume, Chapter 13). In the short run, IGAAD's objectives are to coordinate and facilitate drought related policies and actions. In the long run, other integrative policies could be pursued on a multilateral basis.

OUTCOMES OF INTEGRATIVE ENDEAVOURS

In global politics, the outcome of aggression is not superior to the outcome of negotiation. Countries can maximize their interests by negotiation more than through violence. Conflict resolution by negotiation is a function of time and commitment to peace on the part of the negotiators.

Success in building effective transborder relations depends on the willingness of nations to pledge themselves to practice conflict resolution by negotiating over an extended period of time. It is important to internalize negotiation as an ultimate determinant of conflict resolution rather as a supplementary tool for stalling a war or for sizing up an opponent's predispositions. Negotiation is an end and a means, a 'learning process, constantly renewing and reinforcing the positive elements needed to complete . . . the stages of bargaining'.[30] Countries that have resolved their differences by negotiation, plebiscite and by eschewing violence have succeeded in avoiding costly wars and reaping benefits of stability. Those that resorted to violence and war have gained least, often even in their declared military objectives.

Resorting to negotiation has a ripple effect. Benefits can be gained in enhanced organizational capability, familiarity and acquaintance among negotiating and peace making officials or civil servants of countries concerned, upgrading of skills in conflict resolution, and a conditioning habit for negotiation rather than violence. Countries that opt for airing their differences and staying the course of negotiation always have time for progress.

Since the Derg was overthrown in 1991, Eritrea and Ethiopia have set a new pattern of conflict resolution that will prove beneficial for the region. The EPLF approach seems to be based on an understanding of the futility of war. The organization had promoted regional peace since 1984; unfortunately, its voice was only heard when it demonstrated its formidable military skills by destroying the Ethiopian forces. The EPLF now advocates peaceful resolutions for the whole region. In its fourth regular session (since liberating Eritrea), held in the town of Ghindaa in July 1992, the

EPLF Central Committee declared its willingness to contribute to resolution of regional problems, particularly the Somali crisis. Not only did the EPLF express its willingness to assist negotiations, but the tone of the declaration bespeaks deep empathy for the plight of the Somali people. The Central Committee acknowledged that Eritrea would work for peace and carry its share of the burden in rehabilitating the Horn. The declaration is based on the resolution which the Central Committee issued after its sixth regular session in 11 September 1984.[31]

Furthermore, the fact that the EPLF and EPRDF have peacefully resolved Ethiopia's concerns about access to the sea illustrates the superior outcome of negotiation to war. Access to the sea was the main cause for Ethiopia's war in Eritrea. Under EPRDF leadership, Ethiopia quickly and easily gained unlimited and unconditional access, achieving by negotiation what previous regimes had been unable to win through thirty years of war and bloodshed. The foundation for rebuilding the traditional goodwill that existed between Eritrea and Ethiopia for centuries is now being rebuilt through incremental and patient negotiation. Of course, for these current trends to continue in positive directions, it is important that the regimes and peoples of the region understand that negotiation and interaction as tools for conflict resolution are based on reciprocal understanding and time.

The search for political solutions by peaceful means was also demonstrated when the EPRDF declared in July 1991 its willingness to negotiate a solution to Ethiopia's regional and internal problems. It made its stand clear by declaring that it did not want to add to what the Ethiopian people had already suffered in the previous three decades. The EPRDF made clear that it repudiated violence and war by calling for negotiation among various Ethiopian opposition groups, establishing a transitional government relatively representative of all sectional groups, setting the date for new elections and calling on international bodies to certify the credibility of those elections.

The EPRDF expressed its commitment to democracy by inviting all opposition groups to come and reason together on Ethiopia's future. It is uncharacteristic of any guerrilla organization to make honest efforts to share power and responsibility after it has carried a disproportionate burden of liberating a country. The EPRDF formed the most representative cabinet that could be expected under the circumstances that prevailed when it entered Addis Ababa. It seems to have made an effort to avoid confrontational politics by choosing conciliation and consensus.

The EPRDF also took measures to convince the world that it was committed to democratization and equality. It submitted itself to an honest account of its intentions by calling on nations of goodwill to send representatives to observe the elections and political steps that the organization was undertaking. The EPRDF appears to have endorsed democratic principles for resolving Ethiopia's problems, although it was criticized by some observers.[32]

The declarations and general pronouncements of the EPLF and EPRDF suggest willingness to seek common grounds on which the peoples of the Horn could lay the foundation for peace, stability, and prosperity. Even though such a prospect seems dim in view of current turmoil in Somalia and Sudan, the Eritrean and Ethiopian regimes seem to have analysed the regional situation from the long range perspective. They have accepted the fact that, in the final analysis, the peoples of the region stand to gain by seeking mutual grounds on which to rebuild and strengthen traditional ties. Thus, free transborder movements of goods and people between Eritrea, Ethiopia and Sudan have continued in the last three years.[33]

Pluralism is a tradition in the region, and a valuable organizational resource that could be tapped through the use of credible constitutions. Far more important is the creation of regimes that recognize these traditions and express willingness to be inclusive in representation, governing and in distribution of resources. Today there is hope that such an eventuality may be taking root in Eritrea and in Ethiopia. The war in Sudan is not only a dangerous burden to Sudan itself but a source of dismay among the masses in the region. No ethnic group in the Horn can be abused without the whole region feeling their agonies, whatever their ethnicity or religious beliefs. Collectively, the Horn countries can recover their dignity by contributing to the mending of Somalia. Poor countries can pull themselves to greatness by opting for peace over war.

Notes

1. According to the World Bank, and the UN Development Program, the Horn countries are among the least developed in all aspects of human development needs. World Bank, 1991, *World Development Report 1991: The Challenge of Development* (New York: Oxford University Press) pp. 201–269; United Nations Development Program, 1990, 1991, 1993. *Human Development Program Report 1990, 1991, 1993* (New York: Oxford University Press). (See Basic Data above, pp. xv–xvi.)

2. There was deep ambivalence in Eritrea about secession from Ethiopia until Haile Selassie placed Eritrea under a state of emergency in the summer of 1969. Demands made by Eritrean fighters did not go beyond the right to self-determination. This changed when Haile Selassie's government committed massive atrocities against civilians near Keren. Although the government intensified its military campaign in Eritrea, there were songs indicating the conflict could be resolved peacefully. Prospects for peaceful solution

continued during the brief period of Aman Andom's government when he personally made overtures for negotiation. Aman's 'proposals attracted some interest from the EPLF but disturbed the ELF which put forward some counter-proposals that were unacceptable because they included the possibility of independence' (Rene Lefort, 1981. *Ethiopia: An Heretical Revolution?* (London: Zed Press) p. 72; J. Markakis and N. Ayele, 1986. *Class and Revolution in Ethiopia* (Trenton, NJ: Red Sea Press) p. 117. The Derg extinguished any hope of political solution when it initiated military campaigns against the entire Eritrean population.

3. Bereket H. Selassie, 'The American Dilemma in the Horn'. *In African Crisis Areas and U.S. Foreign Policy.* Bender, J. G. *et al.* (eds) (Berkeley, CA: University of California Press) 163–77.

4. Markakis uses this term to define regimes that mix ideology and massive military prowess in at attempt to eliminate resistance and establish control as they pursue development projects. Inevitably, they end up allocating disproportionate resources to build instruments of control and consolidate their rule. John Markakis, 1987, *National and Class Conflict in the Horn of Africa* (Cambridge, MA: Cambridge University Press) pp. 237–71.

5. Theories of decision-making invoke stable leadership temperaments as important determinants of desirable policy outcomes. Herbert Simon, 1976, *Administrative Behavior* (New York: Free Press) chs 2 and 3; Graham Allison, 1971, *Essence of Decision: Explaining the Cuban Missile Crisis* (New York: Little, Brown) pp. 67–100.

6. Joel S. Migdal, 1988, *Strong Societies and Weak States* (Princeton, NJ: Princeton University Press); Peter B. Evans, Dietrich Rueschemeyer and Theda Skocpol, 1985, *Bringing the State Back In* (New York: Cambridge University Press).

7. Samuel P. Huntington, 1964, *The Soldier and the State: The Theory and Politics of Civil–Military Relations* (New York: Random House) ch. 1.

8. Arend Lijphart, 1968,'Typologies of Democratic Systems', *Comparative Political Studies*, 1(1): 3–33.

9. Neil R. Richardson, 1981, 'Economic Dependence and Foreign Policy Compliance: Bringing Measurement Closer to Conception', in *The Political Economy of Foreign Policy Behavior.* Charles W. Kegley, and Pat McGowan (eds) (Beverly Hills, CA: Sage Publications) pp. 87–110.

10. Ibid. p. 92.

11. Michael Bratton, 'Beyond The State: Civil Society and Associational Life in Africa', *World Politics*, 40 (October 1988), 410–15; Robert Jackson and Carl G. Roseberg, 1985, 'The Marginality of African States', In *African Independence: The First Twenty-five Years.* Gwendolen M. Carter and Patric O'Meara (eds) (Bloomington, IN: University of Indiana Press) pp. 45–70.

12. Harry Eckstein, 1982, 'The Idea of Political Development: From Dignity to Efficiency,' *World Politics,* 34 (July): 451–86.

13. Goran Hyden, 1983, *No Shortcuts to Progress: African Development Management in Perspective* (London: Heinemann).

14. Until the Nimeri and Barre regimes in 1969, regimes in Sudan and Somalia were relatively responsive to popular demands. The exception was the Abboud government in Sudan which overthrew the constitutional regime in

1958. Abboud exercised strong-arm tactics to contain dissent in the South. In the North, the regime refrained from exercising tactics used by garrison regimes. Its pluralist tendencies did not avail as its inefficiency and corruption led to its overthrow by popular uprising in 1966. Subsequent regimes prior to 1969 were constitutional in the North but their Southern policies were characterized by indecisiveness and brutality. *Sudan: A Country Study* (Washington, DC: American University Press, 1982).

15. Numerous examples illustrate the maturity of Ethiopian political culture. The elaborate provision made to facilitate smooth transfer of power is one example. Similarly, fusion of secular and traditional culture was achieved by balancing the role of the Ethiopian Orthodox Christian Church with that of the state. The deep sense of legitimating efficacy felt by citizens towards these institutions did not differ from those cited as examples of developed 'civic culture' Edward Ullendorff, 1973, *The Ethiopians: An Introduction to Country and People* (London: Oxford University Press); Mordecai Abir, 1980, *Ethiopia and the Red Sea* (London: Frank Cass) pp. 42–68.

16. Ullendorff, *The Ethiopians*, pp. 183–201.

17. John Spencer, 1987, *Ethiopia at Bay: A Personal Account of the Haile Selassie Years.* (Algonac, MI: Reference Publications); Patrick Gilkes, 1975, *The Dying Lion: Feudalism and Modernization in Ethiopia* (New York: St. Martin's) p. 63; Christopher Clapham, 1990, *Revolutionary Ethiopia: Transformation and Continuity* (Cambridge: Cambridge University Press) pp. 35–7.

18. Ullendorff, *The Ethiopians* p. 187. This conclusion is a guarded speculation on my part. It is entirely based on the fact that Professor Ullendorff was highly regarded by Ethiopian nobility as an admired chronicler of Ethiopian history, literature and politics.

19. I. M. Lewis, 1961, *A Pastoral Democracy* (London: Oxford University Press) ch. 1. Somalis draw inspiration from Imam Ahmad Ibraahiim al Ghaazi, a religious warrior who conquered Abyssinia and ruled the city of Harar, ransacking Ethiopian churches, monasteries and villages between 1527 and 1543. He preoccupied himself with conversion and establishment of a Somali political state but this did not seem to have been a priority in his scheme of conquest.

20. Referring to Islam as a uniting force in Somalia, Professor Lewis states: 'Despite their common aim of promoting religious as opposed to secular values, the relations between different Orders are characterized by rivalry and centering on the respective religious merits and mystical powers of intercession of their founders' (Lewis, *A Pastoral Democracy* p. 63).

21. Literature on colonial exploitation notes the inevitability of the 'zero-sum' outcome of colonial policies. Invariably, colonial powers became the beneficiaries of such arrangements. Although many conditions required amelioration in the colonies, colonial administrators were averse to promoting genuine economic, educational and welfare redistribution. Peter Worsley, 1984, *The Three Worlds: Culture and World Development* (Chicago: University of Chicago Press); Walter Rodney, 1972. *How Europe Underdeveloped Africa* (Dar es Salaam, Tanzania: Dar es Salaam Publishing House). Andre G. Frank, 1967, *Capitalism and Underdevelopment in Latin America* (New York: Monthly Press).

22. David L. Lewis, 1987, *The Race to Fashoda: European Colonialism and African Resistance in the Scramble for Africa* (New York: Weidenfeld & Nicolson) pp. 1–33, 73–136.

23. This chapter posits that the Ethiopian state made steady progress toward legitimacy until the overthrow of Emperor Haile Selassie, while recognizing that the regime committed grave errors in its diplomatic and military policies with respect to Eritrea. These policies intensified hostilities and contributed to the government's fall in 1974. The Derg's policies, particularly after the 1977 Red Terror, diminished the regime's legitimacy, particularly among Eritreans and Tigrayans. Oromo views of the state after 1974 oscillated between support and disinterest until it became clear in 1991 that the Derg was doomed. Prior to the Derg, Oromo participation in the working of the state was as dynamic, constructive, competitive and deeply integrated as that of any other group. Clapham, *Revolutionary Ethiopia.* pp. 214–19; Lefort, *Ethiopia*, p. 36; I. M. Lewis (ed.), 1983, *Nationalism and Self-Determination in the Horn of Africa* (London: Ithaca Press) pp. 2–3; Oromo disquiet about events in the late 1980s is voiced in a book by Bonnie K. Holcomb and Sisai Ibsa, 1990, *The Invention of Ethiopia: the Making of a Dependent State in Northeast Africa* (Trenton, NJ: Red Sea Press). The book takes bold liberties in manipulating circumstantial facts and incidents, attempting to rewrite Ethiopian history and redefine Oromo experience in that history.

24. Huntington's formulation that 'the sharp increase in political participation gives rise to political instability' is amply demonstrated in Somalia where there was unprecedented level of party formation and destruction, particularly in the 1960s and at the end of 1988. According to Huntington the workings of democracy are uncertain until capable institutions are created to organize, reconcile, regulate and channel multiple political demands. Samuel P. Huntington, 1968, *Political Order in Changing Societies* (New Haven, Yale University Press) pp. 53–9; Similar observations are made regarding causes of the 1974 Ethiopian revolution by L. W. Harbeson, 1979, 'Socialist Politics in Revolutionary Ethiopia'. In *Socialism in Sub-Saharan Africa: A New Assessment*, Carl G. Rosberg and Thomas M. Callaghy (eds) (Berkely: Institute of International Studies) pp. 351–55.

25. Huntington, *Political Order*, p. 66.

26. Immediately after World War II until the eve of independence, the Somali Youth League was the dominant party. Gradually it lost its dominance to the Greater Somali League (GSL). The GSL's platform of a united Somalia with Arabized cultural values appealed even to members of the United Somali Party and Somaliland National League. Instability of party allegiances, personalization of party objectives, and inability of all parties to formulate platforms with national bearing led to constant squabbles and factionalization. By the late 1960s, there were over 60 party organizations: a testimony to the constitutional state's penchant for pluralism and constitutionalism. I. M. Lewis, 1965, *The Modern History of Somaliland: From Nation to State* (New York: Praeger) pp. 289–93; R. Reinehart *et al.*, 1993, *Somalia: A Country Study* (Washington DC: Federal Research Division, Library of Congress) pp. 26–36.

27. K. W. Deutsch, 1964, 'Communication Theory and Political Integration'. In Jacob, Philip E. and James V. Toscano, (eds), *The Integration of Political*

Communities (Philadelphia: Lippincott) pp. 46–74; A. Etzioni, 1965, *Political Unification* (New York: Rinehart and Winston). Joseph S. Nye, *Pan-Africanism and East African Integration* (Cambridge, MA: Harvard University Press).

28.   Nye, *Pan-Africanism.*

29.   *Hadas Eritrea,* 2 May, 1992:2; 1 January, 1994:1; *Eritrea Update,* August 1993:1–2.

30.   Bruce Russett, 1989 and H. Starr, *World Politics: The Menu for Choice* (New York: W. H. Freeman) p. 164.

31.   *Adulis,* Vols 4–5 (October–November 1984): 3–6.

32.   The tone of the criticism is astonishingly harsh. Even more surprising is the impatience of scholars, diplomats, journalists and business professionals in denouncing the EPRDF as uncommitted to democratic participation. Barely a year after the EPRDF drove out the Derg, groups stampeded Ethiopia to observe the 1992 election, looking for democracy in a traditional society with no experience in practising this. That election was the first in Ethiopian history to be called by those who had at their disposal instruments of war and violence without equivocating and postponing for decades. Logistical problems, lack of experience in electoral activities and shortage of trained manpower were not taken into account by observers. Intransigence of groups who were unwilling to give the new regime time to restore order received much attention. The EPRDF's pledge (made in the July 1991 Charter) to respect universal rights in Ethiopia including the right to secession was ignored. African American Institute, 1992, *An Evaluation of the June 21, 1992 Election in Ethiopia. ch. 6;* 'Negat Ba Ethiopia' – Sunrise in Ethiopia – in *Negarit Gazzetta,* 50 (1) (22 July 1991): 38–41.

33.   *Negarit Gazzetta,* 50(1) (22 July 1991): 2–38.

5 Reflections on the Political Economy of Transition in Eritrea: Lessons from Asia's Newly-Industrializing Countries
Okbazghi Yohannes

INTRODUCTION

Recently, I heard Thomas Keneally reiterate themes he had developed in his novel, *To Asmara*, one of which is his genuine belief that the Eritrean national revolution has all the possibilities of creating a good society. This general sentiment is shared by many observers who know the Eritreans and their struggle. At this juncture, it is clear that the economic system chosen by the Eritrean leadership is the market economy. But choosing a system in the abstract is not the same as identifying and strategizing the means by which it is to be structured. Here care must be taken not to confuse ends with means. Such a confusion was, in fact, the hallmark of almost all developing countries in the past. Blaming the system for their failure in prioritizing their national developmental goals and in strategizing the means by which these goals were to be attained, political elites continuously sought refuge in their conversion and reconversion to convoluted forms of either capitalism or socialism. Thus, as Eritrea's economic transition presumably will take on a rough meandering in coming years, the Eritrean leadership must begin a learning process that requires them to make a thoroughgoing assessment of failures and successes of states that have taken the capitalist road of development.

Equally important is a thorough understanding of the complex relationship between economics and politics. The issue of transition mandates a complete understanding of the contours of the political context of development. This involves recognition of what some commentators term primitive cultural accumulation as an integral part of capital accumulation. If genuine development is to occur, the masses of the people will have to be first transformed, to borrow Paolo Freire's words, from being an object of

93

politics into being the subject of politics. This involves progressive construction of a new culture while simultaneously shedding regressive elements of the old one. The cultivation and promotion of participatory political culture and the establishment of democratic leadership and institutions are requisite conditions.

In sum, it is important to note that economics and politics are two strategic components of the same process. One fundamental reason why past revolutions failed was due to the metaphysical understanding of this reality plus the fact that, once in power, elites substituted the politics of order for their revolutionary politics. At this point, then, the fundamental question is: can Eritrea learn to avoid mistakes of past revolutions and translate the paradigm of its possibilities into reality by creating a democratic and prosperous society?

This chapter does not attempt a concrete road map as much as it intends to highlight pertinent lessons that ought to be learned from experiences of some countries regarded as successful capitalist states. It does not represent a systematic investigation of structural dynamics of transition in Eritrea, but rather offers tentative observations and reflections on what ought to be learned.

COMPETING STRATEGIES OF DEVELOPMENT

The Eritrean leadership's explicit commitment to capitalism is certainly a welcome development if only for the simple reason that neither an international contextual situation nor internal structural conditions exist for erection of any other system. Such a commitment to a free market economy, the presumption that the transitional phase of the Eritrean economy will be driven by private entrepreneurial initiatives, does not, however, preclude the indispensability of the state in providing general direction and guidance, in making authoritative allocation of resources and in regulating relationships among competing and conflicting societal forces. This onerous task obviously demands explication of the inner workings, merits and flaws of capitalism.

Construction of systemic capabilities, formation and specification of goals, determination and selection of strategies and providing mechanisms for their implementation and coordination of necessity become major preoccupations of the state. The complexities of these undertakings reveal themselves in the fact that they present contradictory choices and perplexing dilemmas, stemming partly, in the Eritrean case especially, from low levels of social differentiation and high levels of ethnoreligious segmentation, relative scarcity of resources both human and material and the general crisis of international capitalism, and partly from the very transitional character of the Eritrean economy. To be sure, any policy choice poses a dilemma between competing strategies that purportedly help to make tradeoffs among values in ways that balance domestic demands and external imperatives.[1]

These dilemmas stem from ambiguities and contradictory expectations inherent in the nature of capitalism itself. On one hand, there is the presumption that it is naturally appropriate for organization of labour and capital to be determined by the utilitarian application of market forces essentially driven by individual entrepreneurship. On the other hand, the state is required to insert itself in the accumulation process with cross purposes in mind. First, the entrepreneurial class itself needs the help of the state in the form of providing credit facilities, subsidies, tax exemptions or reductions, regulation of foreign competition, building good infrastructure and the like. All these measures can be rationalized in terms of job-creation or broadening the tax base for the state in the long run.

Second, the state must also regulate relationships among members of the entrepreneurial class. To the extent that the state continually receives inputs and pressures from this class whose members have contradictory interests, it is always vulnerable to manipulations by owners of capital who, for one reason or another, enjoy a greater leverage with the state in relation to their competitors. This is one of the fundamental conditions that makes the state incapable of articulating a coherent macro-economic policy.

Third, the state must perform its social legitimation functions, that is, regulate the relationship between those segments of society which supply labour to industry and those segments which own capital. In the context of contradictory expectations emanating from their conflicting perceptions about the proper role of the state in the economy, these segments make conflicting demands on the state. For owners of capital, the politics of order becomes the primary concern since internal political stability and containment of the workforce from exerting pressure on managers of production in the form of increased wages, the right to strike, better working conditions, are viewed by the capitalists as prerequisite conditions for profit maximization.

Conversely, the working class wants the state to be on its side against owners of capital in order to maximize labour's share of industrialization. The state's dilemma is that tilting to either side will have far-reaching consequences. Squeezing hard on labour on behalf of capital accumulation can distort the state's social legitimation functions. Consequently social containment of the workforce by the state will be exceedingly difficult since its capacity to increase labour's share of the economy in the form of transfer payments and increased wages will be short-circuited by its predilections for capital accumulation. Identification of the state with owners of capital risks social instability which is not conducive to the accumulation process which the state seeks to promote.

This line of reasoning can be juxtaposed against the argument that state actions that favour the working class can dampen entrepreneurial initiative and innovativeness. It may even induce the flight of capital while at the same time discouraging the inflow of foreign money. To be sure, every strategic choice involves a risk. State actions, irrespective of their rationalizations and justifications, inevitably produce reactions both internally and externally. It is this reality that makes the transition phase of Eritrea a precarious one. A fundamental lesson we learn from past experience is that a deteriorating economic situation, unemployment and scarcity of economic essentials never foster the growth of democracy. Thus the first task of the Eritrean state is to expeditiously grapple with the economic necessities of life before its political legitimacy is put into question. I do not harbor any illusions about the difficulties facing the Eritrean government at this juncture of its existence; I am simply pointing out the harsh reality that hungry people lack the capacity for rationalization and that this reality must be taken very seriously.

As the preceding paragraphs illustrate, the Eritrean state will of necessity have taken the centre stage of capital accumulation during the initial phase of the transition. It is in the context of this realization that I will devote the rest of this chapter to tentatively stipulating the framework for state actions in the economy. My fundamental purpose is to identify the lessons we can learn as Eritrea is poised to take off.

In the last half century there have been numerous approaches to development which attempt to explain problems of economic transition. The earliest was the modernization paradigm which, drawing on neoclassical economic analysis, dichotomized the world economy into traditional and modern sectors. Here development is postulated as a function of the expansionary process of the modern sector into the traditional one through diffusion of capital and technology and reliance on market forces to promote this process.[2]

The 'modernization' paradigm views such concepts as market efficiency, free trade, comparative advantage and the like as intrinsic to the capitalist system, with some magic power, if left alone, to transform traditional sectors into modern ones. The reductionist nature of its assumptions reveals itself in the fact that political factors are seen as extrinsic to economic development and can only impede rather than facilitate economic transition. In the context of this theoretical orientation, the modernization paradigm maintains that an outward looking or export-led growth strategy is suitable for any developing nation.[3]

In juxtaposition with this analysis, the 'underdevelopment' position, both in its structuralist and dependency versions, argues that the global economy operates in ways that actually distort and underdevelop the Third World. Here capitalism is seen to have inherent tendencies to preserve and even accentuate inequalities between advanced and underdeveloped countries.[4] Insofar as the fundamentals of the 'underdevelopment' position are concerned, given the asymmetrical relationship existing between developing and developed countries, the contemporary international division of labour based on comparative advantage simply legitimizes and institutionalizes structural conditions of exploitation and domination. In this context, the strategy of delinking and inward-looking development becomes the only appropriate one to initiate an endogenously determined and controlled process of development.[5]

Although any systematic evaluation of these competing paradigms is beyond the scope of this chapter, suffice it to say that the 'underdevelopment' position has received relatively wider appreciation in the developing world as many countries have experimented with different gradations of import-substitution industrialization strategy. The results have not been encouraging, however. As a consequence, especially in the wake of the total collapse of the Soviet empire, the inward-looking strategy of development seems to have run its course. We have thus come full circle to the modernization paradigm as almost all developing countries have begun embarking on extensive privatization and marketization. The Asian 'tigers' are often cited as exemplary models for emulation in this regard. Perhaps it is here that Eritreans must stop and rethink before emulating any system. Their history, geography, sociotemporal conditions and the international context under which their development occurred must be systematically and objectively assessed before any imitation of their experience takes place. One should ask, for example, if it is true that the rapid modernization of, say South Korea and Taiwan, has been the result of strict adherence to principles of unfettered capitalism and the outward-looking strategy of development, why have countries like Kenya, Zaire and Ivory Coast, which more or less pursued a similar open door policy, failed to achieve similar results?

A pervasive myth surrounding the Asian pro-capitalist mode of development is implicit in this questioning. In order to dispel this myth, the entire analysis of capitalist development in general must be reintegrated into its historical context. It is crucial to note that all advanced economies, including those of the US, Germany and Japan, initiated and achieved internal growth by first utilizing an inward-looking strategy of development and by varying degrees of import-substitution industrialization. As for the US, Alexander Hamilton articulated a position of economic nationalism as early as 1791 as the only way to attain internal growth and international competitiveness. Hamilton argued that national independence and security were functions of wealth and the latter had in turn to be derived from the internal development of strong manufacturing, because heavy reliance on agriculture would naturally lead to 'a state of impoverishment compared with the opulence to which our political and natural advantages authorize us to aspire'.[6]

According to Hamilton, the transfusion of foreign capital and technology as well as the immigration of labor are functions of internal growth rather than internal backwardness. Necessary factors of production are attracted to a nation not because it is backward or traditional but only because that nation is developing and has sufficiently shown the image of its future by the very forces of modernization it has set in motion.[7] This nationalist economic prescription became the cornerstone of US industrial policy in the nineteenth century.

The outcome of this basic orientation was the adoption of sweeping tariff legislation in defence of home industry and extensive application of what we today call import-substitution industrialization strategy. The strategy proved to be the fulcrum of the transformation of the US from a semi-peripheral economy into a core one. In fact, the results were so impressive that all successive administrations vigorously defended the policy whenever it came under attack by internationally oriented free traders. Thus the history of US capitalism clearly shows that an inward-looking strategy based on internal public subsidization and external protection served as the basis of industrialization. The average duty imposed on foreign imports throughout the nineteenth century was around fifty per cent. It was much higher in certain areas such as iron, steel, cotton and textiles.[8] Economic surpluses exacted in this way were then funnelled into infrastructural development.

Patterns of German and Japanese industrialization were no different. In Japan, a combination of internal factors such as the cultural salience of primogenitural practice which militated against fragmentation of property and in favour of accumulation, and active participation of the state in the economy in the form of what some writers term 'revolution from above' led, not only to rapid modernization of the internal forces of production, but also to the emergence of colossal economic giants (the *Zaibatsu*) which dominated the Japanese economy and foreign policy until World War II. In addition, internal capital formation was aided by favourable external circumstances such as acquisition of colonies which served as sources of cheap raw materials and as market outlets.

The postwar history of Japanese capitalism is no different. In 1948, for example, the US occupation authorities reversed their initial policy of breaking up the *Zaibatsus* as a way of eliminating the economic basis of fascism.[9] The US saw a stake in Japan's reindustrialization, believing that a rehabilitated and prosperous Japan would serve as a procapitalist model of regional integration capable of deterring communist expansion and even enticing China to join the new regional division of labour. Additionally, the US encouraged Japan to produce for export. In this regard, Japanese labour was used as a cost factor as labour's share of the economy was drastically slashed so that Japan could underprice its international competitors.[10] In addition to unhampered access to the US market, Japanese firms were also allowed to participate in Federal government contracts through the Offshore Procurement Program.

Japan's re-emergence as a dominant economy in the postwar era is a function of an export promotion strategy vigorously pursued with US support and under an extremely favourable international environment. In all of this, the Japanese continued to play the pivotal role in formulating comprehensive and coherent macro-economic policies. Today the institutional framework for strategic coordination of the economy is provided by the Ministry of International Trade and Industry, which is in all but name Japan's central planning agency. Its sweeping powers range from regulation of foreign exchange, foreign investment and licensing foreign technology to determination of the geographic location of plants, levels of subsidies and production, and to preventing penetration and domination by foreign companies.[11]

The Japanese experience thus offers ample factual evidence that, without state guidance, coordination and supervision, capitalism can never work as effectively as neoclassical economists wish us to believe. The history of the Asian NICs simply offers additional validation of this already established reality contrary to the much-touted presentation of their success story. Close examination of the history and the international context of their development and their unique geographic location clearly indicate that their achievements are a function of a vigorous implementation of an import-substitution strategy in the 1950s and later of an export-led growth strategy still guided by the state.

Special convergent factors made the capitalist experiment in South Korea and Taiwan particularly successful.[12] First, Japanese colonialism had substantially transformed socioeconomic formations in South Korea and Taiwan. The Japanese built roads, telecommunication systems and even founded universities. One result was that labour was either radically transformed or substantially modified. In the immediate aftermath of World War II skilled and semiskilled labour was abundant in these countries which they quickly transformed into comparative advantage. For example, the relative quality and abundance of labour in South Korea was so attractive that a Chase Manhattan Report could declare that 'the dexterity and aptitude of Korean workers who are available at cash wage rates averaging $.65 a day in textiles and $.88 a day in electronics' were strategic assets.[13]

Second, South Korea and Taiwan made conscious decisions between the values of economic affluence and those of political democracy in favour of the former. The result was the emergence of strong authoritarian developmental states that inserted themselves in the economy in order to organize the abundantly cheap labour on behalf of capital accumulation. Trade unions were repressed and human rights were grossly violated. The facade of stability created as a result of such measures was viewed by foreign investors as conducive to their business ventures.

Third, lying on the periphery of the communist world, these developmentalist states effected relatively good land reform so as to avert any peasant revolutions similar to those that occurred in mainland China and North Korea. In this, they had both the blessing and the unconditional support of the US. As it turned out, land reform became the essential source of extraction and transfer of surpluses from the agricultural sector into the industrial sector fueling the process of accumulation.

Fourth, military Keynesianism was a crucial component of the modernization drive in these countries as the US pumped generous military dollars into their economies in the 1950s and 1960s, enormously accelerating the initial phase of capital formation. The Vietnam war also played a pivotal role in the transformation of these states as they seized opportunities to provide essential goods and services to US forces in the region.

Fifth, the booming global economy and existence of a liberal international trade regime created a conducive context for industrialization. They had unhampered access to the US market for cheaply produced goods. Moreover, as US corporations were attracted to take advantage of labour, the industrialization of South Korea and Taiwan became a 'self-feeding process' with foreign capital flowing in while their finished goods flooded the US market.

Sixth, one crucial factor often peripheralized by analysts is the fact that these states have had an inherent bias toward control of the strategic means of production such as steel, petrochemical industries, shipbuilding and utilities. In the 1950s, for example, Taiwan had the largest public sector outside the communist bloc. To determine the pace and direction of growth, state monopolies provided strategic commodities to other sectors of the economy as cheaply as possible and thus forced them to move in lockstep.

Seventh, the economic flexibility of planning agencies and the leadership in these countries was also important. They have had the capacity to continuously adapt their economies to the changing realities in the global economy. The switch from the import-substitution orientation of the 1950s to the export-led growth strategy of the 1960s is a good example of their extensive adaptability. The shift in orientation and policy was a product of a well-coordinated plan. The realization that the increasing domestic market saturation could not sustain introverted long-term growth and the dwindling in US assistance were driving factors behind this policy change.

The capacity of these developmentalist states to copy and learn from others also needs to be stressed. Like Japan, Taiwan and Korea pushed their firms in ways that compelled them to move up the technological ladder. Companies that targeted high-tech computers, robotics, automation, and telecommunications were given generous tax breaks for their investments in human resource development, research and development, and global brand name identity.

This discussion on the authoritarian developmental states demonstrates that the much-touted success of these countries was not due to unfettered capitalism. Neither the import-substitution strategy nor economic extroversion transformed these countries into industrial powerhouses. It was the convergence of unique circumstances that made their orientations and strategies effective. Failure to understand this reality risks danger. History, geography, international politics and the containment-militarism policy of the US have together been determinative factors.

The fundamental lesson for Eritrea that emerges from this analysis is that the initial drive toward industrialization has always been directed by the state. But there is a qualitative distinction between a state that inserts itself in the accumulation process in semiautonomous fashion and a state which is used instrumentally to advance the interests of those who control the state. In fact, on the basis of this distinction, we can identify three forms of capitalism.

The first form is democratic capitalism like that of Germany. Here the state's primary function is to maintain an equilibrium between capital and labour through continuous adjustment of its regulative and distributive mechanisms. Its mediation role gives the state, at least a semblance of neutrality and impartiality and enhances its legitimacy in a way that renders its policies effective.

The second form of capitalism is patrimonial capitalism as applied in countries like Zaire, Kenya and Ivory Coast. Here the production appara- tuses of society are attached to the state either directly in the form of parastatals or indirectly in the form of personal ownership of assets by government officials in the private sector. In this situation, the state is viewed instrumentally as a means of personal wealth-creation and accu- mulation. The dual effect of this system is that it preempts the emergence of national entrepreneurship and the share of labour is severely curtailed.

The final form is the authoritarian developmental capitalism discussed earlier. Here the state is viewed by those who control it both as an agent of economic transformation and as a source of privileges. The contradictory features of the Asian type of authoritarian developmental capitalism is that it isolates the realm of economics from that of politics. It justifies the maintenance of political stagnation in terms of the economic strides it has achieved which have a trickle down effect.

The above classificatory schema makes the choice for Eritrea clearer. The second choice is not only undesirable, but also dangerous. As for the third, even though it can be rationalized in economic terms if achievable, there are no objective conditions similar to those that existed in northeast Asia in the past to make such a choice palatable. I have narrowed down our choice to the first one. This raises the fundamental question: what can Eritrea learn from the past to build democratic capitalism? It is to this question that I turn in the remainder of this chapter.

AVOID AUTHORITARIAN DEVELOPMENTALISM

If there is anything which Eritrea shares with some of the Asian 'tigers' it is what we call 'the Phoenix factor': rising from the ashes of war. Although difficult to establish a definite correlation between conditions of war and economic growth, some writers include in their analysis the trau- matic experience of these countries as one explanatory factor for their development. If this is correct, and I hope it is, then Eritrea has a huge reservoir of trauma, revolutionary zeal, steeled discipline and strong will that can be translated into tangible economic gains.

Beyond this, the structural conditions and international context that were amenable to the northeast Asian mode of development are virtually non-existent in Eritrea today. The intrinsic coerciveness as part of the industrialization drive in Taiwan, for example, could be justified in terms of the ever present danger of communism. In addition, its obsession with the politics of order and the ability of the state to make tradeoffs between economic goods and political values was underwritten with generous US aid. The temptation to use a similar strategy in Eritrea today can only backfire as it would contribute to the accentuation of the country's eth-noreligous segmentation which is susceptible to external influences and exploitation. Differently stated, any less than democratic means of economic transformation cannot be rationalized in terms of internal or external threat.

In this situation, the best alternative is to rely on democratic urban rural mobilization to make ordinary citizens not only participants in the process of industrialization, but also co-beneficiaries of the product. In this regard, codetermination can be the first constructive step. As applied in Germany, codetermination enables workers to have a say in matters pertaining to levels of employment, expansion or contraction of company activities, etc. This reduces frictions that arise between capital and labour substantially. Eritrea can even go beyond this and encourage worker participation in the ownership of industrial assets.

AVOID ECONOMIC GIGANTISM

As international capital dries up, the task of laying down the foundation of capital formation in Eritrea faces a serious challenge. With its dilapidated infrastructure and uneducated workforce, Eritrea cannot at present offer the necessary attractiveness to foreign investors. Moreover, competition for international capital is such that only those states that already have established credentials or potential for rapid growth will definitely continue to receive the lion's share of international capital. Prospects for international aid are also bleak.

This gloomy description of the existing reality suggests that Eritrea will have to rely on limited internal resources and scanty inflows of foreign money. Under these circumstances, the correct strategy should be one that places the premium on small scale industries geared toward domestic and regional consumption. Even if a good deal of foreign capital could be obtained in the form of loans, it would be extremely risky to embark upon capital-intensive modes of development as many developing nations have done. First, there is no correlation between the size of capital invested in these impressive projects and the number of jobs created as the capital-to-labour ratio tends to be unacceptably high. Failing to utilize effectively the abundance of Eritrean labour, these projects could in the long run prove to be economically unrationalizable. Second, in the absence of a domestically sustainable technological base, Eritrea will be forced to rely on imported spare parts for these projects, thereby accentuating the country's continued dependence on the outside world. Moreover, operating imported technologies by a less trained Eritrean workforce can prove to be costly.

The Tanzanian experience can illustrate the above points. Using state of the art technology, Tanzania built a pulp and paper plant which came into operation in 1985 with generous Swedish aid to the tune of $600 million. Relying on wholly imported spare parts, chemicals and fuel, the mill today operates at a fraction of its 60,000 ton-capacity. Its products cost three to four times more than comparable imports. An environmental nightmare also haunts the country as acid rain generated by the plant is damaging nearby tea plantations which are Tanzania's premier hard currency earner.[14]

In the context of this experience, building technology from the bottom-up, that is, forcing technology and society to move in lockstep, can prove to be effective and cost efficient in the long run. The obvious advantage of starting out with simple technology and small scale production is that technical know-how can accumulate as Eritreans gain the necessary learning curve. In this way the emerging relationship between the levels of technological advance and the knowledge and experience of those who operate the machines become organic.

AVOID DEBT ENTRAPMENT

Reliance on international loans in order to promote internal development is another risky business. In the 1970s, when petrodollars were in abundance, many developing countries borrowed these dollars to finance their industrialization drive. Before long, however, they found themselves entrapped by the money they hoped would provide national prosperity, and consequently their development stalled. Theoretically, it is always possible to borrow money in anticipation that it would be invested in productive sectors. This represents what economists would call intertemporal trade which is the deferment of present consumption in favor of having it sometime in the future. The rationale behind this expectation is that the borrowed money would be invested in projects that would pay off the debt and still generate surplus revenues for society to consume at that time.

In fact, as long as Eritrea participates in the global division of labour, such a form of intertemporal trade is unavoidable. The argument against heavy borrowing is that there is always the temptation to use the loans for capital-intensive development purposes, sometimes investing the money in impressive projects without making valid feasibility studies or cost–benefit analyses. As noted, Eritrea lacks the technological base to sustain any meaningful capital-intensive development. Thus, capital inflow should be directed toward strengthening small or medium size industries.

IDENTIFY STATE DOMAINS

One fundamental factor why most African nations failed to nurture and sustain home-grown capitalism in a larger context of coherent macro-economic policies is the fact that the political elites in these nations evolved an instrumentalist notion of the state. Accordingly, the state is viewed not as an agent of capital accumulation for the common good but as a means of personal wealth-creation and accumulation. Consequently, patrimonial capitalism, defined in terms of patron–client relationships, has come to dominate African economies. The emergent African states, whether self-professed capitalist or socialist, established a multitude of parastatals run by political appointees whose ultimate loyalty is to the political elites. The political managers of these public enterprises and their patrons together siphon off whatever revenues are generated, thereby distorting the process of accumulation and progress. In addition to corrosive elements of corruption and mismanagement, the technical incompetence of these managers makes evolution of any autonomous development virtually impossible.

In this context, ownership of productive assets by the Eritrean state is practically unsuitable to the current stage of Eritrean development. After all, Eritrea shares identical social formations with most African states which suggests that the inherent weakness of Eritrean society makes the latter vulnerable to manipulation, exploitation and control by those who control the state. Thus at this juncture in Eritrean history, the state must clearly identify the areas in which it actively participates in the economy in the form of limited ownership of strategic assets which have national security and those areas where the state plays simply the role of provider of general directions, information and guidance in the context of a larger macro-economic policy.

The above observation requires identification of three general areas. First, renovation and modernization of whatever industrial and business enterprises are left in Eritrea today must be carried out in ways that ensure participation of workers in ownership of these assets in conjunction with private capital. Since these industrial residues do not have perceptible national security values or economic determinacy, the state should stay out. Second, the state must identify specific areas to which foreign capital can be attracted. These must be areas which Eritreans cannot develop and exploit due to lack of capital and technology. In addition, this foreign dominated sector may have to be export-oriented as the foreign firms have the capacity to utilize their oligopolistic position in the global economy to find their own market niches. Properly guided in the desired direction this sector can be induced to generate a spread effect into other sectors in terms of technology and liquidity. Moreover, fear of foreign competition and the resultant internal market saturation or foreign control of it can be judiciously precluded and Eritrea can also benefit from the receipt of foreign exchange earnings. This is exactly what the northeast Asian 'tigers' have done and Eritrea ought to learn from their experience.

Finally, there are areas where active state intervention can be justified especially in the transportation and extractive sectors. Development of an efficient and reliable public transportation system is definitely in the long-term interest of Eritrea. Eritrea is not so large as to require proliferation of private modes of transportation since most people live within walking distance from their work places, at least for now, and they can even continue to use bicycles as they have done in the past. Whatever need exists can be met by publicly-owned-and-operated modes of transportation. Assets necessary for the development of such a system need not be exclusively owned by the central government. In fact, it would be ideal if the system were to be collectively owned by the provinces, the central government and the employees who run the system. In this way, since the major forces in question will have a definite stake in the system in terms of profitability, they will certainly be concerned about its efficiency and reliability.

Numerous additional reasons can be adduced in defence of this position. In the Eritrean context, at this stage in particular, importation of foreign cars represents class profligacy and hence class division. Even in economic terms, importation of cars represents the outflow of much-needed capital and hence a drain on the Eritrean economy. Moreover, curtailment of imported cars can lead to substantial reduction in Eritrea's dependency on foreign oil, another source of capital drainage. Money and energy saved in this way can be effectively utilized in other production sectors. The environmental imperative also militates against importation of cars as, in the long run, they represent environmental costs.

With respect to extractive resources, this sector has been a matter of controversy between developing nations and multinational corporations. It is in Eritrea's long-term interest to avoid future politicization of the extractive sector by clearly defining the parameters of foreign participation and its own role in it. The absence of a technological base and the magnitude of capital outlay needed in this sector may preclude exclusive state ownership. In this context, a state–private partnership can be worked out. The salience of the argument in favor of active state intervention here, however, lies in the fact that the degree and form of state involvement in the exploration, development and exploitation of extractive resources will have determinative implications for the economy as a whole. Any future take-off for the Eritrean economy will partly be determined by the relative availability and price levels of energy resources. There is additional motivation that warrants active state intervention in this sector. Until now, urban society has been wholly dependent on extraction of firewood from the countryside for cooking and related necessities of life, a major contributory factor to the tragic deterioration of the environment. Thus by utilizing its regulative and control mechanisms in the energy sector in particular, the state can be in a position to reorient the urban population toward an alternative pattern of energy uses.

FOCUS ON THE AGRARIAN SECTOR

Above, I alluded to the fact that land reform is requisite for any transition to capitalism. A nation which cannot feed its people is incapable of initiating meaningful development. Not only does the status of being a net importer of food create an external imbalance in terms of capital outflow, but also the inability to produce food internally necessarily precludes the nation from being able to generate agricultural surpluses that can be funnelled into the industrial sector. The foregoing observation suggests that agricultural development must be the major preoccupation of the Eritrean state. Of course, all regions are not equally amenable to similar modes of agrarian development. Thus different strategies applicable to each region must be developed. For example, vegetation is virtually non-existent in the country's Red Sea region, thus the orientation here must be one of developing a fishing industry (see Shaw, this volume, Chapter 13). This can help reorient seminomadic people of the region toward a new pattern of existence and introduces an important diet into Eritrean society. Eritrea can also participate in the regional division of labour as producer and exporter of fish products.

On the other hand, western Eritrea can be transformed into a region of large scale agro-commercial plantations under state guidance and using modern agrotechnology. The region has the potential to provide the basis for primitive capital accumulation. After all, this region had in the past produced most of the fruit, vegetables, oil seeds and cotton for both local and external markets until the 1960s when it was disrupted by war. If economic rehabilitation of this region is achieved, Eritrea can transform its proximity to the Arabian peninsula and its labour abundance into a comparative advantage over its long-distance competitors in capturing a good market share in the region.

Another area which mandates immediate attention is the plateau region. Constituting only twenty per cent of the country's land mass, the region houses over fifty per cent of the total population. Although regarded as Eritrea's bread basket, in recent decades, due to a combination of war requirements and deforestation, its agricultural potential has substantially diminished, with consequent conditions of undernourishment and malnutrition.

The traditional mode of land ownership in the plateau region has been either kinship-based or communal. In either case, the result has been widespread land fragmentation making the inhabitants grossly underemployed and undernourished. To get out of this deleterious cycle of agrarian fragmentation and the consequent impoverishment of the peasants, two strategies can be proposed. The first involves abolition of both the kinship and communal modes of land ownership and promoting, instead, privatization of land in which case land can be freely sold to owners of capital. This would presumably reverse the process of continual land fragmentation and would lead to reaggregation of small plots into large scale holdings until they become agro-commercially viable.

The downside of such a policy is that the process of extensive marketization of land will inevitably produce a massive dislocation of peasants who will then have to drift into urban centres. If this occurs, it will represent the intentional replication of the African experience. The negative implications of such a process can only be counteracted by a concurrent initiation of a state-guided industrialization drive in the cities in order to accommodate the new arrivals. As stated, though, given the absence of either internal liquidity or international capital, the simultaneous pursuance of extensive rural marketization and urban industrialization is beyond the systemic capabilities of the new state and cannot produce the desired results.

Moreover, privatization of the agrarian sector does not necessarily produce an harmonious relationship between nature and society in the countryside. The presumption is that, as capitalism is driven by profit maximization, entrepreneurs may not be willing to sacrifice part of their profits in terms of promoting afforestation programmes. Obviously agrarian rehabilitation of the plateau is impossible without putting up significant portions of the region for vigorous afforestation. To be sure, structural conditions for a rural bourgeois order in highland Eritrea do not exist.

The alternative approach to the above-described strategy of agrarian rehabilitation will be to modify and strengthen communal land ownership. According to the *Deisa* or communal mode of ownership, land was distributed among villagers every seven or so years in order to accommodate new adults. Since land is collectively owned by the village, individual farmers have only possessory right to the land. To ensure fairness, the entire land holdings of the village are divided into three categories: not fertile, semifertile and fertile. Each farmer receives a plot or number of plots from each category. Since parcelization of the land is carried out according to fertility, the method has important geographic implication as these plots are widely dispersed and, as such, is inherently against economies of scale. If this pattern of cyclical distribution and the consequent fragmentation of land is to be halted, villagers must enter into a collective relationship with the land and transform the village into a viable economic unit. That is, since construction of a rural bourgeois order in the Eritrean context is improbable, the alternative will be to promote collective agrarian capitalism. stated differently, only the collective application of labour to the land can make agricultural development in highland Eritrea a sustainable economic option.

In this modified context of the communal mode of land ownership, each village would be encouraged to evolve into an autonomous unit, the produce of collective labour being shared by its members according to the principles of capitalism, and its relationship with the rest of the economy governed by the operatives of the market economy. This method can promote immediate reaggregation of the land into viable large scale units without having to displace any peasant and without consequences of urban congestion. The other advantage is that villages will be willing to set aside portions of their holdings for reforestation. Provided that there is democratic mobilization, education and effective communication, villagers can immediately appreciate the fact that their future survival and livelihood ultimately depend on reestablishing their relationship with nature. The state can help in this regard by providing extension services, education on importance of seed improvement, uses of fertilizers, afforestation services, credit facilities and similar support services.

This strategy, to which I strongly subscribe, is premised on anticipation that villages will over time evolve into a web of autonomous agrarian units whose interdependence is mediated by connection to cities. Farm units become self-sufficient in food production while at the same time supplying agricultural produce to cities. When this occurs, the countryside can provide the basis for surplus extraction in the form of taxes which can then be used by the state to fuel the process of primitive capital accumulation.

CONCLUSION

Operating on the assumption that Eritrea has chosen capitalism as the way of its future, I have attempted to probe the fundamental assumptions of capitalism. I have tried to either implicitly or explicitly validate some of these assumptions and discard others.

The imperatives of development are such that it is crucially important to move away from the economistic understanding of a transition and toward an understanding of the complex relationship of politics and economics. Economic managerialism alone does not produce the desired output. Historical evidence suggests that long-term economic prosperity occurs only in an environment where the political system is capable of building mechanisms that ensure public accountability that militates against the emergence of a self-perpetuating bureaucracy.

A political system that tolerates neither partners nor competitors undermines the very *raison d'etre* of its existence and by extension the crucial context of development. Bernard Shaw's admonition is relevant in this regard: absolute power does not corrupt men; it is rather foolish men in power that corrupt absolute power. Having a popularly elected government and assembly by itself is not sufficient, for these institutions can be undermined, as always happens, by the elite that tries to rule by fiat or decrees. If the political environment is to be conducive to economic development, institutions or parliamentary legislation should be viewed, not as ends in themselves, but as moments in an ongoing process, one marked by a regularized circulation of the elite, celebrating arrival of the new and departure of the old. It is terribly important to note that the endurance and success of any organization ultimately depends on the contributions it makes to the depersonalization of politics and to the institutionalization of the constitutional means of democracy. Failure to understand this political axiom is a dangerous folly.

Notes

1. Steve Chan, *East Asian Dynamism: Growth, Order and Security in the Pacific Region* (Boulder: Westview Press, 1990) p. 36.
2. Robert Gilpin, *The Political Economy of International Politics* (Englewood Cliffs, NJ: Prentice Hall, 1987) pp. 265–7.

3. Ibid.
4. Ibid., pp. 282–4.
5. Chan, *East Asian Dynamism*, p. 37.
6. Robert B. Reich, *The Work of Nations: Preparing Ourselves for 21st Century Capitalism* (New York: Alfred A. Knopf, 1991) p. 20.
7. Ibid.
8. Ibid., pp. 22–3.
9. Thomas J. McCormick, *America's Half Century: United States Foreign Policy in the Cold War* (Baltimore: Johns Hopkins Press, 1989) p. 88.
10. Ibid., p. 89.
11. Chan, *East Asian Dynamism*, pp. 49–50.
12. My discussion of these factors draws heavily on Andrew Leonard, 'Twilight of the Despots: Taiwan Goes its own Third Way', *The Nation*, 13 April, 1992, p. 482. See also Chan, *East Asian Dynamism*, pp. 39–40
13. As quoted in Harry Magdoff, *The Age of Imperialism: the Economics of US Foreign Policy* (New York: Monthly Review, 1969) p. 38.
14. Jennifer S. Whitaker, *How Can Africa Survive?* (New York: Harper & Row, 1988) p. 76.

6 Roots of Famine in Sudan's Killing Fields

John Prendergast

In the market square of El Obeid early one morning, an old man was pulling at the tail of his donkey to get it up. A second man tugged its ears. Two boys joined them and heaved in the middle. All of them failed. The donkey was dying. It was all the man possessed. His cattle had gone in 1984–5, his sheep early in this calamity for virtually nothing. His wife had died under an operation. He had lost everything. Seeing the expression on his face, Sarah Errington, our photographer, impulsively took his hand. It was battered and calloused by work at the wells, where for a pittance he was winding water for the local council. It is hard to know what to say to people who are dying very, very slowly.[1]

The 1980s were a decade of famine, war, and death for Sudan. The statistics of suffering are mind-numbing. The best estimates suggest that more than 100,000 Sudanese starved to death in the drought-stricken Western region in 1984 and 1985. Between 250,000 and 500,000 – no one knows the precise number – perished in the war-torn South in 1987 and 1988. According to the US Committee on Refugees, war and famine have killed at least 1.3 million Sudanese since 1983, when war began again in the South. At least three million Southern Sudanese have been displaced from their homes, as have increasing numbers from the west. Even in parts of Sudan not experiencing conflict, nearly half the people have experienced periods of extreme hunger. Also, at times Sudan has been host to up to one million refugees from Ethiopia and other war-torn neighbours.

Sudanese found no respite in the early 1990s. As the decade opened, nine to 11 million Sudanese were endangered by famine, according to the US Office of Foreign Disaster Assistance. By the beginning of 1994, 1.5 million people were partially or wholly dependent on emergency assistance in the South, according to the UN. Millions more were at risk in the North because of severe shortfalls in food production. In the past decade, tens of thousands died because of delays in providing food aid due to government and rebel obstruction, military strategies which target civilians and productive assets, and the ineffectiveness of donor relief operations.

A field trip to Sudan by this author in late 1991 found that NGOs, UN personnel, and USAID all were unable to accurately assess actual death tolls because conflict and government obstruction kept them out of much of Darfur. But famine was indeed severe. Early rains in many places were followed by extended dry periods, which withered most plant life. Farmers who still had seed left at this point had to gamble whether to plant in an uncertain climate, or instead eat the seed to keep their families alive until the harvest or the next emergency relief distribution. In the event, the 1991 harvest was disastrous, especially in the West.[2]

Four field trips by this author in 1993 discovered even worse conditions. Many displaced communities and towns caught in the war zone were unable to produce for themselves and had not been reached by emergency relief operations, in some cases for nearly a year. A Center for Disease Control team which assessed conditions in four Southern Sudanese towns found malnutrition rates of over eighty per cent, higher than what was found in most of Somalia before the humanitarian intervention in December 1992.

A Famine Early Warning System report describes a situation which might be classified as an emergency, but seems more the norm in parts of Sudan. This excerpt comes from a mid-1991 report on Western Sudan: 'Animals have died, household assets have been sold, and villages are virtually abandoned, leaving behind only some of the old men, women and children. Those who could leave have already done so. Those who remain are running out of coping strategies.'[3]

Behind these statistics lie shattered lives: people caught between armies, fleeing from war, greeted with hostility as they search for scraps of food in unfamiliar towns and villages. Millions are trapped in the same cycle which Catholic Archbishop Gabriel Zubeir Wako of Khartoum described during the 1985 famine:

> War sets in motion a number of deadly anti-social and inhuman forces that will maintain the war mentality in the citizens even in times of peace... Famine is people haunted by the specter of death descending inexorably on them. It is the plight of people longing to fill themselves with the scraps falling from their rich or lucky neighbors' tables.... The hope of picking up a few scraps causes the hunger-stricken to migrate to towns. At their new destinations they discover for the first time that hunger has made them undesirables and social outcasts.[4]

Forty per cent of Sudanese babies are underweight at birth, a figure among the worst in Africa. Children throughout Sudan remain extremely vulnerable. They are the greatest victims of famine related mortality. Malnutrition rates in many areas exceed eighty per cent.[5] Half of Sudanese childhood deaths are caused by diarrhoea-related diseases which could be almost entirely eliminated through improved nutrition and sanitation and simple, inexpensive preventive health measures (see Kelly, this volume, Chapter 12).

CAUSES OF FAMINE IN SUDAN

Four issues at the heart of the creation of famine will be discussed here: war, militia activity, agricultural policies, and World Bank/IMF policies. The role of international humanitarian agencies in perpetuating famine is beyond the scope of this discussion, but is an important factor.

WAR

Conflict in Southern Sudan

The roots of the conflict in Southern Sudan began with the advent of slave trading, which provided the economic rationale for outsider interest. Northern Arab Sudanese merchants joined British and Egyptians in slaving expeditions to the south, leaving an enduring legacy of bitter resentment. In 1822 alone, raiders captured and enslaved an estimated 30,000 southerners. Although outlawed in 1898, slavery still goes on, well-documented in a 1993 International Labor Organization report on world-wide slavery. In the Southern province of Bahr al-Ghazal and the transitional area of southern Kordofan, Arab militias, armed by the government, continue to butcher and enslave thousands of Dinkas and Nubas from neighbouring villages.[6]

British colonial administrators strictly segregated Northern and Southern Sudan from 1925 until shortly after World War II. They hoped to prevent the southward spread of Arab nationalism and anti-colonialism. The South is mainly black; most of its people are followers of traditional religions or Christianity. Northerners are predominately Arab and Muslim, with the exception of scattered African populations and a concentration of over one million displaced Southerners around Khartoum.

For most of the colonial period, Britain banned the teaching of Arabic in the South and discouraged use of Arab names. Christian missionaries (barred by the British from the Arab North) were allocated areas of the South where they could freely proselytize and provide schooling in English. Britain's anti-Arab policies created resentments among Arab Muslims, setting the stage for modern-day discrimination against non-Muslim Sudanese. Arab Muslims, mostly from the favoured Central region between the Blue and White Nile Rivers, have dominated post-colonial politics. Southern leaders say they have been unfairly excluded from decision-making.

Muslim political parties dominated Sudan as it achieved independence in 1955. Already, North–South tensions had led to a mutiny of Southern soldiers, which grew into rebellion against the government in Khartoum. The nation's civilian leaders were ousted in a 1958 *coup* by Northern military officers who favoured military action in the South. Popular protests sparked partly by discontent over the junta's inability to end the war brought down the military government and led to restoration of civilian rule in 1965. But the war continued.

Colonel Jaafar Nimeri led a 1969 *coup* by young officers. In 1972 he signed the Addis Ababa Agreement, granting limited autonomy to the South and ending the first civil war. But after another decade of discrimination against the South and Nimeri's abrogation of the Agreement in 1983, Southern army officers formed the Sudan People's Liberation Army (SPLA), and a second civil war began.

Many Southerners, including most of the political and military elites, believe that the North uses its political dominance to control far more than its fair share of the nation's wealth and government spending. Disputes over natural resources factor into the conflict.

- Southerners opposed Colonel Nimeri's plans to construct the massive Jonglei canal, aimed at diverting more water from the Nile for irrigation in Egypt and the water-starved North. Southerners feared it would disrupt their region's social ecology, by draining the vast Sudd swamp vital to Southern nomadic pastoralists and creating new farming areas which would be reserved for Northern farmers as settlers. Despite southern opposition, the Nimeri government brought in a French multinational corporation to begin excavating in the early 1980s. Since 1983, the SPLA has blocked work on the project.
- Southerners feel the South should benefit most from the large oil deposits discovered in Southern Sudan by Chevron in the late 1970s. Central government plans, vehemently opposed by Southern politicians, would have piped crude oil north for refining and export. At one point, the Nimeri government tried to redraw the boundary between the North and South so as to incorporate the oil deposits in the North, leaving the South out of the planning process altogether. The SPLA brought Chevron's work to a halt in 1983.
- Successive Northern-dominated governments have utilized war tactics which have depopulated areas of the South which border the North.

These are prime agricultural areas, and some suspect a deliberate strategy to clear them for the southward movement of mechanized agriculture by wealthy Northern agricultural interests.7

The aggressive Islamization campaign undertaken by the ruling
National Islamic Front (NIF) further inflamed the conflict, especially in
recent years. At independence, Sudan was at least constitutionally a
secular state. As military ruler from 1969 to 1985, Nimeri gradually
Islamicized the legal system. Islamic laws were introduced in 1983 but not
fully implemented. The democratically elected government of Sadiq al-
Mahdi was reluctant to repeal Islamic law despite its unpopularity with
many Northern and virtually all Southern Sudanese.

General Omar al-Bashir, who ousted al-Mahdi in June 1989, has fully
implemented Islamic law, deepening the South's alienation. The laws in
effect make non-Muslims second-class citizens and curtail the rights of
Muslims who are not fundamentalists. They severely limit the status of
women. Islamic courts now can punish by crucifixion, amputation, stoning,
and flogging. They codify the principle of retaliation, 'an eye for an eye'.[8]

But Sudan's divisions are not simply North versus South, Muslim versus
Christian, and African versus Arab. Many Northerners are non-Muslims;
many Muslim Sudanese are African; and many Sudanese Muslims oppose
fundamentalism and making Islamic law into national law. It is mostly
because differences in ethnicity and religion coincide with gaps in economic, political, and social status that these cleavages lead to violence.[9]

The South is a mosaic of cultures and ethnic groups. Differences have
been exaggerated by divide-and-rule policies of colonial and post-colonial
governments, so that it is quite difficult even in times of tranquillity to
bring a measure of unity to the region. Until the factional split in August
1991, the SPLA had succeeded in being the unchallenged representative of
Southern aspirations by violently repressing all dissent. Successive
Khartoum governments have exploited the perception in parts of the south
that the SPLA is disproportionately led by a group of Dinkas from the Bor
area. Khartoum has armed other ethnic groups in the South to resist what
the government threatens will be 'Dinka dominance'. These militias have
had little success, and command little popular support.

For nearly ten years, the SPLA stated that it was fighting for a unified,
secular Sudan, with peripheral regions in the country having greater representation in the central government. Insurgent commanders Riek Mashar
and Lam Akol rose up against the chairman of the SPLA, Colonel John
Garang, in August 1991. They favoured independence for the South, and
also criticized the SPLA's authoritarian structure and human rights viola-

tions. At the time, *Middle East International* presented the separation issue in the following way:

> The broaching of the independence issue is explosive. The desire for independence is widespread in the South – as is the recognition of the problems this represents. The SPLA has always advocated unity, indeed it fought an extremely bloody war with [another southern faction, Anya Nya II] on precisely this issue, leaving a residue of anger. But anger is great, too, against a North perceived as at best indifferent and at worst permanently aggressive. Separation is an easy issue to exploit in the South.[10]

Outsiders also began to broach the subject of independence in 1991. '[Secession is] no longer so unspeakable an idea,' said a senior US State Department official near the time of the attempted *coup* against Garang. 'We would like to see Sudan remain a viable united entity, but we can't deny that these feelings may be gaining support within [SPLA territory].'[11]

In November and December, 1991, fierce fighting between the two factions displaced over 200,000 people,[12] and killed between two and five thousand Sudanese. Corpses of civilians were reportedly lying on the roads, village grain stores were looted, and cattle raided and killed.[13] Aside from a government offensive during the summer of 1992, nearly all of the fighting in Southern Sudan from 1991 to 1993 was intra-factional combat between Garang's mainstream SPLA and two splinter groups. In 1993 personal rivalries deepened between the various factional leaders but their positions on fundamental issues such as self-determination for the South began to narrow.

Conflict in Western Sudan

During the late 1980s and early 1990s in western Sudan, near-anarchy resulted from conflict with environmental and racial roots. Historically, northwestern Arab pastoralists had followed their migratory routes southward into areas inhabited by sedentary African groups after the latter had harvested their crops. Because of recurrent droughts and increasing desertification, the Arab pastoralists began moving their herds much earlier in search of water and pasture, often destroying the unharvested fields of the African farmers. This resulted in increased conflict between the two groups. London's Panos Institute dubs this and other conflicts of this nature 'greenwars'.[14]

During the 1980s, weapons were supplied by regional governors, Libya, Chadian rebels, governments in Khartoum, and the SPLA. Small-scale localized conflicts escalated into high technology wars of attrition and banditry. Spears and knives gave way to automatic weapons and even attack helicopters. War uprooted villages, displaced families, and provided fertile ground for recruitment of young men to government militias, the SPLA, or even local ethnically-based militias.

The conflict took on increasingly broad political implications during the early 1990s. Libya aggressively sought political and economic integration with the region and control of the border trade; the Sudanese government forcibly attempted to remove any pockets of opposition; and the SPLA tried with little success to get a foothold in the Western region. All of these outsiders appeal to ethnic or religious sentiments as the basis of their message locally, further deepening divisions.

UNEQUAL FOOD AND DEVELOPMENT POLICIES

Historically, government policies toward agriculture in Sudan (as throughout the Horn) have neglected those who have provided most of the food for domestic consumption: smallholder farmers and pastoralists. Government policies have, in several stages, encouraged and subsidized shifts toward larger scale, commercial, often export-oriented agriculture. Internal markets have not emerged which can distribute essential goods and meet the needs of the majority. The result has been, according to Oxfam's former country director in Sudan, the disappearance of subsistence economies throughout much of the country. 'Food insecurity no longer defines one or another period but is a constant condition of the market economy that has come to dominate the country.'[15]

State policies in Sudan, like those in Ethiopia and Somalia, have fostered consolidation of rural landholdings. Thousands of farm families were pushed onto less fertile, over-used lands, and many were left landless. Inappropriate land and agricultural policies undermined many peoples' traditional base of subsistence. They have contributed to dissatisfaction, political turmoil, and famine.

THE ASSAULT ON SELF-SUFFICIENCY

Erratic rainfall is the norm for Sudan, but for centuries smallholder farmers and pastoralists adapted effectively. Their agricultural and livestock practices aimed at minimizing risks rather than maximizing returns.[16] They developed ways to cope with and survive periods of drought and instability:

- Farmers set aside food reserves in productive years;
- Traditional cultures included strong habits of sharing whatever was available through extended families, communities and clans;
- Because rural markets developed slowly, small farmers relied on their own production for a variety of foodstuffs and other essentials, avoiding the risks of wildly fluctuating grain prices in a market controlled by a monopoly of grain merchants;
- Agricultural labourers were paid with grain rather than cash, thus shielding them from grain inflation.[17]

Throughout this century, these community-based coping mechanisms gradually have been eroded. Great Britain introduced large-scale cotton and pump irrigation schemes during the 1920s, working in cooperation with Sudanese large-scale merchants and landowners. During World War II, the British assisted individuals from these groups in greatly expanding production of cotton, sorghum, and millet to meet wartime needs. Much of this expansion was on lands expropriated from small farmers.[18] After independence in 1956, these large landowners used state credit and policies allowing expropriation of land to expand their profitable, mechanized production of food crops further. Meanwhile, Sudan's peasants produced food crops on their own plots by hand and supplemented their incomes by seasonal wage labour. Throughout both the colonial period and early independence, credit and trading terms worked against small farmers. They were increasingly crowded onto marginal lands or off the land entirely. More and more people competed for limited wage employment in agriculture, and few alternatives were developed.

BRUTAL MOVES TO MECHANIZATION AND MARKETS

The Nimeri government in the 1970s introduced yet larger-scale food export schemes financed primarily by Saudi Arabia, Kuwait and other Arab nations. They hoped to make Sudan the 'Breadbasket of the Arab World', providing cheap, abundant food to these wealthy but arid and unfertile nations.

The Unregistered Land Act of 1971 made all land the property of the state, which in turn seized land which had passed down over generations as traditional peasant holdings or grazing areas. The government then leased this at low prices to large-scale investors, some of them from Middle Eastern countries. These investors turned grazing lands into capital-intensive mechanized farms, blocking nomadic routes and ejecting many small landholders.[19] World Bank money was made available for such investment. Safeguards such as lease conditions intended to retain tree belts or create corridors for the nomads' herds were ignored. Many mechanized farmers began to cultivate without permission. After a few years crop yields would fall; exhausted and eroded land would be abandoned, while the lease-holder moved on to repeat the cycle elsewhere. Landless labourers or migrant workers employed on the farm were left behind.[20]

Continuing expansion of large farms and movement of small farmers onto less productive lands put great pressure on forests and scrub. These had been traditional sources of foodstuffs and other resources during drought. During the last decade, Sudan lost an average of 31,000 square kilometres of wooded land per year to deforestation. Studies in the mid-1980s by the National Energy Authority in Sudan suggested that by the year 2000, 77 per cent of all tree cover in the northern regions will have been destroyed. Another study done by Danida, a Danish development agency, found that northern Sudan lost enough forest land to desertification in 1989 alone to supply one-fourth of the nation's wood needs for a year. Environmentalists from groups such as the Worldwatch Institute say that the entire region may soon become a desert.[21]

Since 1917, Sudan's population has multiplied by 6, its cattle by 21, its camels by 13, its sheep by 12, and its goats by 8. If rains were regular, this might be sustainable. But there are dramatic swings of climate. It may be that in certain places the land will not be able to sustain the people and animals that live there. Under today's conditions of war and inequality, Sudan cannot feed itself.

MILITIAS

A primary reason why drought and war in southern Sudan and the transitional zone have led to perpetual famine conditions is the policy of successive governments of creating and arming paramilitary forces along ethnic lines. The result has been a descent into a Lebanon-like anarchy, where each faction needs its own army or militia to survive. Law and order are no longer administered by legitimate state institutions. The rural poor caught up in this power play are ruled by the most feared and powerful, and are often forced to flee their land to escape enslavement or death.

In southern Sudan, an unparalleled period of fratricidal civil conflict is presently unfolding. Thousands have been killed and the region is being indiscriminately stripped of its assets, rendering whole communities totally dependent on international humanitarian aid. The process is abetted and, at times, directed by the NIF regime, using age-old antagonisms to undertake divide-and-rule military tactics.

Civilian populations have become the main military targets. Using the cynical logic of counter-insurgency – 'drain the water to catch the fish' – combatants and their militias have conducted limited, low visibility offensives throughout the 1990s. The objective is to destroy the livelihoods of communities perceived to be real or potential supporters of one's opponents. Villages more often than towns are targeted in low-profile, maximum-destruction, scorched-earth sweeps. Houses are burned, livestock and food are stolen, women are raped, young men are killed or forcibly conscripted, and wells are poisoned. This pattern is followed by all factions and their militia allies and proxies.

The modern militia strategy has its roots in Arab ethnic groups from the western provinces of Kordofan and Darfur, who were initially armed to provide a line of defence against possible SPLA advances. Instead, these militias used their weapons to attack and loot villages of their non-Arab neighbours, seeking to replace their livestock and land lost because of drought and large-scale mechanized farming policies.

In the southwest, the Dinka have been victimized by various Arab ethnic groups armed by the government, primarily because the Dinkas formed the backbone of the SPLA from its inception. The thousands that have left their homes because of the fighting are often attacked and raped, robbed, and enslaved by roving Arab militias operating with support of local authorities and the government army. General Bashir has continuously tried to forge a direct alliance with these Arab militias in the southwest, known as the *Murahaliin*, but because of their traditional alliance with the Ansar (Umma Party supporters), any agreement to work together at any level is tenuous.

Various ethnic groups justify the militias as their only means of self-defence. The government maintains that it needs the militias to sustain peace and order. General Bashir claims that he personally participated in the development of the militia strategy under previous governments. He legalized the militias and incorporated many of them, such as the *Murahaliin*, into the army as paramilitary forces.

WORLD BANK/IMF

The World Bank and the IMF have a long history of collaboration in economic and development planning in Sudan. Although still assisting in mechanized food production expansion, in 1972 the World Bank began pressuring Sudan to increase its main export crop, cotton, because of an externally perceived comparative advantage over other types of agricultural production. By 1978 the Bank had halted all funding for rainfed mechanized food production schemes, offering Sudan a massive rehabilitation plan to rebuild the cotton-producing infrastructure.

Also in 1978, the IMF stabilization plan was implemented. It consisted of drastic currency devaluations, removal of government subsidies on food and other consumption items, revisions in agricultural pricing policies, and privatization (sale to the private sector of many government and quasi-government enterprises, combined with deregulation of agricultural marketing).

The period 1978–85 was the apex of the involvement of the multilaterals, and examining the effects of that assistance is instructive for current analysis. First, the cornerstone of the World Bank/IMF approach to Africa has been to support *productivity increases of primary products for export,* in order that countries like Sudan grow out of their economic malaise. The export-led model of development had severely deleterious effects on the Sudanese economy. The economic, social, and political effects of the export-led growth model in Sudan were becoming increasingly graphic by the mid-1980s. Both the mechanized grain and irrigated cotton schemes supported by the World Bank in Sudan gave the advantage to the wealthiest segments of society with capital to invest, while pushing smallholders off their land by the thousands.[22]

Food production for local consumption fell sharply during the 1980s and the country developed an import dependence on wheat through US taxpayer subsidized commodity aid programmes (which the Bashir regime is attempting to reduce through large-scale wheat production schemes aiming eventually for food self-sufficiency). By the time the 1984–5 famine hit, over a million small farmers were directly at risk of starvation. The government, strapped by growing debt, was unable to purchase any of the over 800,000 metric tons of grain produced by private commercial farmers in eastern Sudan.

A second condition for receiving aid from the multilaterals was *currency devaluation.* The rationale for this component of the structural adjustment package was three-fold: to stimulate export production; curtail import demand; and discourage the black market. Yet despite six major devaluations between 1978 and 1985, the balance of payments, inflation and the budget were not affected as projected. The current account deficit went from 6 per cent of GDP in 1977 to 11 per cent in 1983.

One reason why devaluation failed to improve the performance of exports was that cotton prices declined in the world market. This was no coincidence. Many Third World countries were encouraged to produce many of the same commodities for export by the World Bank and IMF. When combined with constant, competitive devaluations, the result was continuous increases in output and export volumes, but reduced foreign exchange earnings. And of course, cheaper goods in North American and European supermarkets.

Third, attempts to *reduce government expenditure* caused increased suffering and instability. Development and social service spending was halved during the main adjustment period of 1978 to 1985, leading to a decline in nutritional standards and access to health care, clean water, and affordable food supplies. On the other hand, expenditures for general administration and defence more than tripled during this period.

Fourth, to stimulate production, *higher farm-gate prices* were offered to producers. In rural Sudan, wealthy merchants usually absorbed the profits from higher prices, leaving the producing small farmer with no incentive to increase production. The trader's position was enforced by lack of alternative credit sources for small farmers. No coordinated, serious attempts were made to control or regulate this wasteful and destructive speculation.

The World Bank/IMF analysis of the Sudanese economy fundamentally misread what the state really was in Sudan, and appears to continue to do so. State policies do not represent the general interest of the Sudanese people but interests of a few social groups: during the 1980s it was the military, wealthy merchants and landowners, and high-level bureaucrats; during the 1990s, it has been those allied with the NIF. The state's shrinking economic and social basis restricts its ability to act on behalf of the general population, much less specific vulnerable groups.

Stabilization programmes were full of contradictions. Irrigation, highly import-dependent, suffered from import restrictions and foreign exchange shortages and devaluations. Credit was less available because of credit ceilings. 'Thus a devaluation without the backing of considerable foreign exchange for inputs resulted directly in shortages throughout the production structure and led to a contraction of the economy.'[23]

Sudan has the distinction of having the largest arrears to the IMF in the world (over $1 billion). By 1991, the IMF issued a 'declaration of noncooperation' regarding Sudan, which largely results in blacklisting a country from most Western financial aid and credits. Sudan's government continued to negotiate with the IMF in 1992 and 1993. Ironically, their aggressive moves at privatizing the economy were held up to the multilaterals as evidence of good faith in economic policy, but the result of these policies has largely been to allow sympathizers or members of the NIF to purchase state assets at fire-sale prices and further consolidate the power of the current regime in Khartoum.

Since 1978 Sudan's indebtedness has skyrocketed. Total external debt now exceeds $14 billion. Foreign exchange shortages have been chronic. Inflation has remained high and GDP growth rates have become negative. Development expenditures have dropped significantly. Locked into the role of a supplier of raw materials to the world market, the economic results show the risks of an economy based on the export of a few products whose price is fixed externally.[24]

CONCLUSION

Until late 1992 the donor community's response to this complex, chronic emergency was to downplay the human rights element and pursue a massive food band aid, foresaking active human rights pressure, humanitarian diplomacy and broader conflict resolution processes. This has changed of late, as the UN, US, UK and other countries actively engaged in humanitarian diplomacy and ratcheted up the human rights pressure. These interventions are far too little, yet perhaps not too late.

Human rights-guided economic and political pressures must be stepped up further on all combatants, including the possibilities of trade embargoes, border closures, disinvestment, and asset-freezing. This campaign must be carefully coordinated with a well-researched and fully resourced international diplomatic initiative involving a team of seasoned diplomats seconded to a process which receives long-term commitment by major donor countries. Besides a comprehensive peace agreement as its ultimate objective, the diplomatic team should be empowered to negotiate interim agreements on humanitarian access and demilitarization of certain high risk areas.

Massive food aid over the past five years has failed to contain the ever-expanding humanitarian emergency in Sudan. It has, arguably, fuelled it in some places through diversion and parallel currency markets. If one-tenth of the resources used to foot the extraordinary bill for food aid was committed to a high-level peace process through the UN, progress might finally be made toward settling some of the scores which are creating one of the world's worst and longest-running humanitarian catastrophes.

Notes

1. *Daily Telegraph*, 3 March, 1991.
2. UN briefing, Interaction Offices, Washington DC, 13 December, 1991.
3. Famine Early Warning System Bulletin 31 July, 1991.
4. Speech at 43rd International Eucharistic Congress, Nairobi, Kenya, 13 July, 1991.
5. Famine Early Warning System, 'Pre-Harvest Assessment', Washington DC, October 1991.
6. *Middle East Report*, October 1991, p. 3; unclassified US State Department memos, April 1993.
7. Mark Duffield, 1991, 'Absolute Distress: The Structural Causes of Hunger in Sudan', *Middle East Report*, September-October, p. 8.
8. 'News from Africa Watch', 9 April, 1991, p. 9.
9. *Middle East Report*, October 1991, p. 4.
10. *Middle East International*, 13 September, 1991.
11. *Africa News*, 9 September, 1991, p. 2.
12. World Food Programme Report 49 (New York) 9 December, 1991.
13. SEPHA Situation Report 1–30 November (New York) December 1991.
14. Panos Institute, 1991, *Greenwars* (London: Panos Institute).
15. Duffield, 'Absolute Distress', p. 4.
16. Nick Cater, 1986, *Sudan: The Roots of Famine* (Oxford: Oxfam) p. 4.
17. Jay O'Brien, 1986, 'Sowing the Seeds of Famine: the Political Economy of Food Deficits in Sudan', *Review of African Political Economy*, 33, p. 196.
18. Ali Tasier, 1988, 'The State and Agricultural Policy in Sudan', in T. Barnett and Abbas Abdel Karim (eds) *Sudan State, Capital and Transformation* (London: Croom Helm) p. 26.
19. John Clark, 1986, *For Richer, For Poorer* (Oxford: Oxfam) p. 14.
20. Cater, *Sudan*, p. 22.
21. Associated Press Newswire, 3 May, 1991; Worldwatch Institute, 1991, *Annual Report.* Washington DC.
22. John Prendergast, 1990, 'A Famine in the Making in the Sudan', *Wall Street Journal*, 1 January, 1990.
23. Dick Hansohm, 1986, 'The "Success" of IMF/World Bank Policies in Sudan', in Peter Lawrence (ed.), *World Recession and the Food Crisis in Africa* (London: James Currey) pp. 151–2.
24. Ibid., p. 155.

7 Pastoralist Resource Use and Access in Somalia: A Changing Context of Development, Environmental Stress and Conflict

Jon D. Unruh

INTRODUCTION

Turmoil in Somalia in the early 1990s had a debilitating impact on pastoralist activities. Over half the estimated 8.4 million Somalis are nomadic or semi-nomadic herders subject to vagaries of an arid climate. As Somalia's most important agricultural enterprise, pastoralism will continue as the basis for food production (Conze and Labahn 1986:15; Handulle and Gay 1987:36; Markakis 1993:9; Unruh 1993a:308; Lewis 1975:1). Decimation of herds and impoverishment of nomads beyond the capacity of indigenous recovery mechanisms will compromise food production for some time while creating large refugee populations.

Somalia has the greatest proportion of pastoralists in Africa. Prior to war and famine in the early 1990s, 65 per cent of the population participated in nomadic pastoralism, while 80 per cent engaged in livestock raising of some kind (Samatar 1989a:41; Handulle and Gay 1987:36). In the 1980s livestock production accounted for 80 per cent to 90 per cent of export earnings (Laitin 1993:136; Handulle and Gay 1987:36; Bennett *et al.* 1986:10). Pastoralism's importance is largely due to the biophysical setting: large arid and semi-arid rangelands and limited areas suited to intensive agriculture (Laitin and Samatar 1987:22). The focus of Somali nomadic material life is the camel, formerly the principal medium of exchange in the interior; during famine camels outlive less hardy livestock, providing milk, meat and transport to avoid starvation (ibid., 24).

Recent changes in access to dry season and drought grazing and watering locations led to overgrazing, land degradation, ecological stress and reduced options for transhumant herders (ibid., 127; Krokfors 1984:306; Markakis 1993:7; Hurni 1993:20). Land degradation was seen as a serious obstacle to pastoral sector development (Krokfors 1984:306). A deteriorating and shrinking resource base increased discord over access to land and water needed to maintain herds (Markakis 1993:13). Ephemeral coalitions between lineages and their constituent units were created and abandoned in attempts to facilitate access to dwindling resources (Samatar 1993:73). This increased vulnerability for pastoralists during the late 1980s and early 1990s.

As Somalia emerges from these conditions, rangeland livestock production will be essential to feed a growing population off a land resource where pastoralism may be the only sustainable use and one of the few assets possessed and easily exploited by a largely agrarian economy. This chapter examines Somali pastoralist resource use in the context of changing resource access rights. These rights are influenced by, and in turn affect development activities, ecological stress, and conflict. Following a brief description of pastoral systems and important pastoralist-related development efforts prior to the collapse of the Somali state, the chapter focuses on the interplay between development, Somali segmentary social order, and conditions of environmental stress and conflict. This interplay produced the circumstances within which most, if not all, pastoralists found themselves in the late 1980s, replaced by widespread insecurity as the dominant context for resource use options in the early 1990s.

PASTORAL SYSTEMS

Most nomads keep a mix of livestock species to maximize benefits and minimize risks. This exploits variations among species with respect to drought tolerance and vegetation use, and supplies milk, meat, transport, investment, and income (Samatar 1989a:6). Camels comprise about half of most transhumant herds; the other half is mainly sheep and goats in the north and centre, and cattle in the south. Proportions of drought resistant stock (camels, goats) traditionally increased in response to drier climatic conditions (ibid., 28).

Mobility and flexibility are required to exploit meagre range resources, thus production units are small and widely dispersed (ibid., 28). Pastoral economic logic seeks to minimize risk to secure family preservation (ibid., 6; Samatar 1989b:28). Adapted to ecosystems where forage and water are critical parameters, transhumant herding largely depends on dry season forage in reach of watering points (Scudder 1989:6; Johnson

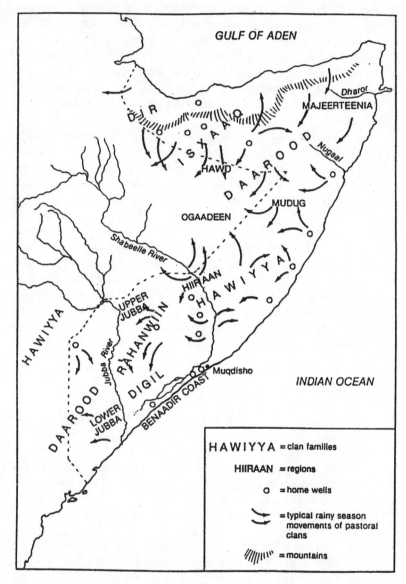

Figure 7.1   Major clan families, regions, and patterns of transhumance (from
            Cassanelli 1982)

1969:5; Breman *et al.* 1979:227). When forage is depleted or access to it and adjoining water supplies is interrupted, the result can be land degradation, livestock die-offs, conflict, and rapid sales as pastoralists seek to realign resource access arrangements, utilize marginal land, and cope with reduced herd viability. Nomadic cooperation, bound by lineage and alliance, traditionally related primarily to confrontation and hostility under ecological conditions in acute competition for scarce resources (Lewis 1961:240). Dependence by several lineage-segments on common pasture and water creates tension, especially when pressure on resources is greater (ibid., 243). Lineage systems and personal relationships provide some insurance against stock loss by the possibility of borrowing animals. This occurs through exercise of rights and obligations and carries assurances of reciprocity (Poulsen 1990:146; Samatar 1989a:40; Ornas 1990:119).

In Somalia six major clan-families and their sub-groups (clans) retain access to most land (Figure 7.1) (Samatar 1993:72; Cassanelli 1982:16). Territories are not distinct but constitute general areas and wells associated with particular groups (Gunn 1990:114). Traditionally, land is not alienated from the clan. If a pastoralist from a neighbouring clan is allowed to use grazing resources, the person is allied with the clan, rather than land being removed from its territory (ibid., 114).

Overlaps exist in territorial orbits of different clans, increasing during droughts as one clan intrudes into another's territory when its own grazing and watering resources become scarce, provoking hostilities (Bennett 1991:31). While cycles of scarcity, intrusion and confrontation have always been part of Somali pastoralism, conflict increased in recent decades due to declining ecological conditions (Bennett 1993:65).

THE DEVELOPMENT CONTEXT

Typically, livestock development attempts in SubSaharan Africa have had two general objectives: increasing animal output for market, and rangeland conservation (Bennett *et al.* 1986:146). Changes in land tenure are usually considered instrumental, with communal tenure seen as a leading constraint. Many programmes involved tenure reforms to reduce multiple resource use and access claims to specific grazing areas (ibid., 146). This disposition to individualization (notable in range conservation projects) operates with a rationale that only under individual tenure will herders use self-restraint in balancing herd size with carrying capacity (ibid., 146). Yet tenure reform has not been effective in either growth of marketable livestock products, or conservation (ibid., 149). One reason is the need for transience in resource use given great spatial variability in rainfall patterns and the quick response needed to exploit a variable environmental base. Thus geographically prescribed land resources normally only have use value for a limited time in any season (ibid., 149). Cyclic transhumant movements between seasonally available water and grazing resources are difficult to connect to individual tenure, which usually requires a technical infrastructure (ibid., 150). Figure 7.1 illustrates major patterns of Somali transhumance.

Rangeland Conservation Efforts

From 1960 to the 1980s Somalia was among the world's most aided countries (Berg 1982:1). Range management was initially pursued as a conservation rather than a development issue. This favoured range resources but not pastoralists, whose resource use strategies can be misunderstood by conservation science (Bennett *et al.* 1986:12). The objective was to stabilize and improve resources to increase quality livestock production and income for pastoralists (ibid., 11, USAID 1979:3). Range resource control and improvement was seen as a bureaucratic activity requiring government intervention (Bennett *et al.* 1986:11). Prior to the Siad Barre administration there were no attempts to introduce range management schemes or improved breeding methods (except a few experimental stations) (Samatar 1989a:41).

There were few attempts to produce forage for livestock (Massey 1989:162). Pastoralists could usually obtain freely what crop residue was available in the dry season. If subsistence farmers grew fodder crops in a good rainfall year, when plenty of free crop residue was available and fewer transhumant livestock arrive in cropped areas for the dry season, they would receive little or no money for a forage crop. Subsistence farmers were unwilling to take this risk. Large farms and plantations did not produce fodder crops for the same reasons. Government subsidy would have entailed construction and maintenance of storage facilities, and a long term commitment for purchase and transport of fodder. This would have aided farmers and pastoralists, but the government pursued other priorities (Unruh 1991:97).

Cooperatives

Under Siad creation of cooperatives was part of the effort to construct a socialist economy. The 1974 Law on Cooperative Development originally aimed to teach nomads to share resources peacefully and efficiently, and allow scientific management of rangeland (Laitin and Samatar 1987:111). The idea was to promote regeneration of grazing lands and creation of new watering holes. Fourteen cooperatives were created, with each participant family allocated an exclusive 500–750 acre grazing area, and common lands available during drought. When these cooperatives were in place the government was to provide health and educational services and a marketing outlet for stock (ibid., 111).

In the late 1970s more ambitious range cooperatives were attempted. With funding from the FAO, the UN Development Program, the Kuwait Arab Fund, and USAID, the Northern Rangelands Development Project got underway in 1977, with the Central Rangelands Development project following in 1979 (ibid., 111; Bennett *et al.* 1986:10). Both encouraged nomads to create associations to discuss rotation of pasture lands, use of grazing reserves, and building of watering points (boreholes), as well as to work with technical personnel for rangeland management. In reality they accomplished little, and there has been little investigation of changes in the pastoral sector by cooperative reforms (Laitin and Samatar 1987:111). Problems included a mismatch between grazing areas assigned to cooperatives and herd needs during drought when mobility was necessary; also contraction and expansion of herds with respect to drought cycles were not modified toward stable, intensified production, even though the rangelands initiatives were designed for this (Bennett *et al.* 1986:13).

By 1979 the cooperative system was beginning to crowd smaller herd owners not members of a cooperative out of certain areas, as grazing lands were increasingly enclosed – even though one objective of the cooperatives was to ensure that nonmembers had access to pasture (ibid., 13). Apart from the cooperative associations, were longstanding grazing associations with indigenous roots in Somali social and political structures (ibid., 13). These fit into the system of village and local government; by 1979 there were 34 associations. Before any assistance was directed to them however, they had to conform to the Rangeland Projects' determination of what was beneficial for livestock production, including grazing restrictions and water development (USAID 1979:3; Bennett *et al.* 1986:14). Different operational rules for grazing cooperatives and grazing associations put these institutions in competition (ibid., 14).

Livestock Trade, Resource Access, and Environmental Stress

Shrinking resources and drought affects terms of trade for pastoralists (Hutchison 1991:131). As land is degraded, resources become scarce and products decline, values can rise (ibid., 131). However with persistent drought livestock quickly depreciate in value at local markets as herders sell enfeebled stock to purchase basic essentials (ibid., 131). Such deteriorating terms of trade for pastoralists are well-known indicators of approaching famine used in early warning systems (ibid., 131, 27). On a larger scale, national and global market forces created a decline in the value of livestock products relative to what can be purchased by pastoralists (ibid., 132). In the twentieth century, the value of livestock products was reduced to between half and one-tenth of their relative values in the previous century; most change occurred in the 1950s and early 1970s. This decrease in value led to very large increases in herd sizes, while impoverishing smaller herd owners (ibid., 132).

The boom in livestock trade to the Middle East in the 1970s raised relative values of livestock products, but Somalia's loss of Saudi Arabia as the principal livestock market in the early 1980s led to a 66 per cent decline in livestock exports (ibid., 84). Livestock trading with Saudi Arabia was heavily dependent on the yearly *hadji* market. As the date of the *hadji* moves with respect to the Gregorian calendar, Somalia's ability to supply livestock was influenced by seasonal availability of good pastures during the fattening period prior to shipment. Thus when the Somali dry season, the *Jilaal*, coincided with the months prior to the *hadji*, livestock exports were at risk (ibid., 84). The Saudi ban on Somali livestock was based on suspected rinderpest infection. While subsequently disproved, a ban on cattle remained while the restriction on sheep and goats was eventually lifted (ibid., 84).

In the livestock export sector a system known as *franco valuta* enabled northern livestock traders to accumulate significant foreign exchange. In the 1970s northern trading families used profits to purchase real estate primarily in Mogadishu; in the 1980s they played a role in subsidizing rebels fighting the government (Laitin 1993:142).

Regulation of market operations in an attempt to control resources worsened terms of trade for many pastoralists, handicapping development efforts (Hutchison 1991:123). The government sought control by establishing the Hides and Skins Association, closing small ports and restricting local and international livestock trade, arguing that private traders were incapable of providing adequate marketing structures (ibid., 134). Trading networks were disrupted and livestock producers and traders were alienated from national efforts to market through the official association. While the economy stagnated a parallel market operated via a network of Somali traders in East Africa and the Middle East (ibid., 134). Often pastoralist self-sufficiency was eroded by modern market mechanisms which transferred responsibility for food security to systems controlled by the state or international agencies. Such dependence has dramatic effects when these mechanisms are disrupted by famine and conflict; it also raises stakes connected with using food as a weapon (ibid., 125).

Increased market benefits associated with cattle production affected livestock production (RMR 1984:36; Gunn 1990:112–117). The proportion of cattle in the national livestock population increased while that of goats decreased during 1952–84 (RMR 1984:36). Increased rainfed cropping and changes in vegetation caused by cutting, grazing, browsing and burning enhanced production of grasses and other herbaceous vegetation and decreased bush and trees (ibid., 36). While this can be beneficial to cattle production in good years due to increased herbaceous biomass and reduction in tsetse habitat (trees and bushes), during drought and famine costs can be high for pastoralists. Browsers (camels and goats) are hardier than grazers (cattle and sheep), have wider forage preferences, and can be watered less. Protein provided by forage trees and bush allows greater utilization of protein deficient grasses and crop residues, which otherwise would be consumed less and with less benefit to livestock (Unruh 1993c:32). A decrease in browsers and vegetation to sustain them can make pastoralists more vulnerable to drought. With prolonged drought, nomads progressively reduce their herds, with cattle being among the first species to go and camels the last. If there is no herd of hardy animals to support them, otherwise minor droughts can have heightened impacts on households that invested heavily in cattle. Thus decreases in browsing vegetation and browsers increase vulnerability to periodic drought, placing pastoralists in a worse situation during famine and conflict when access to grazing lands is disrupted. As well, post-drought restocking efforts important in herd reconstitution begin best with small stock, notably goats, due to their wide forage preferences, short gestation periods compared to cattle, low purchase cost, greater survival capacity, and drought resistance (McCabe 1990a:151; Unruh 1993a).

Improved veterinary services and development of watering sites in areas not previously used during dry seasons due to lack of water improved livestock survivability, and led to increases in herd size of about three per cent per year (Al-Najim and Briggs 1992:358). While the percentage of pastoralists in the total population remained constant, the livestock population has doubled and perhaps tripled since the first meaningful censuses were carried out in the 1920s (Samatar 1989a:41). However improvements in the quantity, quality, and access to range forage through implementation of grazing reserves as the primary approach, were unsuccessful (Al-Najim and Briggs 1992:358). Although marketing facilities (national and international) improved, and animal sales rose, they lagged behind the increment in livestock population because market facilities did not change the social context, where the priority was to sell the smallest number of livestock necessary to maintain and increase herd size, and to obtain cash needs (ibid., 361). Thus sales increases did not reduce pressure on rangelands (ibid., 360). This, together with more constrained livestock movements due to the advance of agriculture and development activities, worsened rangeland degradation as livestock densities surpassed the carrying capacity of many interior regions. Consequently successive droughts had greater impact (Bennett *et al.* 1986:11; Al-Najim and Briggs 1992:357).

Nomadic Settlement and the Drought of the 1970s

Sedentarization efforts began with British and Italian colonial policies to increase the labour pool for plantations, and to prevent conflicts associated with livestock raiding (Hitchcock and Hussein 1987:31). After independence settlement was seen as a means to increase agricultural production, increase employment, meet labor shortages, stem urban migration (enhanced by drought), and reduce environmental degradation by reducing numbers of pastoralists (World Bank 1981:1; Hitchcock and Hussein 1987:31). Thus in the 1970s the government introduced the Agricultural Crash Program, which established farming cooperatives in ten locations promoting rainfed and irrigated agriculture, but this had little impact on agricultural productivity and employment (ibid., 31). Despite efforts by colonial and post-independence governments, until recently little evidence existed of any significant trend toward sedentarization (Samatar 1989a:41).

The drought which peaked in 1974 after four years of poor rains was one of the worst in Somalia's history and caused the deaths of some 20,000 people from starvation and malnutrition related diseases. As well, massive livestock losses were incurred (about 5,000,000 animals) in addition to the loss of tens of thousands of tons of agricultural produce (Hitchcock and Hussein 1987:31). This affected the cooperative movement (Laitin and Samatar 1987:112). The government turned what was planned as a 'Rural Prosperity Campaign' including literacy and sand dune stabilization programmes, into a desperate famine relief effort (Lewis 1975:1; Laitin and Samatar 1987:112; Hitchcock and Hussein 1987:31). However, it used the situation to further the goals of the overall cooperative programme, in essence turning the relief programme into a development initiative (ibid., 38). In 1975, with assistance from the Soviet Union, approximately 120,000 nomads were transported from northern grazing areas to southern fishing and agricultural cooperatives (Samatar 1989a:9; Laitin and Samatar 1987:111; Gunn 1990:13; Samatar 1993:69). While no surveys were carried out prior to site selection, large irrigation projects were funded by the Kuwait Arab Fund and the World Bank to open new lands for these nomads, with the government providing some services and purchasing harvests at a preset price as the sole outlet (Samatar 1989a:34; Laitin and Samatar 1987:111). These were in reality state farms, not cooperatives (ibid., 111). Because crop failure due to drought is more common than livestock decimation, many participants invested in livestock, as a more secure economic strategy (Hitchcock and Hussein 1987:35). By the end of the 1970s the drought had abated and many men left to rebuild their herds, leaving women and children on the farms. Female-headed households, through lack of labour for farming activities, ended up poorer than non-female-headed households (Samatar 1989a:34; Laitin and Samatar 1987:111; Hitchcock and Hussein 1987:33). Resettlement generated severe strains on local tenure regimes and ecology. Resentment by the host population over erosion of land rights, along with problems associated with overgrazing, deforestation, land degradation, and declines in agricultural productivity added to the difficulties (ibid., 38). What began as a relief operation for drought-affected pastoralists ended up as a very expensive program that did not achieve the stated goals of self-sufficiency and development (ibid., 38). The 1977–8 Ogaden war increased numbers of refugees and associated resource problems in resettlement areas. The war and the defeat of Somali forces created a refugee crisis, a domestic political crisis, and an economic crisis, the consequences of which reverberated, up to and beyond the disintegration of the state (Laitin and Samatar 1987:1; Clark 1993:111; Hutchison 1991:83).

Agricultural Development and Pastoralist Resource Use

In the 1980s instability in the north led to development activity being concentrated in the central rangelands and in the inter-riverine area (ibid., 83). This focused on cultivable areas adjacent to the only two perennial rivers, the Shabelle and Jubba. Uncoordinated irrigation development and agricultural expansion along the Shabelle river resulted in serious seasonal water shortages (Roth *et al.* 1987:52). Although the Shabelle receives 90 per cent of its discharge from Ethiopia's eastern highlands (TAMS 1986:I–19) no attempt was made to coordinate water use with that country, with which an adversarial relationship existed. While dry season livestock migrations into the Shabelle basin produced one of

Somalia's highest livestock densities (RMR 1984:69), expanded crop cultivation decreased seasonal flooding and reduced flood retreat pastures
that traditionally served as dry season forage and water areas for nomadic
herds (LRDC 1985:36). This exacerbated problems of locating dry season
forage and water for herders. Along the Shabelle river, and especially near
refugee camps, natural resources are severely stressed by overgrazing and
deforestation (Drechsel 1989).

The Jubba river valley was also to be developed on a large scale to
bring more land under cultivation. Construction of a $780 million dam at
Bardera was to facilitate integrated development of the region (Hitchcock
and Hussein 1987:31; Hutchison 1991:85); this effort was suspended in
the early 1990s. Efforts to increase areas under crop cultivation did not
consider integration of local ecology, livestock systems, or traditional
agricultural methods in the development of a multi-faceted, risk minimizing, drought survival strategy for different production systems dependent
on any single area (Samatar 1989a:45). In particular, many development
and government land use efforts ignored how development activities
affected grazing patterns, and the impact that alterations in such patterns
had on food security for pastoralists. Also ignored was the role of livestock as a fallback food supply for agriculturalists during drought and crop
failure (ibid., 45).

Disruption of nomadic migratory patterns due to location of agricultural
development projects and extended cultivation in river basins and flood-
plains is a widespread problem in arid and semi-arid Africa (Scudder
1989:6; Markakis 1993:4). Such growth usually excludes transhumant
herds which use these areas for dry season grazing and watering.
Unavailable forage in one part of the yearly travels of livestock herders
can have disastrous effects on other areas, because herders must use
already marginal range resources in the dry season (Biswas *et al.*
1987:427; Box 1971:228). As pastoralists leave degraded areas, they may
be obliged to migrate to areas occupied by other herders and farmers, creating overgrazing and conflict as more animals compete for resources that
previously sustained less livestock (Unruh 1991:93). Agreements over
grazing and watering rights can break down as herders cannot gain access
to traditional sites, or find them overcrowded and/or degraded (Biswas
et al. 1987:427; McCabe 1990a:147). Likewise, herders stressed by deteriorating rangeland conditions cannot adequately defend territory from
invading groups. Such degradation makes nomadic pastoralists, their
herds, and the range more vulnerable, with severity of drought impacts
being determined by the prior condition of the rangeland (Campbell
1981:53; Unruh 1991:93).

RESOURCE DISENFRANCHISEMENT AND LAND DEGRADATION

Throughout the Horn disenfranchisement from customary land and water use rights has been a major factor contributing to conflict, instability, and land resource degradation (Hutchison 1991:136; Ornas 1990:121; Homer-Dixon *et al.* 1993:42). Replacement of customary tenure regimes by national tenure systems with changes in tenure security for transient resource users have unexpected repercussions from altered access to resources. As well, changes in customary use arrangements of agriculturalists due to tenure machinations affect pastoralist resource use. Somalia's 1975 Land Reform Act took precedence over customary tenure regimes, and was formulated to give advantage to state enterprises and mechanized agricultural schemes, with limited rights accorded to small farmers and no rights given to pastoralists despite their numerical majority and dominance in export earnings (Roth and Unruh 1990:2; Samatar 1989a:54). All land was declared to be state owned and administered by the Ministry of Agriculture (ibid., 53). Arable land could be leased from the government but pastoralists could no longer claim access to land they previously depended upon (Gunn 1990:112). Land registration was cumbersome, required much time and money for small farmers, was centralized in Mogadishu, and was easily manipulated by well-connected officials and their associates. This allowed non-locals to gain title to large tracts of land customarily used by small-scale cultivators because the latter could not compete in terms of the political and capital mobilization necessary for registration (Samatar 1989a:54). Dislocated small-scale cultivators shifted to more marginal land resources.

Small-scale cultivators on both rainfed and irrigated land commonly allowed pastoralist access to forage (grazing, fallow, and crop remnants) and water resources, based primarily on connections within the pastoralist community which made such arrangements mutually beneficial. Operators of large scale, mechanized and intensive agriculture, were much less willing and able to allow similar arrangements.

A frequent use of newly registered large holdings was as 'fodder farms'; land, usually in the Shabelle river valley, was enclosed and guarded, and pastoralists charged for access to natural pasture. This led to violent conflict as nomads were unwilling to pay for what they previously used freely. Traditional access to restricted or scarce resources was primarily based on membership in a lineage or religious community capable of defending such rights against competitors. This is a fundamentally different concept than that of territorial ownership, use, and access where geographic boundaries establish where rights of one group begin and those of another end (ibid., 50). Sections of the 1973 Unified Civil Code abolished traditional clan and lineage rights of use and access over land and water resources (Hooglund 1993:161).

The national land tenure system was unrelated to traditional arrangements practiced by small farmers and pastoralists (Unruh 1993b:3; Roth and Unruh 1990:2). As a result, multiple tenure claims were more common in the 1980s. The national registration programme had steps intended to avoid this but they were often ignored (Unruh 1993b:3; Samatar 1989a:50). Land tenure dispute resolution mechanisms were inadequate to resolve competing claims. Such mechanisms embraced a variety of means of mediation that were frequently in jurisdictional conflict (Roth *et al.* 1987:28; Samatar 1989a:50). For small holders and pastoralists the most immediate forms of resolution were traditional methods: settlement by personal negotiation; involvement of farmers' committees; intervention by community religious leaders; and, less often, violence. Local administrations also took part in resolving land disputes, as did the Ministry of Agriculture at various levels, and the legal system (Roth *et al.* 1987:28; Samatar 1989a:50). Resolution methods of different tenure systems were not reconciled and frequently operated in incompatible ways.

THE SOMALI SEGMENTARY SOCIAL ORDER, LAND USE, AND CONFLICT

Background

Genealogy is the main organizing principle of the Somali social system, characterized by competition and conflict between clans, lineages and their segmented units with each level of segmentation defining rights, obligations, and relative standing of persons (Laitin and Samatar 1987:29, 31; Clark 1993:110; Samatar 1993:71,31; Poulsen 1990:139; Gunn 1990:114). Multiple layers of alliance reveal different levels at which competition occurs and the need for security exists (Bennett 1991:31). Because each person is a member of several lineage segments or subgroups which have alliances with lineage segments of other clans, political allegiance is constantly shifting. A pastoralist's situation in regard to needed resources and other factors determines the relative importance of various identities (Bennett 1993:31). Segmentation and structural instability are common in pastoralist societies, due to the considerable territory required for grazing (Laitin and Samatar 1987:158; White 1990:241; Bennett 1993:20, Storas 1990:138). Traditionally the primary unit for Somali social and political action is the *diya*-paying unit, several families (200–2000) of an immediate lineage unified by a collective obligation to pay or receive compensation for infractions such as homicide (Laitin and Samatar 1987:30; Lewis 1961:127; Ofcansky 1993:198). Among the more sedentary inter-riverine population descent has given way partially to territoriality as an organizational framework (Laitin and Samatar 1987:29).

Power in Somalia operates by temporary coalitions and alliances between lineages and their divisions, facilitated by diffusion of political authority, lack of stable and formally defined political roles, and virtual autonomy of herd-managing units that comprise an extended family or group of families (Samatar 1993:93, Doornbos 1993:100, Lewis 1961:127; Compagnon 1992:10). Such organizational flexibility, or 'low investment politics' is a general feature of east African pastoral communities and is appropriate to highly variable, unpredictable natural environments (Dyson-Hudson 1985:166). Alliances can fragment into competitive units as soon as conditions that necessitated them cease to exist, or more favourable arrangements present themselves or are desired, i.e., as when new or alternative grazing and watering areas are required (Samatar 1993:93; Markakis 1993:8; Lewis 1961:127). In such a system there are no permanent enemies or friends, only relevant contexts in the endless shifting of affiliations that is among the more important hallmarks of Somali pastoral clan politics (Samatar 1993:93). Such arrangements serve pastoralists poorly in interactions with the state (Markakis 1993:1, 8).

While the government exercised central authority through the military and civilian bureaucracy, most Somalis had more loyalty to their lineages (Laitin and Samatar 1987:30); pastoral ethics of clan socialism continued to operate, sometimes exacerbated by urban settings (Laitin and Samatar 1987:46; Compagnon 1992:10). One political consequence of the Siad regime was intensified clan identification (Hooglund 1993:163). In the decade before the collapse of the state, animosities between clans grew to clan-based insurgent movements, which became opposed to the government (Ofcansky 1993:187; Compagnon 1992:11). Yet there was no significant coordination or cooperation between various armed fronts (ibid., 10).

THE SOCIAL ORDER, LAND USE AND CONFLICT

Access to land and water for individual households customarily is based on lineage membership, making agreements between clan units decisive. In fragile environments, this is important in preventing land degradation and ensuring long-term range productivity (Ornas 1990:121; Samatar 1989a:38; Poulsen 1990:143).

Thus pastoralist households have access to social-ecological zones of changing size and shape, depending on transient agreements between various lineage segments and relative ecological endowments of different grazing locations (Helander 1986:96). These zones represent perceptions of both social and biophysical space where the correlation is not one to one. In other words, pastoralists must consider tradeoffs associated with moving to good pastures where bad social relations exist versus areas with good social relations but poorer grazing and all variations between these (ibid., 97). Thus, genealogical relations, seasonal resources and personal relations combine to govern herding and migration decisions (ibid., 106).

RESOURCE DETERIORATION, INACCESS AND CLAN ARRANGEMENTS

As more land was removed from customary use in the 1980s, environmental and resource issues gained importance for pastoralists. Herders increasingly lost access to resources. Where access agreements failed due to increased competition, they used areas previously avoided either because they were contested, or held by several lineage units in reserve for dry season and drought grazing. This generated conflict, as did using grazing land without permission. With less scope for agreements, pastoralists employed aggressive encroachment and defence (Lewis 1961:248).

Conflict over resources has repercussions as old transgressions and latent hostility are aroused with new scope for expression (ibid., 246). This has significance at higher lineage levels, i.e., involving more people, because the clan system lacks a concept of individual culpability (Samatar 1993:93; Helander 1986:101; Fadal 1984:74; Lewis 1961:45). Transgressions are seen as the responsibility of all the perpetrator's kin; revenge or compensation may be sought from any lineage member. Localized conflict can escalate into wider resource access problems between lineages and segments thereof (Helander 1986:101), influencing intra- and inter-clan alliances (Lewis 1961:45). From the late 1980s, increased propensity for disagreements over grazing and water to escalate and become part of larger conflicts exacerbated insecurity. Minor conflicts over grazing territory or watering points easily triggered responses among groups opposed in the wider conflict. Also, such groups were more prone to discord over resource access than otherwise (Laitin and Samatar 1987:162).

CONFLICT IN AGRONOMICALLY HIGH POTENTIAL AREAS

In the late 1980s spatially limited, fertile, well watered areas such as the Shabelle river basin became increasingly unstable. Both pastoralist and agriculturalist refugees arrived, fleeing insecurity and food shortage as their coping strategies were exhausted. This exacerbated crowding and competition for resources, aggravated in northern Somalia by government forces who poisoned wells in rural areas (Laitin 1993:137). Hostilities increased as the social cohesiveness of past resource use arrangements broke down.

These high potential locations had long been occupied by agriculturalists and seasonal concentrations of pastoralists, in addition to refugees from earlier droughts and wars. Local fuelwood sources were depleted to the point where long-distance transport of wood and charcoal was both a necessity and a thriving business and cooperative pursuit prior to the collapse of the state. From the late 1980s transport of fuelwood and food to these areas became problematic due to deterioration of roads, land mines, and general insecurity.

As decreasing food and fuel combined with perceptions of a worsening economic situation and political and ethnic rivalries, confrontation erupted into violent conflict. Figure 7.2 illustrates for southern Somalia that the most intense armed conflict was along the Shabelle river valley, the most agronomically endowed area.

COLLAPSE OF THE SOMALI STATE AND SUBSEQUENT PASTORALIST DECISION-MAKING

The pastoralist segmentary social order is vulnerable to external manipulation, which occurred under Siad Barre (Laitin and Samatar 1987:46). Politicians found it convenient to disburse scarce resources through clan structures, as ethnic support determined political success (ibid., 46). Interclan rivalries were exploited, and clans were rewarded or punished collectively (including distribution of development projects) to obtain objectives and divert attention from an increasingly unpopular and vulnerable regime (Samatar 1993:93; Laitin and Samatar 1987:159; Bennett 1993:67). Mass desertions from the army by forced conscripts provided more weapons to opposition groups (Hutchison 1991:85). In 1990 all aid programmes were halted, imports and exports ceased, and hyper-inflation made the currency worthless. For a country dependant on international welfare the consequences were devastating, with conflict, starvation, malnutrition

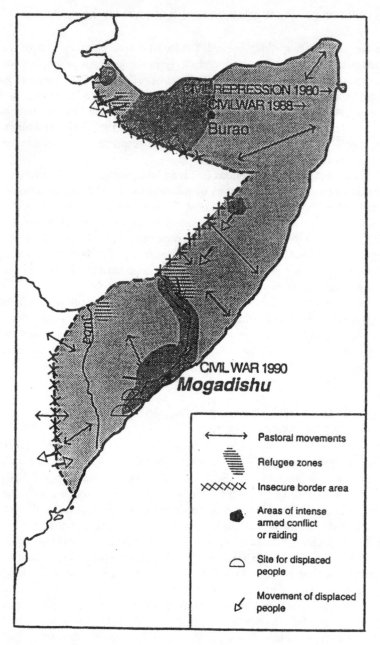

Figure 7.2   Armed conflict and displacement (from Hutchinson 1991)

and epidemic diseases widely reported (ibid., 85). Interclan conflict progressively limited the government's reach until, ultimately, streets of the capital were ungovernable (ibid., 85).

Deliberately poisoned wells, destruction of reservoirs and grazing areas, machine-gunning of herds, and indiscriminate bombing of cities in the territory of opposition clans killed thousands of people and hundreds of thousands of animals (Hutchison 1991:116; Hooglund 1993:154; Clark 1993:111). The army confiscated food destined for refugees; foreign relief aid was diverted to support the military (Hutchison 1991:126) and used as a weapon against opposition groups. Disaffection generated by these and similar policies conducted against important lineages and subsequent organized armed resistance led to collapse of the regime and the state (Clark 1993:112). Subsequent power struggles among clans and region-based groups over resources and the spoils of state led to civil war. Clan militias eventually divided the country up into twelve zones. Persistent drought forced many Somalis from home areas in a desperate search for food, exposing them directly to violence (ibid., 112).

Violence is affected by acquisition of modern weapons (Hutchison 1991:115). Emptying of Somalia's armories into the general population, along with arms from Ethiopia's crumbling army (Clark 1993:112), obliterated damage limitation (Hutchison 1991:105), heightened violence and shifted the magnitude and nature of conflict. These weapons allowed bandits to disrupt and loot relief supplies, escalate famine's severity and force 800,000 to 900,000 Somalis into exile in neighbouring countries, while over a million internally displaced persons fled to urban areas (OFDA 1993:1; Clark 1993:113). About 4.5 million people required external food aid, including approximately 1.5 million at severe risk of starvation (OFDA 1993:1; Clark 1993:113). This led to the UN-authorized Unified Task Force military intervention intended to secure delivery of food and other supplies (OFDA 1993:1; Clark 1993:109).

Nomadic resource use during widespread unrest operated in a context of considerable fluidity, with coalition cohesion regarding land and water becoming increasingly confused, transient, and less meaningful as modern weapons undermined traditional authority of clan elders (ibid., 112). This combined with a multiplication of conflict episodes complicated by increasing instances of both clan and non-clan related banditry, sometimes indistinguishable. Nevertheless clan divisions, often operating in traditional decentralized fashion, influenced violence (Ryle 1992:162; Clark 1993:110). As pastoralists armed themselves for protection, confrontation became more frequent in the search for resources and insecurity became the dominant context for decision-making.

For those still possessing herds, such decisions functioned from a combination of perceived biophysical, social, and conflict zones, all geographically defined. With instability the dominant element, resource access was pursued within much shorter planning horizons, with enormously increased possible processes and conceivable outcomes brought on by the general turbulence (Hutchison 1991:90). While decisions for pastoralists increased, spatial and temporal disarray in the socio-biophysical mix meant that expected outcomes did not have the certainly they might have previously.

Conflict zones can be seen as comprised of perceptions of security threats of specific frequency and severity. Such perceptions are shaped by information on conflict zones and events, in the form of personal experiences, related experiences, and reports involving fact, speculation and rumour. They can influence decisions to: migrate more or less often; slaughter animals; travel to clan homelands or other destinations; time movements differently; and fragment herds among family members according to the animals' age, sex or species to exploit specific ecological and social resources, or according to each species' ability to handle worsening conditions (Samatar 1989a:38).

Conflict plays a large role as pastoralists seek to identify combinations of threats, opportunities, risks and trade-offs in decision-making (Ornas 1990:118; Hutchison 1991:145). Reaching socially and biophysically secure areas may require travel through unsafe areas; during widespread conflict, confrontation can have high costs because, in addition to loss of life, stock loss does not carry with it the possibility for compensation from the perpetrator's clan as it might have otherwise (Laitin and Samatar 1987:21). While relationships between social and conflict zones might in some cases be straightforward (such as not using grazing areas belonging to a lineage segment opposed to one's own in the larger conflict), relations between conflict and biophysical options might be harder to predict. Conditions of formerly biophysically favoured locations may be uncertain while migration with herds entails new conflict-related hazards such as land-mines and poisoned or destroyed watering points (USIP 1993:2). These may require moves to riskier locations; aperiodic movements of nomads and herds increase enormously during conflict as herders set off to lesser-known pastures in last ditch efforts to save stock (Warshall 1991:107).

Typical strategies (selling animals, dependence on others in the community for assistance) were less of an option given the total economic breakdown and subsequent disintegration of community cohesion (Bennett 1991:103). Other options, unsual in more secure circumstances (raiding, invading cropped areas for forage, fleeing to Ethiopia, incorporating feeding centers into survival strategies), were employed. In the late 1980s nine refugee camps were established in Ethiopia, in territory of Somali pastoral clans (Ryle 1992:160). They provided refuge, food and water; in some cases they were incorporated into seasonal migrations with clan members going there in the dry season because of unavailability of grazing areas due to conflict (ibid., 163).

While pastoralist decision-making during insecurity seeks to maximize chances of household survival, it can contribute to unsustainable collective consequences (Samatar 1989a:63). Through long-term vegetative degradation and aggressive confrontation to attain resources, the foundation for resource use strategies in peaceful contexts is compromised. Overexploited vegetation, especially trees, can require long recovery periods. Increasing contention over diminishing resources can confuse what might constitute acceptable resource use arrangements. The result is continued disorganization until a shared sense of purpose becomes part of pastoralists' lives again, and/or part of the strategic vision of leadership at the local, regional, or national level (ibid., 63).

FUTURE OF PASTORALISM

While rehabilitation of the pastoralist sector will necessarily play an important role in Somalia's recovery, it also presents a dilemma. Although pastoralists are the majority, there is some doubt whether anything close to a traditional pastoral strategy can continue in Somalia and elsewhere in the Horn (Laitin and Samatar 1987:127; Fadal 1984:84; Hutchison 1991:101; Baxter 1993:143; Morton 1993:30; Poulsen 1990:147; Bennett 1991:41). Environmental stress, and restrictions on migrations and resource access will likely limit access to the material base for such a strategy (Krokfors 1984:306; Markakis 1993:1). Disintegration of economic and social tenants of traditional pastoralism in Somalia have been underway since the colonial era (Fadal 1984:71; Bennett *et al.* 1986:150; Samatar 1989a:45). As elsewhere, traditional pastoralist society has not managed well the changes thrust upon it (Bennett *et al.* 1986:150). Underlying causes include introduction of modern forms of transport, employment possibilities in the Gulf states, development of productive forces in cities, progression of money-commodity relations in the pastoral economy, market demands for livestock products and a subsequent drive to increase production, breakdown of traditional social and economic ties to family and group, clan rivalries, conflict, the role of central authority, and development programmes such as veterinary services and water development (Fadal 1984:76; Hutchison 1991:102; Poulsen 1990:148). These influences substantially weaken the ability of pastoralism to reproduce itself (Fadal 1984:79).

From a development perspective, settling pastoralists permanently into exclusively farming or fishing pursuits has not been successful (Samatar 1989a:42). Sedentarization may be especially impractical considering the limited spatial extent of Somalia's arable lands and that farming areas are already crowded. Development efforts must recognize that some form of pastoralism will be essential to Somalia's ability to feed a growing population from a land base with few alternative uses. Arrangements involving Somali-generated adaptations to resource use changes including variations of agropastoralism and multiple access and use of spatially-limited arable lands should be explored. New models of resource tenure must be designed to meet a changing pastoral production system (Bennett *et al.* 1986:150). New approaches must recognize that no development initiative or technological system will remove drought and that herding as a drought avoidance strategy will remain a central objective of many pastoralists (Samatar 1989a:67).

RESTOCKING PASTORALISTS

For such adaptations to evolve, restocking is a near-term priority. However drought, conflict, famine and subsequent food distribution programmes undermine traditional restocking mechanisms (McCabe 1990b:147). These are usually based on contributions of animals by fellow stock-owners with whom exchange relationships and assurances of reciprocity exist (McCabe 1990a:156; Hitchcock and Hussein 1987:31). Animal loans to destitute pastoralists in refugee camps do not carry the same assurance. Once social exchange networks are disrupted, return to pastoral life is difficult. Better recovery mechanisms must be designed for refugee pastoralists, given their generally reduced capacity for recovery (Toulmin 1987:130; Moris 1988:287).

Evaluations must assess the capacity and rate with which pastoral production systems can rehabilitate themselves without external intervention and compare expected rates of recovery with external intervention and associated costs versus costs of prolonged famine relief (Toulmin 1987:130). However recovery does not occur in isolation. Several production systems, each with many participants, may attempt drought or famine rehabilitation simultaneously, most likely in spatially limited 'agronomically high potential' areas. Recovery rates of various production systems may or may not be compatible. For example, indigenous rates of recovery for pastoralism may entail lengthy year-around occupation of farming areas which are also important in sustaining large agricultural and urban populations. Incompatibilities in land use can lead to conflict and accelerate land degradation, reducing further the productive capacity of scarce land resources (Unruh 1993a:306). Intervention must be based on more than single production systems. Approaches to restocking must build on traditional institutions to rebuild herds in culturally relevant ways to ensure efficiency. Such mechanisms are part of coping strategies that have evolved to meet challenges of existence in precarious environments given in-place cultural, ecological, and socio-political constraints and opportunities.

References

Al-Najim, M. N. and J. Briggs, 1992. 'Livestock development in Somalia – a critical review', *GeoJournal*, 26:357–62.

Baxter, P. T. W., 1993. 'The 'new' east African pastoralist: an overview', *Conflict and the Decline of Pastoralism on the Horn of Africa*, J. Markakis (ed.) (London: Macmillan).

Bennett, J. W., 1984. 'Political ecology and development projects affecting pastoralist peoples in East Africa', Research Paper 80 (Madison: Land Tenure Center).

Bennett, O (ed.), 1993. *Greenwar: Environment and Conflict* (London: Panos Institute).

Bennett, J. W., S. W. Lawry and J. C. Riddell, 1986. 'Land Tenure and Livestock Development in Sub-Saharan Africa', AID Evaluation Special Study No. 39 (Washington DC: US Agency for International Development).

Berg, E., 1982. 'Encouraging the Private Sector in Somalia', Report prepared for USAID (Washington DC).

Biswas A. K., Y. F. O. Masakhalia, L. A. Odero-Ogwel and E.P. Pallangyo, 1987. 'Land Use and Farming Systems in the Horn of Africa', *Land Use Policy* 4:419–43.

Box, T. W., 1971. 'Nomadism and Land Use in Somalia', *Economic Development and Cultural Change*, 19:222–8.

Bremen, H., A. M. Cisse, M. A. Djiteye, W. T. Elberse, 1979. 'Pasture and Forage Availability in the Sahel', *Israel Journal of Botany*, 28:227–51.

Campbell, D. J., 1981. 'Land-Use Competition at the Margins of the Rangelands: An Issue in Development Strategies for Semi-Arid Areas', Planning African Development, G. Norcliffe and T. Pinfold (eds) (Boulder: Westview).

Cassanelli, L. V., 1982. *The Shaping of Somali Society* (Philadelphia: University of Pennsylvania Press).

Clark, J., 1993. 'Debacle in Somalia', *Foreign Affairs*, 72:109–23.

Compagnon, D., 1992. 'Political Decay in Somalia: from Personal Rule to Warlordism', *Refuge*, 12:8–13.

Conze, P. and P. Labahn, 1986. 'From a Socialistic System to a Mixed Economy: the Changing Framework for Somali Agriculture', *Somalia: Agriculture in the Winds of Change,* P. Conze and P. Labahn (eds) (Saarbrucken: Schafbrucke Publishers).

Doornbos, M. 1993. 'Pasture and Polis: the Roots of Political Marginalization of Somali Pastoralism', *Conflict and the Decline of Pastoralism on the Horn of Africa,* J. Markakis (ed.) (London: Macmillan).

Drechsel, P., 1989. 'Soils and Reforestation in the Central Rangelands of Somalia', *Arid Soil Research,* 3:41–64.

Dyson-Hudson, N., 1985. 'Pastoral Production Systems and Livestock Development Projects: an East African Perspective', *Putting People First,* M. M. Cernea (ed.) (Oxford: Oxford University Press).

Fadal, M. O., 1984. 'The Ongoing Process of Gradual Disintegration of the Traditional Social and Economic Systems of Pastoralism in Somalia', *Proceedings of the Second International Congress of Somali Studies.* T. Labahn (ed.) University of Hamburg, 6 August, 1983 (Hamburg: Helmut Buske Verlag).

Gunn S. (1990) 'Somalia', *The Peasant Betrayed.* J. P. Powelson and R. Sock (eds). (Washington DC: Cato Institute).

Handulle, A. A. and C. W. Gay, 1987. 'Development and Traditional Development in Somalia', *Nomadic Peoples,* 24:36–43.

Helander, B. 1986. 'The Social Dynamics of Southern Somali Agro-pastoralism: a Regional Approach', *Somalia: Agriculture in the Winds of Change,* P. Conze and P. Labahn (eds) (Saarbrucken: Schafbrucke Publishers).

Hitchcock R. and H. Hussein, 1987. 'Agricultural and Non-agricultural Settlements for Drought-afflicted Pastoralists in Somalia', *Disasters,* 30–39.

Homer-Dixon T, J. H. Boutwell and G. W. Rathjens, 1993. 'Environmental Change and Violent Conflict', *Scientific American,* February, pp. 38–45.

Hooglund, E., 1993. 'Government and Politics', *Somalia A Country Study,* H. C. Metz (ed.) (Washington DC: Library of Congress, Federal Research Division) Fourth edition.

Hurni, H., 1993. 'Famine in Somalia: Fate or Failure?', *Journal of Soil and Water Conservation,* 48:20–1.

Hutchinson, C. F., 1991. 'Short FEWS: An Action-oriented Famine Early Warning System', *Famine Mitigation.* Proceedings of a workshop in Tucson, 31 July–2 August, 1991 (Tucson: Office of Arid Lands Studies, University of Arizona).

Hutchison R. A. (ed.) (1991) Fighting for Survival: Insecurity, People and the Environment in the Horn of Africa. Based on study by B. C. Spooner and N. Walsh, IUCN, Gland.

Johnson, D. L., 1969. *The Nature of Nomadism: A Comparative Study of Pastoral Migrations in South Western Asia and Northern Africa* (Chicago: University of Chicago Press).

Krokfors, C., 1984. 'Environmental considerations and planning in Somalia', T. Labahn (ed.), *Proceedings of the Second International Congress of Somali Studies,* University of Hamburg, 1-6 August 1983 (Hamburg: Helmut Buske Verlag).

Laitin, D. D., 1993. 'The Economy', *Somalia A Country Study,* H. C. Metz (ed.) (Washington DC: Library of Congress, Federal Research Division) Fourth edition.

Laitin, D. D., and S. S. Samatar, 1987. *Somalia Nation in Search of a State*

(Boulder: Westview Press).

Land Resources Development Center (LRDC), 1985. Land Use in Tsetse-Affected Areas of Southern Somalia (Surbiton, UK).

Lewis, I. M., 1961. *A Pastoral Democracy* (London: Oxford University Press).

Lewis, I. M., 1975. *Abaar: the Somali Drought*. Emergency Report 1. International African Institute.

Markakis, J., 1993. 'Introduction', *Conflict and the Decline of Pastoralism on the Horn of Africa*, J. Markakis (ed.) (London: Macmillan).

Massey, G., 1987. *Subsistence and Change* (Boulder: Westview Press).

Massey, G., 1989. 'Agropastoralism and Agropastoral Society in South-central Somalia', *Journal of Developing Societies*, 5:137–74.

McCabe, J. T., 1990a. 'Success and Failure: the Breakdown of Traditional Drought Coping Institutions among the Pastoral Turkana of Kenya', *Journal of Asian and African Studies*, 25:146–59.

McCabe, J. T., 1990b. 'Turkana Pastoralism: a Case against the Tragedy of the Commons', *Human Ecology*, 18:81–103.

Morris, J., 1988. 'Failing to Cope with Drought: the Plight of Africa's Ex-Pastoralists', *Development Policy Review*, 6:269–94.

Morton, J., 1993. 'Pastoral Decline and Famine: the Beja Case', *Conflict and the Decline of Pastoralism on the Horn of Africa*, J. Markakis (ed.) (London: Macmillan).

Ofcansky, T., 1993. 'National Security', *Somalia A Country Study*, H.C. Metz (ed.) (Washington DC: Library of Congress, Federal Research Division) Fourth edition.

Office of US Foreign Disaster Assistance (OFDA), 1993. Somalia–Civil Strife (Washington DC: Agency for International Development).

Ornas Af, A. H., 1990. 'Pastoral and Environmental Security in East Africa', *Disasters,* 14:115–122.

Poulsen, E., 1990. 'The Changing Patterns of Pastoral Production in Somali Society', *From Water to World-Making*, G. Palsson (ed.) (Uppsala: Scandinavian Institute of African Studies).

Resource Management and Research (RMR), 1984. *Somali Democratic Republic Southern Rangelands Survey*, Vol 4, Part 1, London.

Roth, M. H. Lemel, J. Bruce, and J. Unruh, 1987. 'An Analysis of Land Tenure and Water Allocation Issues in the Shalambood Irrigation Zone, Somalia'. Project report (Madison: Land Tenure Center, University of Wisconsin).

Roth, M. and J. Unruh, 1990. 'Land Title, Tenure Security, Credit and Investment in the Lower Shabelle Region, Somalia' (Madison: Land Tenure Center).

Ryle, J., 1992. 'Notes on the Repatriation of Somali Refugees from Ethiopia', *Disasters*, 16:160–68.

Samatar, S. S., 1993. 'The Society and its Environment', *Somalia A Country Study*. H. C. Metz (ed.) (Washington DC: Library of Congress, Federal Research Division) Fourth edition.

Samatar, M. S., 1989a. A Study on Drought Induced Migration and its Impact on Land Tenure and Production in the Inter-Riverine Region of Somalia (Rome: Food and Agriculture Organization of the United Nations).

Samatar, A. I., 1989b. *The State and Rural Transformation in Northern Somalia 1884–1986* (Madison: University of Wisconsin Press).

Scudder, T., 1989. 'River Basin Projects in Africa', *Environment*, 31: 4–32.

Storas, F., 1990. 'Intention of Implication – the effects of Turkana Social

Organization on Ecological Balances', *Property, Poverty and People*. P. T. W. Baxter and R. Hoog (eds) (Manchester: University of Manchester Press).

Tippetts Abbett McCarthy Stratton (TAMS), 1986. Genale Irrigation Rehabilitation Project: Feasibility Study. Annex I, Natural and Human Resources. (Mogadishu: Ministry of Agriculture).

Toulmin, C., 1987. 'Drought and the Farming Sector: Loss of Farm Animals and Post-drought Rehabilitation', *Development Policy Review*, 5:125–48.

United States Institute of Peace (USIP), 1993. Special Report II on Somalia (Washington DC: United States Institute of Peace).

United States Agency for International Development (USAID) (1979) Somalia: Central Rangeland Development. AID project no. 649-0108 (Washington DC).

Unruh, J. D., 1991. 'Nomadic Pastoralism and Irrigated Agriculture in Somalia: Utilization of Existing Land Use Patterns in Designs for Multiple Access of 'High' Potential Areas of Semi-arid Africa', *GeoJournal*, 25:91–108.

Unruh, J. D., 1993a. 'Restocking Refugee Pastoralists in the Horn of Africa', *Disasters*, 17:305–320.

Unruh, J. D., 1993b. 'Post Famine Rehabilitation of Agricultural Production Systems in Southern Somalia: Resource Tenure Issues in 'High Potential' Areas'. Paper presented at The Fifth International Congress of Somali Studies, 1–7 December, Worcester and Boston, MA.

Unruh, J. D., 1993c. 'An Acacia-based Design for Sustainable Livestock Carrying Capacity on Irrigated Farmlands in Semi-arid Africa', *Ecological Engineering*, 2:131–48.

Warshall, P., 1991. Cash, Cows, and Camels: the Fate of Livestock in African Disasters. In: *Famine Mitigation*, Proceedings of a Workshop in Tucson, 31 July–2 August 1991 (Tucson: Office of Arid Lands Studies, University of Arizona).

White, C., 1990. 'Changing Animal Ownership and Access to Land among the Wodaabe (Fulani) of Central Niger', *Property, Poverty and People*, P. T. W. Baxter and R. Hoog (eds) (Manchester: University of Manchester Press).

World Bank, 1981. Somalia Agricultural Sector Review. Report No. 2881a-SO. Eastern Africa Regional Office, Northern Agricultural Division, Nairobi, Kenya (Washington, DC: International Bank for Reconstruction and Development).

Young, L. A., 1985. 'A General Assessment of the Environmental Impact of Refugees in Somalia with Attention to the Refugee Agricultural Program', *Disasters*, 9:122–33.

8 Disaster, Relief and Political Change in Southern Ethiopia: Developments from within Suri Society

Jon Abbink

INTRODUCTION

The early 1990s saw substantial changes in the Horn, especially in terms of politics and socio-economic organization. Previous dictatorial structures chaacterized by political stagnation and economic crises were brought down by demands for democratization, economic restructuring, ethno-regional rights and state independence. The process of change in Ethiopia after demise of the Mengistu regime in 1991 resulted in a remarkable turn toward 'ethnicization' of political and public life under a Transitional Government (TGE) led by the former rebel movement Ethiopian Peoples' Revolutionary Democratic Front (EHADIG, in its Amharic and Tigrinya acronym). Explicit recognition of ethnic groups or 'nationalities' as units on which to base political parties and regional administrative structures is being incorporated in the new constitution and being adopted in education and language policies. Whether positive or negative, its future effects on development policy execution, through the Ethiopian government or through foreign NGOs, will be significant.

For some observers, these changes in state structure and national discourse hold an example for other African countries, while for others – recalling violent ethnic clashes of the past – they are a recipe for disaster (cf. Walle 1993). Be that as it may, this new discourse on national identity, ethnic group relations and the 'development effort' will shape future social and politico-economic developments, if only by creating new ideological realities.

In the past few years, the new decentralizing approach affected some ethno-regional groups more than others. Larger ethnic groups have (often forcibly) been involved in political and ideological struggles to redefine their 'identities' within a new national political arena, the boundaries of which are still contested. But other groups remain at the margins. Recent discourse on change and development has been mainly confined to ideological squibs related to the TGE's ethnic policy-approach and to the criticism of its various rivals such as the OLF (Oromo Liberation Front), the AAPO (All-Amhara Peoples' Organization), the COEDF (Coalition of Ethiopian Democratic Forces), or the SEPDF (Southern Ethiopian Peoples' Democratic Front). Less attention has been paid to *local*-level perceptions and aspirations of average inhabitants not involved in party or ethnic politics. Here, first hand data – even on large 'nationalities' like Amhara, Oromo, Tigray, Sidama, Wolaita, Afar, etc. – are indeed scarce.

In this chapter, I describe responses to recent socio-ecological crisis and political process among the Suri, an agro-pastoral group in Ethiopia's southwestern Käfa Region. Data come from fieldwork done after the change of regime in 1991. Effects of natural disaster as well as political changes are considered in order to trace the recent history of a group only marginally involved in national politics. Even at this level however, important points about national politics, ethnicization and group relations arise.

The Suri number about 24,000,[1] live in a remote border-area of Ethiopia and Sudan, and are perhaps even less touched by 'outside forces' than the famous Yanomamö, described by Chagnon (1992) as one of the world's last 'true' tribal peoples. News about the Suri is never reported anywhere, not even in the Ethiopian press.

In past decades, the Suri witnessed serious ecological and societal crises. They faced drought, crop shortages, cattle disease, and violent confrontations with neighbouring peoples, leading to severe disruption of traditional modes of subsistence and serious reduction of their population. As they were at Ethiopia's politico-economic margins, they were not provided with substantial external aid from either the government or international aid agencies. Through various strategies like temporary migration, increased hunting and gathering, exploitation of gold resources and investment in, and use of, automatic weapons for attack and defence, a group response to societal survival was formulated. It culminated in full recovery of the economic and socio-cultural fabric of their society, but at the cost of increasing isolation and violent conflict with all their neighbours, including the former Derg administration as well as the new EHADIG authorities.

The Suri, as a relatively homogeneous and solidary population, must be considered as one interacting part in the wider natural and socio-political environment, i.e., not only must determining factors in their eco-niche be taken into account but also those of the regional-political context of the Ethiopian state, of which they and most of their neighbours nominally have been a part since 1898. Both spheres impinge on each other and consideration of developments after 1991 are of interest to evaluate changes in a long-term perspective. Part of the story of their successful 'indigenous' recovery is indeed that of their changing political relations with other ethnic groups and agents in their area.

THE SURI ENVIRONMENT AND SUBSISTENCE SYSTEM

It is of course impossible to speak of ethnic or tribal groups as if they were 'primitive isolates', but the Suri can be described as a relatively remote and untouched population. Their area is one of the most inaccessible and neglected parts of Ethiopia. It was nominally conquered in 1898, when the army of Ethiopian emperor Menilik II passed southward to the borders of British-held territories (Sudan and Kenya). Even today, after ninety years of nominal incorporation in the Ethiopian state, there are no government offices, no services, no transport facilities, no police or army posts in the Suri area (National Atlas of Ethiopia 1988: 35, and local information in Maji), and economic exploitation of the area is marginal. The advantage of this isolated position has been that the Suri were not bothered for taxes or other civil duties.[2] They neither have (and never had) *k'ebeles* (local administrative units) or peasant associations, and are virtually autonomous in the maintenance of internal social order. Because of this image of remoteness, however, they have been sought out by foreign tourists seeking 'exotic tribes'. The appearance and peculiar behaviour of these tourists during the 1980s (paying Suri for photographs, trying to buy or swap their artefacts, etc.) has had negative effects on the Suri, who now are wary of all outsiders.[3]

The Suri consist of two subgroups: Tirma and Chai.[4] Research was done among the latter. The Suri linguistically belong to the Southeast-Surmic language group (within the 'Nilo-Saharan' family), about which little information is available.[5] They practice shifting cultivation of sorghum and maize (on a fairly primitive technological level), some gardening, transhumant pastoralism, and hunting and gathering.

Environmental Conditions

The Suri eco-niche – a limited natural environment with which they interact to find most of the products to sustain themselves – is a semi-arid lowland zone, between 500 and 1000 metres in altitude,[6] covering about 4400 sq. km, which, obviously, is not fully inhabited everywhere.

According to the National Atlas of Ethiopia (see note 6), rainfall is between 800 and 1200 mm per year. The average is certainly below 1000 mm, and the pattern is rather unreliable, especially further south from the Dizi mountains. Rain is insufficient for permanent, intensive agriculture, and – as the drought-and-famine crises of the 1980s show – even for shifting cultivation of maize and sorghum. Most soils are fertile but rocky, and hardly suitable for plough agriculture. Vegetation cover consists of bushed shrubland, wooded grassland and remnants of riparian wood or shrubland along the Kibish River. The tse-tse fly is not widespread in the area, which means that, in principle, conditions for cattle-keeping are good. Game animals were, until about two decades ago, abundant but have diminished due to ferocious hunting by local people.[7] One perennial river, the Kibish, crosses the Suri area from north to south, flowing down from the Maji mountains to the area of the Nyangatom people (who have a different language and culture). Five to ten kilometres west is a smaller river, the Kiba. Between these two rivers, the best Suri grazing land is found. There is no flood-retreat cultivation along the river banks, as among the Mursi people east of the Omo. At the end of the dry season (March–April), there is a problem of water and pasture shortage, with staple food supplies often precarious.

Ethnic Relations

Neighbouring the Suri are the Nyangatom in the south, the Dizi and Me'en in the north-east, the Anuak in the far northwest, and east across the Omo river the Mursi (only the latter are closely related to them in language and culture).

Suri oral tradition maintains that they arrived in the lower Kibish and the Tirma range (a hill area north of Shulugui) at least fourteen generations ago,[8] coming from the lower Omo River Valley, via the Dirga and Gherghetto hills. When they moved into their present habitat (including the now vacated part close to Shulugui), they did not find other people there; their Nyangatom neighbours (part of the 'Karimojong-cluster' and closely related to the Turkana) arrived later. With the Nyangatom (or 'Bume' as they call them), the Suri have always had a very tense relationship, although in times of relative peace the two groups had ritual bond-friendships and exchange partners. When moving to the north fringe of the Kibish valley, the Suri encountered the Dizi, long-settled agriculturalists in the highland zone. They established a ritual bond with them, under which the Dizi would perform a rain-ceremony for the Suri if they suffered from lack of rain in the valley. There is also a tradition that chiefly families of both groups are related and cannot intermarry. The groups were therefore traditionally on good terms.

With the Anuak, the Suri have no positive relations whatsoever, unless one considers the recent trade in automatic rifles (in the Dima area) as such. With the Mursi they intermarry and exchange cattle and other resources. They are seen as similar to the Suri. Also with the Me'en (also a Surmic-speaking group, with historical and cultural affinities) there was some intermarriage, but now the groups avoid each other because of conflicts. There is only significant contact between the agro-pastoral Bodi-Me'en (across the Omo River) and the eastern Suri who live below the Sai mountain, east of the town of Maji.

In the early years of this century, northern immigrants (Amhara, Oromo, Tigray, Gurage, and others) arrived, in the wake of the imperial army led by Emperor Menilik II's general Ras Wolde Giorgis, who founded Maji town and also temporarily subdued (or thought he did) the Suri in adjacent lowlands. The area was then one of adventurers and traders who, from their base in Maji, roamed the lowlands to buy, exchange or rob cattle from pastoral peoples like the Nyangatom, Dassanetch and Suri. Some northerners became influential local figures who carved out political spheres of influence extending well into the Toposa and Turkana country, then nominally British. Before settlement of colonial boundaries with the British (1905–1920), the northern Turkana area, for instance, was effectively the territory of the highland-Abyssinians led by *gerazmach* Aberra, from Tigray.[9] Turkana oral tradition (see Lamphear 1992:155–6, 162) knows him as Apara.

In this century, the Suri oriented themselves to regional markets, especially Maji and Jeba, the two earliest highland villages founded in 1898, lying a three- to six-hour walk from their area. There they sold cattle and goats, and bought small trade items (cloth, salt, razor-blades, iron tools, grain). They also traded with Sudanese Balé and occasionally Murle people (livestock, beads), but their main orientation was toward Ethiopia (evident from their exclusive use of Ethiopian currency). Also, in Haile Selassie's time, the Suri were (for a few decades) administered by Ethiopian officials, who founded police posts and appointed district representatives in two small settlements in the area. While Ethiopian authorities were present, there was no effort to 'assimilate' the Suri. In terms of the hegemonic cultural ideology of the highlanders, the Suri were perhaps looked down upon – being seen as 'nomads', 'without religion', etc., and authorities tried to discourage them from 'going around naked' and from inserting their large lip- and ear-plates. But the reverse was also true: the

Suri had a disdain bordering on contempt for the highlanders. From their point of view, the latter were marginal to their society. Thus, mutual differences were recognized, with no party expecting them to disappear.

Despite contacts with various groups, the Suri have almost no proficiency in any other language than their own. If they have a second language it is, especially among the Tirma, Balethi, spoken by the closely-related Balé people. Some speak Nyangatom or Dizi; Dizi women who marry Suri men stop speaking Dizi and their children only learn Tirma-Chai. The Me'en, Anuak, or Murle languages are not spoken. Among the Chai, about thirty-five people speak Amharic, most of them former soldiers recruited by force or trickery for the National Army under Mengistu.

On the basis of environmental and ethnic relations it can be concluded that the Suri eco-niche is not a stable set of natural conditions, but is highly sensitive to differing patterns of rainfall, wild and domestic animal movement and human use of and competition for limited resources. It is difficult to sketch a clear picture of the resource base and number of people in the early decades of this century (just before the Northerners arrived, changing the political set-up with trade, slave-raiding, cattle-rustling and a newly imposed administrative structure). But population distribution and settlement patterns at that time showed less density and less intensive resource use (e.g. of pasture, cultivation sites, trees and bush for firewood and building).[10]

Transhumant pastoralism, shifting cultivation of sorghum and maize, gardening and hunting and gathering still form the core of Suri subsistence. Fields for sorghum and maize (for which there still is sufficient unused bushland) are cleared and burned every year, although one plot may serve for two or three years. Technology is elementary: they only use machetes, hoes, and iron-pointed digging sticks. No other inputs (apart from collective labour, in exchange for sorghum beer) are known. As noted, the lower Kibish Valley provides excellent pasture for cattle. The Suri, recognizing herds as their security and future, invest any surplus in acquiring cattle. Cattle are not only used as food (blood, milk, occasionally meat) but also for clothing and utensils, constitute the main wealth transferred at marriage and have a role in many rituals. Also, the Suri keep goats and sheep. Leaves and fruits from various trees and shrubs are gathered especially by women and children. Women plant cabbage, pumpkin, gourds, peppers, and cassava – the only root-crop, but a major food resource. Hunting has always provided a good additional, though irregular, source of animal protein. In the early 1970s, Suri hunting was seriously restricted by the creation of the Omo National Park.[11]

THE FAMINE CRISIS

Over the past two centuries, the Suri suffered badly from drought and famine. Their oral traditions indicate that cattle epidemics were not unknown but it appears that they were less devastated by the big rinderpest epidemic and famine of the 1890s than other southern peoples, like the Tishana-Me'en, Dizi, Mursi or Dassanetch. The most recent serious cattle plague was the anthrax epidemic in the early 1970s (probably imported from Sudan), which made large tracts of traditional grazing area around Mount Shulugui and along the Tirma Range unusable. Also in the 1970s, drought caused severe crop failure and cattle death especially among the Chai (the Suri section east of the Kibish River). David Turton mentioned this crisis in his studies on the Mursi (cf. Turton and Turton 1984: 187). In these years, the Suri subsistence base was slowly undermined; numbers of cattle and people declined, crop yields were small, and gathering roots and fruits could not yield sufficient nutrition to sustain the population. Also, the Suri were earlier prevented from hunting in Omo National Park, which was guarded by (at that time, better armed) game wardens. Thus, the Suri had neither food-reserves (grain or cattle) nor sufficient weapons, i.e. they could not retaliate for cattle raids from their neighbours (mainly Nyangatom).

In 1984 the rains failed again. The ensuing drought and famine period of 1984–85 forms the baseline for this analysis, although it must be emphasized that it had its precedents in a decade of crisis. In 1984–85, more Suri were dying because traditional responses of increased hunting and gathering, emergency selling of stock animals and raiding did not work and people were already weakened by preceding crisis years. Informants recall this period as the worst in recent history. In these years, the Suri lost several thousand people from all age-groups, and as the victims could not all be buried, corpses were left in the bush, covered with tree-branches and leaves. A possible contributory factor to the crisis, the increase of fatal contagious disease (intestinal infections, diarrhoea), cannot be assessed at the present state of knowledge, but was probably important (see Kelly, this volume, Chapter 12)

Following traditional crisis-responses, several Suri groups migrated north to the Tulgit area, a Dizi border area west of Jeba town, to find new forest/bush resources, new grazing or cultivation lands, and to be near the town. Some 1000 to 1200 Tirma (Suri living west of the Kibish River) crossed into Sudan to exchange cattle for grain with local Balé and Anuak people and to find new cultivation sites on the southern fringe of the Boma Plateau. (A similar Tirma migration occurred early in this century.) For the same reasons, the Chai moved closer to the Maji foothills, considered a Dizi area. For the Chai-Suri especially, an additional reason to move north was the persistent threat of the Nyangatom (see below).

Meanwhile news of the crisis reached local administrators in Maji, and eventually the Jimma and Addis Ababa offices of the Ethiopian Relief and Rehabilitation Commission (RRC) were notified. With World Vision International, an emergency famine relief programme was set up late in 1985. Planes landed at a small airstrip in the Kibish area (constructed by missionaries in the 1960s), and corn and grain were distributed. No camp was set up: the Suri collected their grain and returned to their homesteads nearby. Many lives were saved and, as in the similar Mursi case described by the Turtons (1984), no long-term dependency relationship was created between donors and recipients.

The Suri had no indigenous conception of outside 'aid' or 'development'. Aid by external groups was initially neither expected nor understood. There were traditional ways of appealing to bond-friends among neighbouring ethnic groups – a kind of 'structural reciprocity' – but, significantly, this did not work in the 1980s.

The Suri attitude toward outside agencies - which they only knew in the form of the Ethiopian government and a short-lived missionary effort in the 1960s–early 1970s[12] – was sceptical and distant. They had had no contact with relief organizations when World Vision and the RRC stepped in.[13] While they eagerly accepted grain given to them, they noted that it was a short term non-reciprocal event, and that they ultimately would have to rely on their own meagre resources and get whatever they could by their own effort.[14]

When the donors left after some months, natural and material conditions had not substantially improved. Crops were poor, cattle were scarce, game resources outside the Park area were being seriously depleted, and no new inputs in terms of sowing grain, draught animals, etc. were supplied. Recovery of their subsistence base was thus left to the Suri themselves.

INTER-ETHNIC CONFLICT, 1984–93

The other major contributory factor to crisis, coinciding with subsistence problems in Suri society was that of inter-ethnic movements, especially in the Ethio-Sudan-Kenyan border area. In roughly the same years that famine affected them, violent conflict emerged with the Nyangatom, their immediate neighbours. Several factors explain Nyangatom aggression towards the Suri: (a) pressure from Turkana people in Northern Kenya, who have steadily moved north, due to persistent drought, scarcity of grazing lands in their own habitat, and perhaps to political harrassment by Kenyan authorities. Several serious clashes with both parties were reported over the past decade, up to today; (b) high Nyangatom population growth and need for more grazing and cultivation sites, c) the southern Sudanese war. In 1982–4, the Toposa in Sudan acquired automatic rifles from either Sudanese government troops or illegal traders and traded them to the Nyangatom, their brethren and allies. Also, the Nyangatom bought them from traders and more recently may have gone as far as Malakal to get training and free weapons from government forces.[15] This gave the Nyangatom a decisive edge over their traditional enemies the Suri (called by them 'Nyikoroma', hill-dwellers). They pursued them in their home territory, causing a disproportionate toll of human life among the Suri and loss of many cattle and small stock and of traditional grazing areas near Mt Shulugui.

One might even argue that this ecologically- and demographically-motivated movement and its violent effects were the prime cause of star-vation, because it undermined traditional Suri ability to respond to drought and crop-failure crises based on their own resources (i.e. cattle, hunting-gathering, short-term migration). These developments forced them to con-centrate in larger, more defensible villages, and (over-)exploit a more limited area. This resulted in relative crowding, depletion of bush resources for firewood, huts and cattle corrals, and in a fall in yields of cultivation sites (shorter fallow). The Nyangatom threat finally also induced the Suri to settle in their present locations along the upper Kibish, about 40 kilometres north of their core area.

Although most have now (1994) lived for six to seven years in the Dizi border area, many Suri see this as exile: their real 'homeland' is near Mt Shulugui, the place, as they say, where their main rituals (like the long-awaited age-set initiation ceremony) should be held. But although they claim (ideologically, so to speak) that they want to return there, they realize that it may already be too late. The Nyangatom have settled at the base of the Shulugui mountain and now urge district authorities to recog-nize a new Nyangatom *k'ebele* on former Suri territory. They have also a strong EHADIG contingent there, partly made up of their own people.[16]

In the meantime, the Suri's northward push into fringes of Dizi (and perhaps Me'en) territory continues. Whether they will settle in the high-lands and adopt cultivation, is another matter; so far no Suri (either indi-viduals or family groups) have moved out of Suri country permanently (for one insignificant exception, see note 14).

ADAPTIVE RESPONSE AND REGENERATION, 1988–92

In February 1988, during my first visit, the Suri were still suffering from effects of drought and famine. However, in late 1991, they had substantially recovered: many young children, large villages, large fields of sorghum and maize, herds restored to a remarkable degree compared with the 1985 situation. Migrant Suri even returned from Sudan to Ethiopia. Another indication of regained strength was that most adult males had an automatic rifle, the new symbol of power and male status. Next to the Nyangatom, the Suri thus became the best armed group in the area, and were (and still are) a serious threat to peace and security in the Maji area.

One secret of their recovery was increased exploitation of a unique resource: gold. Lower parts of the Maji-Kibish and the Upper Akobo areas, especially in and near streambeds, have small deposits of gold which can be extracted by panning. This practice was known among Dizi and Anuak people. The latter mined gold near northern tributaries of the Akobo (Dima) river. Nobody knows exactly when this practice started, but it was probably during the Italian occupation (Italians sent prospecting teams to the area and set up a branch office of their mineral exploration company COMINA near the Akobo). The Suri say they became familiar with the practice about twenty years ago. But as mining is very hard work, often done for several weeks, outside the Suri area proper in a kind of no-man's land, they had never fully exploited this resource before. Neither did they use gold for any purpose within their own society. Only external demand – traders in Jeba and Maji – finally urged them to take up gold-mining in the drought years. It yielded substantial cash with which they bought tools, food, and cattle, and, later, weapons. For 4.5 grams of pure gold (the work of a few weeks' mining, including travelling), they received about 300 Ethiopian *birr* (in 1986–7, U\$ 149), the price of one cow or bull, or two heifers. In 1991, the price was about 15 per cent higher, in mid-1993 again 5–10 per cent more. Thus, especially in 1986–90, there was something of a native goldrush to the Akobo area. Gold was (illegally) sold not only to town-traders but also to Anuak people up north, who gave them cattle, bullets and Kalashnikovs in return (obtained from Sudanese army depots). Interestingly, the Suri never invested proceeds from gold in cultivation (i.e. in ploughs, draught animals (oxen), tools, other crop seeds like t'eff or wheat, in permanent housing, etc.) but only in these two elements allowing them to reinforce their hold on their traditional eco-niche: cattle and guns. The Suri saw the need to arm themselves in order to *re-assert* claims to their own traditional area in the face of efforts by, especially, the Nyangatom, to monopolize resource niches (water sources, bush tracts and grazing land) in the southern border area near Shulugui. In other words, they wanted to 'restore the balance'. But the newly acquired weapons also tempted Suri to raid cattle from the Dizi, on whose lands they had steadily encroached since 1985. In 1991, there were at least four big raids on Dizi settlements, in which close to a hundred Dizi were killed. In 1992 and 1993 this continued, while Suri armed youngsters killed several old Dizi chiefs and also defenceless Dizi girls carrying water or firewood, or farmers returning from fields. Numerous cattle were stolen and property destroyed. Trade routes between Maji and Jeba were constantly threatened, and people moving to markets (village people, Tishana, Dizi) were ambushed, robbed and killed. In 1993 conflict escalated further so that large numbers of southern Dizi, tired of random killings, left their home areas to go north. Government action, either from the Derg or the EPRDF-led government, has been slow in coming but finally a crack-down of EHADIG-forces on the Suri at the end of 1993 seemed to have muted Suri aggression.[17]

In sum, gold and use of violence not only helped the Suri to survive their subsistence crisis, but also to obtain new power. By investing and using automatic rifles their recovery turned out to be *too* successful, so to speak.

Even though violence may be checked in the near future, at present it allows them to restore their way of life as they see fit. It is unlikely that the Suri – as sometimes expected by government or NGO representatives – will make a transition to sedentary cultivation. The Turtons (1984) described such a settlement move by a part of the Mursi, who in a comparable period of crisis went to live as cultivators in the Mago highland area. But nowadays, this experimental settlement (where no cattle could be kept due to tsetse) has largely been abandoned: most Mursi returned to the plains.[18] The Suri, like the Mursi, are reluctant to live as farmers in the highland zone, especially if there is an option to regain a foothold in the pastoralist economy. Like the Mursi, the Suri see themselves as a free herding people. Whatever cultural reasons there are for it, this attitude makes some economic sense: not only are the Suri relatively free from administration and tax-imposing government officials, they also can, in good years, accumulate much more wealth[19] than, say, the Dizi or the Me'en, because of their substantial numbers of cattle. In addition, with their new weapons, the Suri also regained access to the last plentiful sources of game meat in Omo National Parks'. They were not disturbed by the Parks' game wardens, who feared Suri fire-power, although in 1993 an EHADIG-force was stationed there, which will discourage large-scale hunting. Of course, Suri weaponry also enabled them better access to gold, exploitation of which they have tried to monopolize, pushing out the Dizi.

SOCIAL AND POLITICAL EFFECTS OF CRISIS

The main effects of drought, famine and political upheaval on Suri society can be noticed in three domains.

Socio-economic Organization

Initially, in the worst famine period, domestic units became more independent, with solidarity between agnates, clan members or fellow villagers eroding as resources declined. Also, a 'split' in domestic groups occurred: males and females operated more independently of each other. Related to this were changes in labour organization – between males and females and in labour-tasks themselves – most of which proved to be shortterm. Male household heads were more mobile, hunting, visiting the relief distribution point, selling cattle in various places, begging for food (e.g. among the Dizi), and going to gold-mining places.[20] Clearing and planting declined, as seeds were used for consumption. Women and young children spent more time gathering. Women seemed less affected by famine. The number of female victims was lower than that of males. In recent years, as the Suri recovered, this led to increased polygamous marriages (also because of 'levirate' marriage: a man taking the wife (wives) of a deceased brother or other close agnatic relative).

Trade with highland villagers increased after 1985. First, the Suri offered goats and cattle, in return for grain. Second, the role of gold as a commodity rapidly gained importance. In Maji and Jeba traders were happy to buy gold, which could be resold at a profit elsewhere. Increased market exchange, however, did not draw the Suri into the regional money economy. They used it to funnel resources into their own society, not to acquire other commodities except for salt, razor-blades or cloth. It was neither extensively used as measure of exchange, 'saving' or value within their own society: it was mainly seen as a medium for dealing with outsiders.

Internal Political Relations

A notable long-term effect was a change in the balance between generations within Suri society: elders (in Suri: *bara*, or in general, *kumin*) versus youngsters and younger married men (*tègay*) and junior elders (*rora*). Although the three *komoru*, or 'ritual leaders', retained their prestigeous (hereditary) position, their effective influence declined. Their advice on raiding, location of new fields or villages, control of ceremonial duelling contests, or on occasional government directives or proposals, was listened to but not seen as binding. Their mediatory functions were still called upon (during group conflict or public meetings) but their authority or 'executive power' (already poor in the traditional system) was reduced to virtually nothing in the years of crisis.

To illustrate, we look in some detail at a central Suri ritual, ceremonial male duelling (*sagine*). This is done with poles (*dongen*, sg. *donga*) of tough *kalloch*i wood (*Grewia mollis Juss.*), 2.10 to 2.40 metres in length. Contestants are young men of the *tègay* age-grade (unmarried) from different territorial settlements and/or clans. They hold several matches and return-matches over a period of a few months every year. The short fights have to be supervised by referees (*oddá*). In functionalist terms one might maintain that these contests 'regulate' internal tensions generated between competing village communities in Suri society, in allowing young, ambitious men, eager to start life as independent household heads to show their strength and virility in a socially accepted manner (this aspect is explicitly recognized by nubile Suri girls). There is certainly more in it than this, but in fact the actual level of violence (harrassment, assault, theft, murder) within Suri society is low. However, the important point is that the *sagine* institution has undergone notable changes in the past six to seven years. First, frequency of contests has much increased. They are held almost every two to three weeks over a period of three to four months after the main sorghum harvest (September–November, and after that as well (e.g. in January and in the first rains in April–May). Second, influence of elders (including the *komoru*) and referees over contesting parties has diminished: nowadays, young men continue as they like, and after one party has 'lost' a contest, they grab their Kalashnikovs and start shooting (usually, but not always, in the air) to show their irritation. Suri elders say the game has lost much of its former attraction and its meaning is being eroded.

The increase in the number of contests is, from the perspective taken here, a predictable result of two underlying factors: a) mounting *external* pressure on Suri society from neighbouring groups, especially the Nyangatom, which has made them nervous and agressive but also unable (yet) to vent this agression against the Nyangatom without risking heavy losses, and: b) population pressure and decreased resources in a limited area. Resource use and population growth (at least 3.5 per cent per annum in the last four years[21]) have led to visible degradation of their immediate environment. Village communities live much closer to each other and must take each other's fields and bush resources into account, as they exploit the same places for gathering, firewood, washing, water, etc..

Relations become more competitive, leading to inter-community rivalry, expressed *partly* in *donga* contests.

The fact that young men have taken over the *sagine*-proceedings indicates their newly gained power-base (guns, cattle) within Suri society. Gold exploitation enables them to assert independence from fathers or other older agnates (who wish to use their labour as long as possible): they do not have to wait so long to start building up their own herd, or to marry.

A related effect is the increased self-confidence of the Suri after having recovered from crisis. This is what village people and the Dizi mean when they say the Suri have become 'arrogant', 'saturated' (Amharic: *t'egabeñña*). One sees this in the expression of violence with automatic weapons, which has had a kind of cultural effect in itself, tending to stimulate a 'cult' of the gun among Suri youngsters.

Inter-group Relations

Although gold-mining enabled the Suri to gain cash and expand cattle herds, this has not led to repossession of former areas of settlement close to the Nyangatom area – which would have eased the abovementioned demographic and ecological pressures. The system of inter-ethnic relations is as strained as ever. One might associate this development with the TGE's new ethnic policies but, as is clear from the preceding analysis, deteriorioriation started well before the change of government. The Suri are also still one of the least politicized groups in Ethiopia, having avoided the heavy ideological pressure on ethnic identity development, etc., through their isolated position and limited exposure to highland culture. Remarkably, although they know from experience what the highland socio-cultural model of life implies, they are not in the least drawn to it. There is a persistent, largely sceptical and negative, image of highland Ethiopians (in Suri: *Golach*, which includes Amhara, Tigray, Gurage, Oromo) as opposed to their own self-image as proud, independent cattle-herders with distinctive customs like female lip-plates, body decoration, ceremonial duelling, and specific initiation rituals. Change of government has not significantly modified this attitude. The EHADIG is seen as another representative of highland society.

While the TGE's policy is to stimulate ethnic group self-organization and representation on local and regional levels, in the case of the Suri this cannot be easily applied. While the Me'en formed a self-organization (not a 'party') under EHADIG auspices, the Suri have no interest in this. Neither it is likely that they will join the Käfa Peoples' Democratic Movement, which has a Dizi academic as one of its leaders. In the Maji area, there are serious debates about boundaries, compensation for past raids and killings, resource exploitation and secure trade routes. As long as outstanding disputes (on recent Suri expansion into Dizi lands, their killing of Dizi leaders and ambushing trading parties in an area jointly used by all groups) are not solved, it is difficult to see how regional-ethnic autonomy could work. In such conditions, government troops are needed as intermediaries maintaining a semblance of law and order.

Thus, the Suri – and the other groups – do not share in the newly propagated political discourse on ethnic group identity. They follow pre-existing, socio-ecologically rooted, group images, which are partly complementary and partly antagonistic, and which emanate largely from regional-level political group relations and from daily economic concerns.

Traditional mediatory channels through elders and established ritual mechanisms seem to have lost their importance and consensus between ethnic groups has given way to confrontation. As this also seriously impairs trade and exchange relations, each group unwittingly develops the need to rely on its own resources, and to aim at a false self-sufficiency (cf. Abbink 1994). This response is not simply due to deterioration of the natural environment in itself - because in earlier times, conflicts and crises were more or less contained and concluded in temporary, ritually sealed, reconciliation. Such a response is decisively aggravated by the uncontrolled spread of modern arms, creating an unpredictable, insecure political environment. As such regional problems of proliferation of arms cannot be solved easily – except by massive disarming – this instability will remain and continue to reinforce traditional tensions and overexploitation of precarious resource bases for increasing numbers of people. Paradoxically, for the new political models of ethnic autonomy and representation to work, a new framework of inter-ethnic mediation would be required, to be organized along the lines of traditional arrangements, de-emphasizing the usurped power of youngsters with guns. Development schemes would have to stimulate joint involvement of various ethnic groups (because there is no numerically and territorially dominant group in the Maji area).

One development project is currently underway among the Suri – it could be seen as another effect of the serious crisis of 1984–5. This is the 'Surma rehabilitation project', set up by the Lutheran World Federation and the Ethiopian Evangelical Church Mekane Yesus. From 1989 to 1993 they were in a base camp in Tum, the small district capital of Maji zone. Late in 1993, another base was being built in Tulgit, at the north fringe of the Suri area. While the project has missionary aspects (e.g., translating the Bible and other Christian texts into Suri) the aims are to open a clinic, improve cultivation techniques, give veterinary services, and eventually a open a primary school. While medical services have up to now been provided to the Dizi and the Tum townspeople, the Tulgit project will be geared chiefly to the Suri. It will certainly attract a number of Suri youngsters but whether it will lead to basic changes in the Suri way of life is doubtful.

CONCLUSION

The Suri have been able to get out of their crisis by timely exploitation of gold as a cash resource, which was 'invested' back into their transhumant pastoral economy, in the form of cattle and weapons. The were able to regenerate their reproductive powers in a double sense: more cattle (either bought or raided) allowed a quick upsurge in marriages and births; and acquisition and use of weapons which permitted self-defence and expansion at the cost of others. Availability of automatic rifles also led to changes within Suri society itself: generational tension, territorial disputes, and rivalry between Tirma and Chai sub-groups. An unintended effect of Suri self-rehabilitation is that the role and use of arms has acquired a cultural momentum of its own, with far-reaching effects on Suri social structure and on ethnic group relations (cf. Abbink 1994).

The perhaps atypical recovery of the Suri – which temporarily decreased their inter-dependence with other groups in the ethno-system – does not solve problems of long-term vulnerability of their environment and way of life (this is not something foremost in the Suri mind; they seldom speak of the famine of the past and think the weapons give them an enduring power base). The main problems of the Suri eco-niche remain:

1. Unreliable rainfall, affecting pasture and bush resources;
2. Unstable relations between expanding, competing ethnic populations in a partially shared area with limited resources;
3. Unpredictable (national) government policies;
4. External threats due to regional conflicts spilling over into adjacent areas (Northern Kenya, Southern Sudan). When state influence (administrative, military or police presence) is relaxed, local conflicts will be played out increasingly by force. A political-administrative emphasis on ethnic group identities and boundaries will, most likely, not ease group tensions in Maji area, where groups have traditionally been partly dependent upon each other.

While this chapter indicates that disaster-affected people can develop their own adaptive response to subsistence crises, and that external aid should be geared to that, it is far less certain what must be done if this response is formulated, so to speak, at the expense of others.

Obviously, indigenous views should be considered, *including* the 'target' group's possible inclination to reject aid if it has perceived draw-backs. Sustainable development programmes, insofar as they have any long-term chance in a still unfavourable macro-economic setting, should be grafted upon serious consideration of local conditions and, in this case, implies recognizing Suri wishes to maintain their agro-pastoralist economy; taking into account short-term migratory patterns; recognizing environmental limits and possibilities for agricultural crops and tech-niques; respecting the central role of women in family life and in most subsistence activities; and acknowledging gathering plants, roots, nuts and fruits as important components in their food portfolio. If 'cultivation pro-jects' are envisaged, examples should be provided in irrigation agriculture along the Kibish, but with crops the Suri prefer. Obviously, improvement is required in transport, educational and medical facilities, giving the Suri a choice to eventually participate in the regional or national economy. This applies to the (multi-ethnic) region as a whole.

There must be a response to eventual Suri desires to enter into more close relations with other groups or government agencies, but they should not be forced into a marginal economy which destroys the remarkable measure of self-reliance and cultural stability they now possess.

Acknowledgements

I thank Dr David Turton, editor of *Disasters – Journal of Disaster Studies and Management*, for permission to use material first published in that journal in 1993 (*Disasters*, **17**(3): 218–25). Generous support by the Royal Netherlands Academy of Science (KNAW) and the Netherlands Organisation for Scientific Research in the Tropics (WOTRO) for my fieldwork in Ethiopia (1991–3) is gratefully acknowledged. I am also very grateful to Suri friends for help and hospitality, among them Barhoyne Wolesirba, Wolekibo Wara, and especially Londosa Doleti. Finally, I thank the Institute of Ethiopian Studies at Addis Ababa University for its interest and assistance.

Notes

1. This figure is based on census work in 1991–2. Existing statistics on the Suri/Surma are scarce and unreliable. The local administration in Maji keeps no population records for them. In 1985, World Vision International made a preliminary census and came to an estimated, but inflated, figure of about 35,000. This was during the famine.

2.   I exclude here the Bale or Balethi people who might be considered a third Suri group (see Lyth 1947). They are closely related, especially to the Tirma and number about 8000. However, most live in Sudan east of the Boma plateau.

3.   The Suri have repeatedly stolen unattended things from tourists. They see the tourists' behaviour as unresponsive, exploitative and non-reciprocal and basically do not understand what they want. In the meantime, the security situation in the area (late 1993 – early 1994) has deteriorated so much that to visit the Suri as a tourist would be near-suicidal (see Abbink 1993). Organized excursions were halted several years ago and a new effort in October 1993 failed. For a kind of 'tourist view' of the Suri, see Beckwith and Fisher (1990;1991), interesting but in several ways inappropriate accounts.

4.   See T. Girard, report of abortive Suri survey, *SLLE Reports* (Addis Ababa) no. 4 (1993):10–24, and G. Dimmendaal on the Suri/Mursi and related groups, ibid., 26–7. Cf. J. Abbink, 'Suri-English Basic Vocabulary', *Frankfurter Afrikanische Blätter*, forthcoming.

5.   For these data see the *National Atlas of Ethiopia*, pp. 7–8, 10–12, 18.

6.   Also, Western tourists with a permit obtained from Addis Ababa's Ethiopian National Tourist Organization (for thousands of US dollars) hunted in the area, much resented by local people.

7.   This was the longest genealogy I could find (among the Chai Suri).

8.   Information from Abba Fanta Yimer, a senior resident of Maji (July 1993). He was a soldier in the area shortly after Aberra's exploits in the early decades of this century.

9.   Cf. Viezzer (1938) and Rizetto (1941) for the earliest reports on the Suri area.

10.   See Turton (1987) for a study of the effects of the Omo National Park on the Mursi.

11.   A mission with a small airstrip and a clinic was built in Merdur in the Tirma area. It was abandoned in the 1970s when the Ethiopian government accused all American missionaries of being CIA agents. The buildings and materials were later destroyed and used by local people.

12.   Even in this emergency period, several unfortunate incidents troubled relationships between Suri and outside agencies. One instance was the following: in Jeba village a government shack contained bags of powdery poison for treating crops. The Suri learned of this and believed it to be flour that was being withheld from them. One night they stole the bags and when they later used the contents to prepare flour porridge, several people died. They then blamed the village people and the administration for trying to poison them.

13.   There had been some half-hearted rehabilitation attempts by the RRC and World Vision International, meant to introduce farming in the Kibish area but these were unsuccessful. Another attempt was made in 1985 when about five hundred Suri were taken outside the area to be 'trained in farming' (see Abbink 1992). This was also a failure, as 85 per cent of the migrants returned to their area of origin; the high rate of return migration also indicates that the Suri were successful in gradually restoring their traditional subsistence base in their home area, on which they knew they would depend in the future.

14. Some of this information was confirmed to me 'by Professor Serge Tornay (Université de Paris, Nanterre), foremost expert on the Nyangatom, in private conversation in Addis Ababa (January 1992) and in subsequent letters.
15. The EHADIG force in Maji have no Suri members.
16. In November 1993, a large-scale battle between Suri and EHADIG forces erupted, after Suri killed some EHADIG soldiers. EHADIG patience and restraint had already been severely tried when the Suri shot and killed one of their men in April 1993 and later defiantly exhumed and burnt the corpse. The night-long battle left many Suri dead and may have been a turning point in relations of the Suri with other groups in the area.
17. As mentioned in two recent films about the Mursi, *The Land is Bad* and *Nitha* (D. Turton and L. Woodhead, Granada Television, 1991).
18. This wealth is, however, not converted or reckoned in money but in terms of reproductive powers (family) and social standing (alliances) within their own society.
19. Suri (after the Kibish food distribution point was closed) continued to visit Dima refugee camp (for Sudanese refugees) to obtain food. It was located on the Akobo river, a two-day walk north, and was a major training and support base for the Sudan People's Liberation Army (SPLA), supported by the Mengistu regime. Retreating SPLA troops pillaged the camp in June 1991.
20. Based on field census data 1991.

References

Abbink, J., 1990. 'Tribal formation on the Ethiopian fringe: toward a history of the 'Tishana'.' *Northeast African Studies*, 12(1): 21–42.
Abbink, J., 1991. 'The Deconstruction of 'Tribe': Ethnicity and Politics in Southwestern Ethiopia', *Journal of Ethiopian Studies*, 24:1–21.
Abbink, J., 1992. 'Settling the Surma: Notes on an Ethiopian Relief Experiment,' *Human Organization*, 50(2): 174–80.
Abbink, J., 1993. 'Ethnic Conflict in the 'Tribal' Zone: the Dizi and Suri in Southern Ethiopia', *Journal of Modern African Studies*, 31(4): 675–82.
Abbink, J., 1994. 'Changing Patterns of Ethnic Violence: Peasant–Pastoralist Confrontation in Southern Ethiopia', *Sociologus* (in press).
Beckwith, C. and Fisher, A., 1990. *African Ark. Peoples of the Horn* (London: Collins Harvill).
Beckwith, C. and Fisher, A., 'The Eloquent Surma of Ethiopia', *National Geographic*, 179(2): 77–99.
Chagnon, N., 1992. *Yanomamö. The Last Days of Eden* (New York: Harcourt, Brace, Jovanovich).
De Waal, A., 1989. *Famine that Kills: Darfur, Sudan, 1984–1985* (Oxford: Clarendon Press).
Ethiopian Mapping Agency, 1988. *National Atlas of Ethiopia* (Addis Ababa: EMA).
Lamphear, J., 1992. *The Scattering Time. Turkana Responses to Colonial Rule*, (Oxford: Clarendon Press).

Lyth, R., 1947. 'The Suri Tribe', *Sudan Notes and Records*, 28:106–114.

Office of the Population and Housing Census Commission, 1988. *Analytical Report on Keffa Region*. Population and Housing Census 1984 (Addis Ababa: Central Statistical Authority).

Rizetto, F., 1941. 'Alcune notizie sui Tirma', *Annali d'Africa Orientale Italiana*, 4:1201–11.

Turton, D., 1987. 'The Mursi and National Park Development in the Lower Omo Valley', D. Anderson and R. Grove (eds). *Conservation in Africa: People, Politics, and Practices* (Cambridge: Cambridge University Press).

Turton, D. and P. Turton, 1984. 'Spontaneous Resettlement after Drought: an Ethiopian Example', *Disasters*, 8:178–89.

Viezzer, C., 1938. 'Diario di una carovana di missione geomineraria di Bonga-Magi-Tirma dell'Ovest etiopico', *Rassegna Mineraria Mensile*, 17:404–425.

Walle Engedayehu, 1993. 'Ethiopia: Democracy and the Politics of Ethnicity', *Africa Today*, 40(2):29–52.

9 From Famine to Food Security in the Horn of Africa

Patrick Webb

INTRODUCTION

Policy-makers in the Horn face three great challenges at the turn of the new century: first, to bring long-lasting conflicts to a durable conclusion; second, to define and implement government policies that are demonstrably non-discriminatory in regional or ethnic terms, such that much of the basis for past conflicts is removed; third, to stimulate economic growth that is not wrecked by periodic crises and is therefore able to raise and stabilize purchasing power and food consumption among vulnerable households. Arguably, of these challenges, the third may prove most difficult.

The food situation in sub-Saharan Africa as a whole is getting worse, not better. The continent's gap between domestic supply and demand of staple foods, growing since the early 1970s, is projected to reach 50 million tons by the end of the decade; the Horn countries alone will likely account for almost 20 per cent of that deficit (von Braun and Paulino 1990; WFP 1991; Aylieff 1993). Governments and international donors have responded by emphasizing goals of raising domestic food supply and seeking food security. However, negative trends in per capita food production in many countries continue to make improved household food security an elusive goal.

This chapter examines some causes and effects of acute food insecurity in the Horn, focusing on Ethiopia, and discusses policy and programme initiatives that might be pursued to address such problems within the search for sustainable growth (see Campbell, this volume, Chapter 10). The central argument is that while a focus on raising agricultural production lies at the heart of future growth in famine-prone countries, conventional subsistence-oriented self-sufficiency goals are no longer appropriate.

Concern with growth in food supply must not detract from the increasing relevance of non-farm income and employment constraints where central policy objectives are enhancing household food security and reducing household vulnerability to periodic income collapse. In coming years improved food security in Ethiopia, as elsewhere in the Horn, will likely be secured through a location-specific mix of three key policy and programme instruments: namely, sound policies for economic growth with a particular focus on agriculture, employment creation through labour-intensive public works, and stabilization of food entitlements for the poor in famine-prone areas through effective early warning and emergency relief.

THE THREAT OF FAMINE DESPITE PEACE

The last quarter of the twentieth century is one of the most traumatic periods in the Horn's turbulent history, marked by major famines (leaving millions dead), numerous revolutions, multiple droughts, and steady erosion of food security. All contributed to cumulative erosion of the effectiveness of food production, distribution and consumption systems.

In Ethiopia, these upheavals culminated in 1991 in a change of government and policy direction. After seventeen years of centralized decision-making and economic control, national policies developed rapidly in favour of market liberalization, dismantling parastatals and disengagement of the public sector from economic management. Steps were taken to improve democratization, rule of law and relations with enemies such as Somalia and Eritrea. As a result, international donors slowly became more willing to invest development capital as well as support 'social safety-net' programmes for softening the blow of macroeconomic reforms. These measures, coupled with reallocation of resources away from military spending towards rural development, were essential first steps in eradicating famine.

But are they sufficient to prevent another famine? Peace is certainly a precondition for successful economic growth. Prospects for Somalia and Sudan remain bleak while internal military conflict is the norm. It can be argued that with an end to war in Ethiopia and macroeconomic reforms in place, the Ethiopian economy will grow itself out of vulnerability. The market, freed from its former strait-jacket, will provide the food (through domestic production and imports) and income necessary to meet minimum requirements. Famine will simply disappear.

Yet, absence of war is not in itself sufficient guarantee of food security. There are two main reasons for this. First, vulnerable households are not great competitors in the market-place. They often do not have the resources (or credit) to grow more food even if they wanted to sell a surplus on the market. Access to oxen, seeds, hired labour and tools depends on availability of capital which is in short supply in rural areas.

What is more, transport and marketing infrastructure required for the smooth flow of food, capital and labour are still absent. Costs of increasing food production are rising fast along with input prices. Thus, even with growth the chronically poor will remain vulnerable to climatic or economic shocks for many years to come.

The second reason is that the problem itself is changing. On the one hand, new elements must be considered. Rapid urbanization, growing urban food insecurity, demobilization of huge armies, regional fragmentation of decision making attendant on democratization, and continued economic uncertainty cast the famine problem in a new light. There are 'new' groups of vulnerable people competing for external assistance as well as market shares, new structural problems to be addressed by policy and project action and new roles for institutions to be considered.

On the other hand, with population growth exceeding three per cent per year the number of vulnerable people continues to grow. In 1993 between 10 and 15 million individuals (over ten per cent of the population) were vulnerable to famine (Ethiopia 1992; World Bank 1993). By the year 2000, Ethiopia's population will reach over 70 million (OPHCC 1991). Even if the relative share of vulnerable people does not change, the absolute number of individuals requiring assistance is becoming hard to manage.

While it is easy to explain these problems in superficial terms of war or drought such reductionism is unhelpful to policy-makers. Parts of Rwanda and Malawi suffered near-famine conditions in recent years, as well as long-term undernutrition at chronic levels, without direct agency of drought or war. By contrast, millions suffered massive famine in Ethiopia in regions far removed from the fighting or epicentres of drought (Webb, von Braun and Yohannes 1992). The problem is not so simple that it can be resolved by stopping wars and foreseeing drought. Causes of food insecurity, and policy initiatives required to tackle them, are more complex.

CAUSES OF FOOD INSECURITY IN THE HORN

The genesis of food crises (with their severest expression in famine) must be understood as an interaction between environmental, economic and policy variables, both in the short and long term. A narrow focus on any single element does not fully address the problem. On the environmental side, there is no doubt that drought is a primary agent of famine in Africa. For example, mean annual rainfall declined in western Sudan by 7 per cent between the 1960s and the 1970s, followed by a further 18 per cent decline in the 1980s. At the same time, variability around the trend increased from 16 per cent in the 1960s to 32 per cent in the 1980s (Teklu, von Braun and Zaki 1991). Such trends may represent the negative swing in a long-term cycle that will be reversed in the future. However, not only is solid evidence of predictable cycles lacking, the current relationships between rainfall, production, prices and consumption are so strong that actions against drought and degradation are needed immediately.

Food consumption in drought-prone regions is highly-correlated with domestic production, itself closely linked to rainfall. In 1984, rainfall in Ethiopia was 22 per cent below the long-term national average and more than 50 per cent below average in the worst-affected regions (Webb, von Braun and Yohannes 1992). A 10 per cent decline in rainfall below Ethiopia's long-term average results in a 4.4 per cent decline in national cereal production (ibid.); in Sudan, a similar 10 per cent decline in rainfall causes a 5 per cent decline in domestic production (Teklu, von Braun and Zaki 1991).

So drought is important; food supply constraints must not be overlooked. However, one year of drought does not usually cause famine. The droughts of 1984 were preceded in Ethiopia and Sudan by at least two years of below-average rainfall. Thus, household vulnerability to famine had already increased through depletion of food stocks and capital assets. The asset base of poor households in northern Sudan, for example, declined by some 80 per cent during 1983–85, but regained by only 20 per cent in the next three years (ibid.). Subsequent droughts found a much more vulnerable population.

However, production failures caused by drought, even those lasting several years thereby contributing to accelerated resource degradation, do not become famines unless other conditions are propitious. Such conditions include

(a) lack of improved technology and inputs, which prevents the food insecure from realizing existing yield and output potentials; (b) high rates of environmental degradation, regained by only 20 per cent in next three years (ibid). Subsequent droughts found a much more vulnerable population.

However, production failures caused by drought, even those lasting several years thereby contributing to accelerated resource degradation, do not become famines unless other condition are propitious. Such conditions include:

(a) lack of improved technology and inputs, which prevents the food insecure from realizing existing yield and output potentials;
(b) high rates of environmental degradation, which limit sustainability of any productivity gains that are achieved;

(c) lack of alternative rural and urban employment opportunities, which limits non-farm incomes;

(d) fragmented markets due to poor infrastructure and/or policy con straints, which contribute to steep price rises and rapid purchasing power collapse;

(e) limited access to education, which hinders human capital improve ment and keeps birth rates excessively high;

(f) severely underdeveloped financial markets, which impede stabiliza tion of consumption;

(g) poor health and sanitation environments.

These conditions are characteristic of poverty at both national and household levels. Wherever they are concentrated, prevalence of drought, locust invasion, or armed conflict will likely lead to famine where national ability to respond in time is weak. Moreover, just as pre-conditions of food insecurity lay foundations for famines, famine itself contributes to greater food insecurity by destroying material and human assets, thereby laying survivors open to years of further uncertainty. Thus, a proximate cause of famine is low and variable income among the poor. When food supplies are low, for whatever reason, it is their purchasing power which is most seriously impaired (due to cumulative effects of conditions outlined above), and it is therefore they who suffer first and most intensely.

But if poverty lies at the root of food insecurity, then policy failure has much to answer for. Famines of the 1970s and 1980s played a major role in raising food security high on the political agenda of many countries. But real progress towards sustained food security has been slow. Much blame for this lies with excessive state interference in macroeconomic activity and deficiencies in public policy.

For example, exchange rate regulations, export taxes, monopolistic marketing systems and producer price regulations have all been turned against the rural economy. Inappropriate policies not only undermine rural growth prospects but can have other effects. For example, prohibitions against domestic trade (between provinces) and against free labour markets in Ethiopia in the 1980s prevented the equalizing power of market forces found in other countries.

In Ethiopia, Sudan and Uganda, chronic lack of public investment in rural infrastructure makes a market-oriented response to food scarcity (as well as efficient famine relief) difficult. Long-term neglect of infrastructure in the 1960s and 1970s led to major problems in the 1980s and 1990s. Similarly, well-developed rural infrastructure stimulates the non-farm rural economy, permitting poor households to diversify income sources.

Africa's rural poor typically obtain 30 to 40 per cent of their total income from non-agricultural sources, ranging from under 10 per cent in eastern Zambia to over 50 per cent in western Kenya (von Braun and Pandya-Lorch 1991).

Thus, food insecurity and famine are inseparable from poverty, in turn inseparable from deficiencies in public policy as well as environmental shocks. A narrow focus on production variables (food supply) is inappropriate to full understanding of how food insecurity develops. Narrow promotion of subsistence-based agriculture as a means of tackling massive household food insecurity is therefore equally inappropriate. Growth in domestic food supply will, of course, be central in any development agenda. But increasing relevance of non-farm income and employment among rural households implies that a subsistence-oriented approach to national food security may actually leave increasing numbers of the poor vulnerable to hunger. What, then, should be the policy approach to tackling food insecurity in the coming decade?

A STRATEGY FOR IMPROVED FOOD SECURITY

Three policy and programme priorities are proposed as foundation stones for reducing household food insecurity in the 1990s: sound policies for economic growth with a focus on agriculture; employment creation through labour-intensive public works; stabilization of food entitlements for the poor in famine-prone areas through improved early warning, developed financial markets and appropriate emergency relief.

Each instrument is dealt with in turn below. It should, however, be understood here that successful implementation of any strategy depends on an end to armed conflict, evolution of participatory government, and good governance. Reference to governance or participation does not imply a particular political dogma or procedure. Rather it means, (a) an efficient use of resources that is accountable, (b) allocation of resources in a transparently non-discriminatory fashion in regional and ethnic terms, and (c) participatory planning and control of resources at a decentralized, local level.

Efficiency and accountability are important in their own right, but are essential for productive relationships between public and private sectors. Accountability is essential to prevent economic mismanagement and to build trust among private sector operators in long-term public commitments and contracts. It is also crucial to participatory interaction between government and its constituents; namely, rural smallholders.

Transparency in political decisions on where to spend resources (as well as where to raise taxes), is important in defusing many concerns that lead to civil conflict. Regional and ethnic strife often revolves around perceptions (real or otherwise) of discrimination by central authority. Part of this problem can be addressed by improving the information base upon which decisions are made. It can also be helped by broad discussion of the rationale underlying long-term development objectives.

Decentralization of decision-making and resource control can improve the value of actions taken and local accountability. Improved popular participation in decisions and in resultant actions lies at the heart of successful development. Little effective development can be achieved while political and military conflicts drain human and capital resources and hamper appropriate government policy-making (von Braun, Teklu and Webb 1993). That said, peace and good governance alone do not bring about food security; responsibility for that lies largely in the effective design, funding and implementation of programmes outlined below.

Policies for Agriculture-led Growth

In the long-run it will be successful development (as opposed to relief) activities that eradicate threat of famine. This requires not just economic growth, but growth that removes roots of chronic food insecurity. National and regional governments, as well as donors, must make strong commitments to allocate sufficient resources towards sustainable poverty alleviation in Africa. With its huge dependence on agriculture, improved food security across Africa, as in Ethiopia, depends on a strategy of agricultural growth. Successful investments in agricultural growth have been made over many years in countries such as India and China, where famine was once a threat to life. These investments focused on promoting technological change and commercialization in smallholder agriculture.

The continued primacy of agriculture in the Horn's economic development is not in question. Agricultural growth plays a key role in generating employment and income, as well as food, in rural areas, and the need to reverse downward trends in smallholder productivity must remain a priority, especially in countries facing land-locked borders, highly variable inter-annual production and severe foreign exchange constraints (Tshibaka 1990; Hazell and Anderson 1991).

While opportunities for bringing new land under cultivation compensated for slow yield growth in the past, continued attempts to expand agricultural land will entail ever larger investments, accelerated deforestation and land degradation, and, ultimately, falling yields (Delgado and

Pinstrup-Andersen 1993). Productivity increases must be sustainable in the long-term. Growing food demands must be met without compromising the ability of the total stock of resources (natural and human) to meet larger demands in the future.

A number of complementary avenues must be explored by government and donors in collaboration with local communities; for example, promotion of agricultural growth through technological change (including yield improvements) and commercialization. Adoption of improved technology is one key to long-term famine prevention, both through its potential to enhance agricultural productivity and through its related capacity to increase rural employment.

For example, Ethiopia's aggregate food output could be raised through increased application of chemical fertilizer in favourable regions. Ethiopia uses less than 10 kg of fertilizer per hectare, compared with 60 kg in Zimbabwe and almost 200 in China. Yields of maize, sorghum and rice can increase five-fold given adequate fertilizer and moisture. Fertilizer distribution is one tangible action that is almost certain of results.

Irrigation is widely considered to be an expensive option. Yet, Ethiopia again mirrors the rest of Africa in that its irrigation potential is huge and almost untapped. Irrigation can increase and stabilize yields, expand area cultivated and increase incomes. In many regions, small-scale, farmer-controlled irrigation in which water resources are appropriately-priced and managed deserves closer consideration.

Improved seeds continue to make an important contribution to hunger alleviation and not just in the staple food crop sub-sector. A recent evaluation of fourteen programmes of agricultural research in Africa since the 1980s found positive rates of return ranging between 15 and 40 per cent (Oehmke and Crawford 1992). Yet, breeding new varieties of non-grains as well as grains with characteristics such as high-yields, drought and pest resistance, and higher micronutrient-density (iron and zinc) remains a high but largely unfulfilled potential.

It remains unfulfilled largely because of a declining trend in donor and government support of agriculture. During the early 1990s, for example, US assistance to agriculture in developing countries was less than one half (in real terms) than it had been in 1988 (von Braun *et al.*, 1993). A similar, though less dramatic, decline in assistance to agriculture was posted by the World Bank (a decline of 25 per cent over the same period). Most other international and bilateral donors have shared in this negative trend. This is unfortunate, because it can take up to ten years to develop a productive new strain of crop; thus, lack of investment in agricultural research today translates into lack of food tomorrow.

It is also unfortunate because potential for greater productivity in Ethiopia is high. Wealthier farmers can obtain drought-year cereal yields three times higher than poorer farmers in the same community (Webb and Reardon 1992). This points to a potential for growth even at current levels of technology. The difference in current performance is linked to greater and more timely labour inputs, higher seeding densities, and more effective and timely use of plough technology. Agricultural growth must, therefore, be fuelled by better input availability and policies that stimulate the labour market, rather than restrict it as was the case in the recent past.

Recent macroeconomic reforms are likely to improve the incentive structure for, and returns to, agriculture, thereby stimulating increased food supply. Such agricultural growth will depend on appropriate investments in market infrastructure. Poorly developed infrastructure coupled with unfavourable market conditions contributed greatly in the past to purchasing power collapse. Price explosions occurred during the 1980s because weak inter-regional links prevented localized demand from generating increased supply. Consequently, while market liberalization is crucial, investments are required in physical infrastructure before markets can play their expected role. This is where public works can play an important role.

Labour-intensive Public Works

The transport and marketing infrastructure required for the smooth flow of food, capital and labour are still lacking. Costs of raising food production are therefore rising almost as fast as the heralded benefits of structural adjustment and, since most poor smallholders are net purchasers of food, they are affected by higher food prices perhaps more as consumers than as producers. If real effective demand is to be enhanced among the poor, who are increasingly dependent on the labour market for their meagre income, attention must be paid to diversifying their employment opportunities.

Provision of infrastructure necessary for increased market participation at reduced transactions costs and well-targeted transfers of resources to vulnerable parts of the private sector are public sector functions. Where these can be achieved cost-effectively by labour-intensive means there exists a dual opportunity for effective poverty-targeting and employment generation.

Public works can play a vital role as a reserve employer of labour by supporting the purchasing power of the poor, firstly through targeted income transfers, secondly by transferring management skills, and thirdly by generating physical assets upon which long-term development depends.

Ethiopia has a rich experience of such projects. Most food aid to Ethiopia (which receives roughly 25 per cent of all food aid to sub-Saharan Africa) is channelled through the World Food Programme (WFP) which uses 20 to 30 per cent of the total to support Africa's largest food-for-work (FFW) program (Aylieff 1993). From 1980 to 1990, WFP contributed over US$ 230 million to labour-intensive projects aimed at rehabilitating farm and grazing lands through reduced soil erosion and improved soil and water management (Webb and Kumar 1993). In practice this meant soil bunding, contour terracing and afforestation. The programme's most recent phase, costing US$ 78 million, aimed at improving 2.6 million hectares of degraded land by offering 27 million workdays per year. At the same time, up to 80 per cent of the food aid not used by WFP is channelled to NGOs (Aylieff 1993). In 1984, few NGOs were active in FFW but by 1993 the number had risen to more than thirty (Berhanu and Aylieff 1992).

Drawn by this momentum, the Ethiopian government is more committed than ever to a national public works programme. The country's Emergency Code (akin to India's Famine Codes that formalize central and local government responsibilities in the event of crises), and the donor supported Social Safety Net (to protect the poor during structural adjustment) both rely strongly on the principle of public works.

Project evaluations of public works in Ethiopia have been largely satisfactory, particularly from the stand-point of short-term support of food consumption. Where project wage rates are set sufficiently low in relation to prevailing market rates, public works schemes attract only the poor and are thus 'self-targeting'. However, the targeting of the absolute poor can be improved, since past programmes tended to rely on a fixed wage rate whose value attracted relatively less-poor households. This results in scarce resources being spread too thinly.

Targeting is important because even where everyone is poor in absolute terms, there are important differences between the ability of households to cope with famine. Among the poorest households in Ethiopia surveyed by the International Food Policy Research Institute (those with annual per capita income less than US$ 50), 48 per cent sold farm assets to survive, compared with only 5 per cent of wealthier households (with a per capita income of US$ 100 per annum) (Webb 1993). Similarly, less than half of the wealthy were forced to consume less than one meal per day during famine, while almost 65 per cent of poorest households reduced consumption to that level.

Wealthier households participated in FFW in the 1980s and early 1990s at the same rate as the absolute poor (Webb and Kumar 1993). This argues for more innovative and effective ways of using food aid resources, including self-targeting through low wages and monetization of food to generate cash wages and non-wage inputs. Attention must also be paid to technical elements of projects. Public works are not easy instruments to use. Technical, institutional and financial constraints are immense. While they may be labour-intensive, public works are also management-, material- and motivation-intensive. Close attention must be paid to the supply of non-wage inputs, to genuine community participation in project design, to monitoring the real purchasing power of the wage received, and even to contemplating privatization of some operations (von Braun, Teklu and Webb 1991). But, recognition of real constraints does not invalidate the argument that a proven targeted income-transfer mechanism should be used wherever possible.

Attention should also be paid to multiplying positive effects of income transfers by combining them with other, non-employment-based interventions such as credit schemes, health activities and direct food transfers to the destitute. Not everyone can work for a wage, or respond to higher producer prices and market liberalization. It is these people who need to be targeted separately with consumption protection and stabilization measures. In this way the artificial divide between emergency relief and development activities can be effectively bridged. Public authorities must mobilize the construction, repair, and maintenance of public assets as well as protect the poor against acute food insecurity. Households need to invest in income growth and diversification to protect themselves against acute food insecurity. It would be appropriate to assist both through labour-intensive technologies where possible.

Consumption Stabilization

While agriculture-led rural growth must be the bedrock of long-term development, with employment-generating projects providing a bridge between long-term asset creation and short-term income transfer, there remains a need for a strategy aimed at stabilizing consumption of the poor in food-deficit regions of famine-prone countries. Such a strategy needs to encompass both food supply stabilization and the stabilization of access to food for the poor. Regardless of how fast other policies are implemented, food crises will continue in the 1990s. This calls for a long-term commitment to timely and coordinated public intervention.

Governments and donors came late to the realization that costs of responding to famines can be much higher, both in human and economic terms, than costs of attempting to prevent crises in the first place. It has been shown, for instance, that in Indian states like Bihar, Gujarat and

Rajasthan famine relief expenditure for crisis years of the 1960s represented between 40 and 100 per cent of these states' annual development budget (Torry 1984). Similarly, drought relief activities in southern Africa in 1991–92 cost the US over US$ 730 million, compared with USAID's Development Fund for Africa budget for 1992 of US$ 800 million – for the entire continent (Interaction 1993). As a result, questions are now being asked about how to improve the active preparedness of both nations and households. Active preparedness by the state means preparing for a crisis while simultaneously working to prevent it. Such a strategy has three principal components: first, capability to record and diagnose distress signals and alert appropriate institutions; second, pre-establishment of explicit targeting and intervention strategies to cover population groups most at risk; third, development of local institutional capacity to organize an effective response. These functions rely on clearly defined central and local government responsibility, strong political and technical backing for legislation that supports action by government structures, and appropriate financial backing for large-scale preparation and intervention.

The first step involves improving early warning systems. Much effort has been put into developing and fine-tuning information systems relevant to crisis prediction but improvements are still required. First, greater refinement is possible in analysis of non-production data. Conventional yield and output estimates are too crude to serve as indicators for expected consumption shortfalls among the poor. Greater disaggregation is needed in analysis of data on prices, markets, daily wage levels, dietary changes and anthropometric measures in order to improve regional predictive capabilities and district-level 'disaster potential' mapping.

The second required improvement is stronger ties between early warning and early action, possibly dictated by legislated famine codes. In Ethiopia and Sudan, there was no lack of warning about the 1984–5 famine long before it assumed unmanageable proportions. Yet, lack of financial and administrative capacity for responding to warning signals reduced the relevance of both the signals and the agencies involved. In other words, early warning was a necessary but not sufficient condition for preventing famine in both countries.

The success of famine intervention in Africa rests on the political, financial, and bureaucratic capabilities available, and currently these are limited. For successful implementation, local government institutions need to be strong and efficiently supported both financially and technically by the central authority. Governments should be planning for the next famine in Ethiopia or Somalia while investing in programmes to prevent its occurrence.

Public intervention to minimize food shortfalls assume many shapes. At one level, stabilization of prices and food supply can be achieved through an open trade policy combined with improved rural roads. Yet, private trading and stockholding cannot be relied upon for famine prevention, especially when purchasing power is eroded. More direct public intervention to protect food security should be based on advance preparation of interventions aimed at human capital preservation and asset preservation. These must complement, not supplant, private response strategies (Webb 1993; Davies 1993).

Food aid will continue to represent a major element of any such package. Ethiopia and Sudan have become highly dependent on food aid in the past ten years. There were three major waves of food aid into Sudan during the past decade: 1984–5, 1988 and 1989. In most cases, food arrived too late to prevent mass migration but it did prevent deaths on an even greater scale. One drawback was that everyone was eligible to a quota of food, thereby spreading resources too thinly and reducing the aid impact to the severely distressed (Teklu, von Braun and Zaki 1991). Ethiopia has received even more aid than Sudan since 1984, with imports exceeding one million tons in 1988–9 and 1991–2. Recent surveys suggest effective targeting since households consuming only one meal a day during famine received more food aid than those consuming three meals, and woman-headed households received at least as much food as those headed by men (Webb, von Braun and Yohannes 1992). However, universal eligibility again diluted amounts available, and an average of only 180 kg was received per household in the worst year – sufficient to maintain a family of six for only two months.

What is more, evidence from Ethiopia suggests that food resources alone have a limited impact, even for famine mitigation (Webb and von Braun 1994). Households may need emergency support, but they also need income and asset support to stand on their own feet. Other useful forms of non-food emergency relief include transfer of assets (often on credit) such as livestock, seeds and farm equipment. Distribution of assets is designed to accelerate post-famine rehabilitation of the economy, thereby shortening periods of chronic food insecurity. A short-term support package of food or cash may be required to protect such asset distributions until the subsequent harvest has been gathered.

Given the multiple causes of a food crisis, and its dynamics, project interventions must carefully consider the type, scale and sequencing of individual public actions. Programmes such as food aid distribution, asset distribution, technology transfers and labour-intensive public works can work simultaneously as long as they are coordinated to complement each other rather than compete.

CONCLUSIONS

Given scarce resources for addressing famine, investment may be best concentrated in a few priority areas such as technological change and commercialization in agriculture, labour-intensive public works, and targeted consumption stabilization. The positive complementarities of these priorities are promising and an appropriate macroeconomic and political environment would allow high returns to both public and private investment in these areas.

Success depends on improved technical and participatory design, complementing non-food resources with food, better communication with participants about local priorities, improved and decentralized management and supervision, and integration of implementation with sound monitoring and evaluation. Equally important, the experience of poor Ethiopian households shows that more than one intervention may be needed at a time. Just as there is not universal manifestation of famine, there is no universal solution. A diversity of instruments is often required to multiply the positive short-term income transfer effects of any single programme. Thus, food distribution or employment programmes can be designed as one part of a food security package adapted to different regions that goes beyond reliance on a single intervention.

Public-sector administrative and financial capacities for coping with famine, and for investing against it, remain weak in most parts of the Horn, especially at regional and district levels. But, the same is true of private capacities. Thus, the transition from famine to food security and from centrally-controlled to free market economies will be fragile for years to come. The danger of a famine striking before Ethiopia has grown out of its poverty cannot be discounted. This calls for strengthened cooperation between public and private sectors. It also requires all policies and programmes to be based on a more thorough understanding of the rural economy. A widely-held belief in the uniformity of rural households prevents attention being paid to distributional consequences of policy and programme interventions. As a result, households most vulnerable to famine are sometimes overlooked. Sustainable food security requires that such households become a focus of attention, not neglect.

References

Aylieff, J. 1993. *Statistical Summary of Food Aid Deliveries to Ethiopia 1977–1992.* Food Aid Information Unit (Addis Ababa: World Food Programme). Mimeo.

Berhanu, Aytenew and J. Aylieff. 1992. *Inventory, Map and Analytical Review of Food and Cash-for-work Projects in Ethiopia*, (Addis Ababa: Draft Report to World Food Programme). Mimeo.

von Braun, Joachim, Raymond Hopkins, Detlev Puetz and Rajul Pandya-Lorch, 1993. *Aid to Agriculture: Reversing the Decline* (Washington, DC: Food Policy Report. International Food Policy Research Institute).

von Braun, Joachim, Tesfaye Teklu and Patrick Webb, 1991. Labour-Intensive Public Works for Food Security: Experience in Africa. Working Papers on Food Subsidies No. 6 (Washington, DC: International Food Policy Research Institute).

von Braun, Joachim, Tesfaye Teklu and Patrick Webb, 1993. 'Famine as the Outcome of Political, Production and Market Failures', *IDS Bulletin*, 24(4):73–8.

von Braun, Joachim and Rajul Panda-Lorch, 1991. Income Sources of Malnourished People in Rural Areas: Microlevel Information and Policy Implications. Working Papers on Commercialization of Agriculture and Nutrition No. 5 (Washington, DC: International Food Policy Research Institute).

von Braun, Joachim and Leonardo Paulino, 1990. 'Food in sub-Saharan Africa: Trends and Policy Challenges for the 1990s', *Food Policy*, 15(6):505–17.

Davies, Susannah. 1993. 'Are Coping Strategies a Cop Out?' *IDS Bulletin*, 24(4):60–72.

Delgado, Christopher L. and Per Pinstrup-Andersen. 1993. Agricultural Productivity in the Third World: Patterns and Strategic Issues. Paper presented at the AAEA/IFPRI Pre-Conference Workshop on Post Green Revolution Agricultural Development Strategies in the Third World: What Next?, Orlando, Florida, 30 July 1993.

Ethiopia (Transitional Government of Ethiopia). 1992. *Study on the Social Dimensions of Adjustment in Ethiopia* (Addis Ababa: Ministry of Planning and Economic Development). Mimeo.

Hazell, Peter B. and Jock R. Anderson, 1991. *The Green Revolution Reconsidered: The Impact of High-Yielding Rice Varieties in South India* (Baltimore: Johns Hopkins University Press for the International Food Policy Research Institute).

Interaction, 1993. *The Relief-Development Continuum* (Washington, DC: American Council for Voluntary International Action).

Oehmke, James and Eric Crawford, 1992. The Impact of Agricultural Technology in Sub-Saharan Africa: A Synthesis of Symposium Findings. Report to USAID. (Washington, DC) Mimeo.

Teklu, Tesfaye, Joachim von Braun and El Zayed Zaki, 1991. *Drought and Famine Relationship in Sudan: Policy Implications*. Research Report 88, (Washington, DC: International Food Policy Research Institute).

Torry, William I., 1984. 'Social Science Research on Famine: A Critical Evaluation', *Human Ecology*, 12(3):227–52.

Tshibaka, Tshikala B., 1990. 'La Croissance de la Productivite Agricole en Afrique', *Transformation Structurelle de l'Agriculture Africaine*, Sommaires de l'IFPRI sur les Politiques Agricoles et Alimentaires No. 5 (Washington, DC: International Food Policy Research Institute).

Webb, Patrick, 1993. 'Coping with Drought and Food Insecurity in Ethiopia', *Disasters*, 17(1):33–47.

Webb, Patrick and Thomas Reardon, 1992. 'Drought Impact and Household Response in East and West Africa', *Quarterly Journal of International Agriculture*, 31(3):230–46.

Webb, Patrick and Shubh Kumar, 1993. Food/cash for Work in Ethiopia: Experiences during Famine and Macroeconomic Reform. Paper Prepared for the IFPRI International Policy Workshop on Employment for Poverty Alleviation and Food Security, 11–14 October 1993, Airlie House, Virginia, USA.

Webb, Patrick and Joachim von Braun, 1994. *Famine and Food Security in Ethiopia: Lessons for Africa* (London: John Wiley & Sons).

Webb, Patrick, Joachim von Braun and Yisehac Yohannes, 1992. *Drought and Famine in Ethiopia: Policy Implications of Coping Failure at National and Household Levels*. Research Report 92 (Washington, DC: International Food Policy Research Institute).

WFP (World Food Programme), 1991. *1991 Food Aid Review* (Rome: WFP).

World Bank, 1993. *Ethiopia: Toward Poverty Alleviation and a Social Action Program*. Agriculture and Environment Operations Division. Eastern Africa Department. Green Cover Report (Washington, DC: World Bank) Mimeo.

10 Disastrous Pasts, Sustainable Futures? Land and Peasants in Ethiopia[1]

John Campbell

Is it reasonable to assume, as some analyses of peasant agriculture have, that with peace, stability and a reasonable stake in managing their own resource base, peasants can alter and possibly reverse long-term agricultural and environmental decline in the Ethiopian highlands?

To this way of thinking, the crisis of highland agriculture, from which has emanated a series of increasingly frequent and devastating famines, is linked primarily to policies of the Ethiopian state: notably (i) its prosecution of war and pacification programmes; (ii) a regressive and extractive agricultural policy; and more specifically, (iii) nationalization of land and trees which laid the foundation for extensive resource mining by peasants. If correct, collapse of the state following overthrow of the Peoples Democratic Republic of Ethiopia (PDRE) in 1991 should have provided the necessary condition for recovery!

Phrasing the problem in this manner throws into sharp relief fundamental aspects of the crisis afflicting the highlands which need careful thought as Ethiopia begins reconstruction and development. For example, what is the situation with respect to peasant agriculture and the environment? What are the priorities for sustainable and equitable development of highland society (one which recognizes and supports rural livelihoods *and* generates food and revenue for other sections of Ethiopian society)? What role will the state, peasants, pastoralists and other communities play in resolving the crises?

In this chapter, I identify and examine some of the long-term processes underlying *highland society*. The focus is on highland communities because, until their needs and livelihoods are addressed, neither environmental nor broader issues of resourcing economic reconstruction are likely to be resolved. Towards this end, section (i) reviews available data on environmental degradation in the north-central and eastern highlands. Section (ii) provides a brief overview of centrally directed, aid-financed development projects. Section (iii) looks at the situation of highland peasants, and specifically at the extent and nature of rural poverty. Finally, section (iv) examines policy options in a context likely to be characterized by limited development assistance and continued political and social fragmentation.

PARAMETERS OF ENVIRONMENT FOR DEVELOPMENT

While information on causes and processes of environmental degradation in Ethiopia is sketchy, clearly the problem is an old one. Current agricultural and settlement practices are not responsible *per se* for the present extent of land degradation, rather causes must be sought in the cumulative effect of agriculture over previous centuries during which time a long, slow process of erosion has gradually outstripped soil formation by a factor of approximately 6:1, i.e. at 5–10 tons/hectare (Hurni 1983; Wood and Stahl 1989: 9). Loss of the 'A' soil horizon, and subsequent loss of humus, drastically reduced ability of crops to root and ability of remaining soil to retain moisture (even with inorganic fertilizers) and increased soil erosion.

Central to this process, particularly in the past century, have been: (i) growing population movement south and west out of the northern highlands (accompanied in part by subjugation of indigenous nomadic and pastoral peoples); (ii) sedentarization of the population on arable land based around ox, plough and cereal crops; (iii) continuous population growth; (iv) consolidation of subjugated land and people through a hierarchic political system monopolizing land and oxen; and (v) periodic drought.

The inter-relation between dynamic social factors and drought has had an important influence on Ethiopia's tremendously varied ecological system, and indeed on the wider regional environment and ecology of northeastern Africa whose varied societies have a long history of adaptation to and reciprocal impact on an physical environment characterized by extremes of altitude, rainfall, soil type, vegetation, temperature (Anderson and Johnson 1988; McCann 1988a).

Before examining relations between socio-cultural practices and environment, it is useful to observe the extent of land degradation and its impact on highland populations (Wood and Stahl 1989: 9–14; Belshaw 1989). Much of Ethiopia has a 'dissected' terrain, 79 per cent of slopes exceed a 16 per cent grade and at least one third of all slopes exceed a 30 per cent grade. Potential for erosion is enhanced by nearly the entire range of traditional agricultural practices: (i) fine tilling of soil, with a final ploughing down-slope to facilitate drainage; (ii) mono-cropping; (iii) lack of vegetative cover during rains; (iv) use of crop residue and animal dung for fuel rather than for soil cover; and (v) insecurity of land tenure. Further, seasonal rains are often intense and erosive.

Historical evidence of population growth is scanty (McCann 1988a: 2–7; McCann 1990). It is clear that the plough allowed higher population densities than pastoralism, and highland soils are fertile by African standards. The population is concentrated in highland areas (88 per cent), and available evidence indicates steady growth at least since the mid-nineteenth century which resulted in periods of localized migration into low-lying areas. Serious soil erosion was in progress long before, although increasing population pressure on resources probably accelerated it.

Rates of soil loss have been calculated for several types of land/land-usage but provide only indicative measures (Hurni, cited in Wood and Stahl 1989:14): average national soil loss is approximately 12 tons/hectare (ha); this masks considerable diversity of rates ranging from 400 tons/ha where there is no ground cover or conservation measures, to 42 tons/ha on arable land, and 5 tons/ha on pasture. A recent study of land degradation estimated that in the highlands,

> which cover some 54 million ha, erosion has led to serious degradation of 14 million ha and moderate degradation on 13 million ha, while for over 2 million ha the soil depth is so reduced that the land is unable to support civilisation (Wood and Stahl 1989:14).

Not only is one-half of the highlands degraded, with serious consequences for agricultural production, but lowland areas are subject to increasing problems compounded not only by the spread of the plough to more fragile soils, but also because increasing livestock numbers and lack of rainfall are resulting in soil compaction which reduces fertility and animal fodder. *A cycle of extensive land-use is set in motion in both highlands and lowlands as yields and fodder decline and require new use of economically marginal land.*

Shallow soils arising from erosion lack ability to retain moisture for root development and are subject to low and variable cycles of rainfall. This further exacerbates erosion and loss of soil fertility. While only a small decline in overall rates of rainfall is evidenced for the past twenty-five years, it is the *accumulation* of several years of poor rainfall which creates drops of food production and famine (Webb and von Braun 1989).

Equally important, and frequently overlooked, has been the impact of a *rapidly rising population*. The 1984 census, the first undertaken, revealed that Government had consistently underestimated population by 20 per cent as a basis for development/economic planning. This meant that despite fairly rapid growth in agriculture of 1.9 per cent p.a. leading up to the early 1970s, it was exceeded by population growth of approximately 2.2 per cent p.a.[2] The immediate effect of rapid population growth in a situation in which land was controlled by landlords was mitigated partly by seasonal migration, reliance on off-farm work, voluntary re-settlement, etc. In the short term, increasing numbers of poorly endowed households were established on outlying, marginal lands; this had longer term consequences both for the population (starvation) and environment (degradation) in the face of persistent drought (McCann 1990).

Estimates have been made for the effect of some of the above-mentioned factors on agricultural production (Webb and von Braun 1989: 70; Wood and Stahl 1989:12; Belshaw 1989: Annex IV) thus: (i) a 10 per cent decline in rainfall is correlated with a drop in cereal yields of 9.8 per cent; (ii) present levels of burning dung reduces cereal yields by 10–20 per cent ; (iii) soil erosion is reducing cereal yield by 2 per cent p.a., etc. Further declines in food production and food availability will occur as peasants are forced to more marginal lands and/or as fallow and crop rotation periods are reduced (Cohen and Isaksson 1988; Webb and von Braun 1989:54–9). Current grain production shortfalls in normal years are estimated at 500,000 metric tons, an increase of 150,000 tons since 1980. Unsurprisingly, per capita daily food availability mirrors declining production, dropping from 580 grams per day in 1961 to 420 grams per day in 1984.

CONSERVATION EFFORTS AND PEASANTS

It is hardly surprising, therefore, that the Ethiopian government and international agencies became active in conservation. Continued population growth and drought increased pressure on local resources reducing size of land holdings, increasing cultivation of marginal lands and pasture, and resulting in extensive mining of common property resources for food, fuel, fodder and shelter. As agricultural productivity falls new pressures arise for land to provide subsistence, which in turn lead to renewed pressures on resources, migration and a search for alternative forms of supplementing agricultural incomes. Highland areas were the first affected by these pressures during the latter nineteenth century and population pressure sought a release to lowland areas which are still being brought under the plough. In all cases growing demands placed upon land – in lieu of improvements in farming technology or agricultural practices – mean continued degradation of the local resource base.

Prior to the 1974 revolution, attempts to improve land, rural technologies and agricultural practices were stymied by effects of complex systems of private and freehold land tenure, absentee landlords, local administrators (*balabats*), and vested Church interests (Cohen and Weintraub 1975: ch. 2; Hoben 1973; Cohen and Koehn 1977). The precise mix of tenure was often regionally specific, and analysts frequently differentiate traditional, pre-revolutionary land tenure patterns between those of the north-eastern highlands from those introduced by the Imperial state in southern regions. Controversy concerns the concept of land, and particularly land ownership, with recent evidence arguing against the feudal model of outright ownership of or title to land in favour of a series of effective claims on income and juridical rights arising from land, and specifically from households who till the soil.

The fundamental issue then and now *is access to land* – for cultivation, pasture, fodder, fuel, etc. – *and water* by peasants and pastoralists and recognition that various local communities whose livelihoods depend on land have a long history of overlapping/nesting rights of access to local resources (see Unruh, this volume, Chapter 7). Locally negotiated understandings have, over time, altered through various factors such as continued population growth and changes in cropping practices and in tenure systems which benefited certain communities (McCann 1990), and interventions by the Ethiopian state (often to the detriment of pastoralists and peasants).[3] The nature of local rights of access varies considerably in the highlands between localities, communities, and ecologies.

In the 1960s and early 1970s agricultural production was low due to limited integration of peasants into the national economy (by poor infrastructure and transport), constraints on production arising from the land tenure system, and instances in which landowning classes blocked or otherwise 'hijacked' benefits which could accrue to peasants through limited experiments with mechanized agriculture, improved seed, credit, etc. (Stahl 1973; Cohen 1975; Ege 1988).[4] For peasants, access to land (through descent or land redistribution) was less important to household agricultural production and well-being than control over animal traction and other productive resources (labour, seed, equipment; McCann 1988b). The pre-eminent issue was land ownership and absence of secure tenure for most peasants; without secure tenure tenants were unwilling to invest in soil conservation.

Despite accelerating pressure on land and natural resources relatively little was accomplished in resource conservation. For instance, in 1974–5 the Ministry of Agriculture (MoA) achieved only: 10.5 million seedlings raised, 2000 ha planted, 1000 kilometres (km) terraced, and roughly 1000 ha planted in community forest (CF). Further, quality of community forestry was considered to be poor with low seedling survival rates and poor maintenance.[5]

Conservation work accelerated rapidly following the 1974 revolution due largely to introduction of new forms of rural political organization called Peasant Associations (PAs) and because nationalization placed land under nominal authority of the PAs. Impact of nationalization probably varied by region: in the north existence of village and kinship tenures meant that a larger proportion of peasants already held land privately; in the south there were more landless share-croppers due partly to large numbers of absentee landlords and private estates. Transfer of 'land to the tiller', as the nationalization programme was called, equalized land hold-ings among peasants and provided the administrative basis for rural reform (Rahmato 1985; Pausewang 1983). Initial redistribution of land and aboli-tion of tithes and taxes to landlords resulted in increased food production which tended to be consumed by rural households. Reform did not, however, address problems of distribution of agricultural capital (espe-cially ownership of oxen) or access to improved rural technology. Given the continued increase in population and the subsequent re-imposition of taxes and crop marketing quotas, this meant that constraints on produc-tion/subsistence, and therefore on the local resource base, remained unchanged.

PAs undertook a range of political, agricultural and administrative tasks under the direction of central government. *Establishment of PAs lay the foundation for effective rural development*, including food-for-work (ffw) projects. At the same time the new government began promoting collec-tivization (Stahl 1989). Pressures to join service and producer co-opera-tives, low producer prices, controls over private marketing/trading, potential relocation to new villages and/or settlements all created new problems and pressures on peasants who now faced a far more organized and efficient state apparatus which broke down rural isolation, integrating peasants into a modern national political economy (Pausewang 1988).

The 1973 and 1977 famines also provided an impetus for conservation work through large increases in food aid – imported grain and cooking oil – and its use as a payment for labour, replacing 'voluntary' labour previously relied upon for conservation campaigns (Holt 1983; ILO 1986). Escalation and extent of conservation activities through use of food aid, administered under ffw projects, is easily observed. During 1983/4 the MoA using ffw: raised 65 million seedlings, planted 18,000 ha of land, terraced 9500 ha, while PAs planted 11,000 ha in CF using 361 nurseries. Conservation targets expanded arithmetically though implementation lagged well behind. Between 1976 and 1985 600,000 km of bunds were constructed on culti-vated land; 470,000 km of hill-side terraces were built; and 80,000 ha of steep slopes were closed for regeneration (Belshaw 1989: Annex IV).

The bulk of the food for this work was provided through the World Food Programme (WFP) within which the European Community was the largest single donor (Maxwell 1986:15). Up to 1986, ffw accounted for approximately 29 per cent of total food aid (5 per cent of which was sold to provide direct financial support to ffw projects) and 71 per cent of food aid was distributed as emergency rations. While undoubtedly filling important relief and development needs, Ethiopia's dependence on food aid has made it the largest ffw programme in Africa (second largest in the world after India), with conservation work expanding to 117 water catchment areas in nine administrative regions (Lirenso 1986). Eighty per cent of this work took place in highland regions with the most extensive deforestation (Wollo, Eritrea, Shoa, Tigray and Hararghe). Conservation objectives were able to be increased because ffw eased demands placed on rural labour conscription by providing payment for all aspects of conservation-related work. Substitution of a payment in place of 'voluntary', but in effect compulsory, labour allowed major escalation in the number of work-days on which households could be recruited. In 1982–5, the voluntary programme accounted for about 30 million work days, increasing to approximately 50 million work-days through use of food for work Kohlin estimated that 150 million work days may have been required to complete planned conservation work in 1986/7, which in turn would have meant that each of the 6 million rural households affected would have supplied labour for approximately 25 work-days per year for conservation work alone (1987:30). In Wollo, household heads provided on average 92 days/year – women working approximately 69 days/year – for ffw, far above the 30 person days per family per year assumed to be realistic for conservation work (Kohlin 1987:30).

Food-for-work activities are supposedly curtailed or suspended during planting and harvesting, periods of peak demand for labour.[6] Limited evidence indicates that food payments represented a good 'wage' in real terms, and that no major disincentive existed for short-term agricultural production in terms of depressing local food prices, etc. (Maxwell 1986; Holt 1984:196–8).[7] Despite the potential benefit of employing surplus agricultural labour in ffw projects, a potentially important negative repercussion may be the requirements for PAs to commit scarce productive land to community forest and hill-side closures to which households no longer have access, and for bunding which can reduce the amount of arable land by 10 per cent. The impact of ffw is likely to be of a different nature from a concern with short-term disincentives, and escalating demands on household labour (either directly, through compulsory or paid conservation work, or indirectly, through participation in PA affairs, etc.) must be seen within a wider politico-economic perspective.

Agricultural labour requirements, the wider implications for rural households of government policy, and the extension of food for work schemes, suggest a different set of conditions for evaluating conservation work. These are: (i) short-term effects of removing arable land from household access; (ii) a 5–15 year period before peasants see initial benefits from an investment in conservation; and (iii) implications for resource conservation of government economic policy, especially the issue of land 'ownership' and of agricultural taxation/investment. Little or no systematic information has been collected on these issues, though fragmentary information discussed below suggests what may be occurring.

Prior to 1991, conservation activities were organized through MoA *woreda* and district offices which planned, monitored and co-ordinated all work (Admassie and Gebre 1985). Extension officers organized labour informally through local co-ordinators in each PA, who in turn selected and supervised work teams who were paid food for work. This highly centralized system removed decision-making from local PAs,[8] ensuring that conservation work conformed to agricultural policy and land-use directives.

The bulk of land allocated for afforestation lay within PAs; gazetted forest land and tree plantations over 80 ha were designated as state forests and PAs were required to undertake conservation and afforestation work on them. All rural land was owned by the state[9] and access has been controlled by PAs responsible for differentiating between different types of land use (community forest (including hill-side closure), village/housing land, perennial crops, communal grazing and private cultivation plots) and supervising its use.

Total land administered by each PA was restricted by legislation to 800 ha. Land available for household cultivation (through usufruct not private ownership) has ben allocated amongst registered households by the PA on the basis of the total land available, number of households, and household size. Up to 80 ha was set aside for community forest and, in the face of rapidly rising population (between 2.6–2.8 per cent nationally), communal grazing areas declined due to demands for cultivable land for households.

NGO afforestation work operated in the same manner as WFP/MoA projects (Evans 1989; McCann 1987a). Though more flexibility is possible in site selection, work arrangements and possibly in selection of species for planting, all activities are organized through the PA and on land reserved for community forest or hill-side closure. This means that virtually the same result occurs: *communal resources are developed at the expense of household needs.*[10]

POVERTY, RURAL LIVELIHOODS AND DEVELOPMENT

In many areas use of scarce PA land for community forestry constrains peasant access to cultivable land and to pasture. Repeated attempts by PAs to deal with pressures for access to land by re-distributing cultivable land to growing numbers of households underlines the seriousness of the problem.[11] The effect, however, is a continuous *reduction in the size and increase in the number of land holdings* per household. Table 10.1 indicates one index of this process, the close relationship between areas of land shortage – primarily highland PAs – and large (probably increasing) numbers of households without access to oxen. This situation is documented throughout Shoa, Hararghe, Wollo, Gojjam, Sidamo and elsewhere (e.g. Pausewang 1988; Rahmato 1985).

Closer examination of specific highland areas, however, reveals an underlying complexity to this process relating to the interaction between land, population growth, and the active role played by peasant associations.

Table 10.1   Resource poverty: the distribution of oxen and land in north-central Ethiopia12

Province	Woreda	Peasant Association	Percentage of households without oxen	Average size household holdings (ha)
Wollo	Ambassel	Haiq (H)	20	n.a
		Highland PAs	n.a.	0.96–1.1
		Lowland	—	2.2–2.3
Shoa	Ankober	Denki (L)	40	2–2.5
		Lalo (L)	34	n.a.
		Mesabit and Gedeber (H)	46	0.075
		Endode (H)	25	1.25
	Tegulet	Segatner Jer (H)	18	(2.0)
	Ada	Debra Zeit (L)	9	—
		Debra Birhan (H)	31	—
Gemu Goffa				
	No. Omo	Dawe Sake (H)	40	0.75
		Edo Bolasso (H)	30	0.75
National average			29	n.a.

(H = Highland; L = Lowland)

Table 10.2   Resourbe poverty: Deder and Babile Woreda, Hararghe Province

Woreda/Service Cooperative	No. PAS	Average plot size	Member households	Non-member house-holds (%)	Members without land	Female HH-head
Babile						
Kito	5	2 ha	1301	429 (33%)	n.a.	120
Tula	5	2 ha	730	321 (44%)	n.a.	58
Deder						
Legacheffe	5	0.8 ha	1615	119 (07.3%)	337 (22%)	124
Lelisa	3	0.8 ha	669	285 (28.5%)	17 (01.7%)	93
Burka Telila	3	0.8 ha	1796	56 (03.2%)	30 (01.7%)	92

In Table 10.2, data on two woredas in Hararghe, Deder (in the eastern highlands) and Babile (on the western edge of the Ogaden) are presented which illustrate the impact of rapid population growth in a context in which continued land redistribution by PAs to households and for communal use resulted in declining land holdings, and to growing numbers of local households left without access to cultivable land. Reasons for this can best be illustrated by looking further at Deder. In Deder Service Cooperative: (i) population growth was estimated at 3.8 per cent p.a. over a 12 year period, placing huge pressures on the PAs to find land to allocate; (ii) this led local PAs to allocate communal pasture, but still left 200 households without land; (iii) a further reallocation led to the sub-division of holdings, often by a father for his married sons. Growing pressure for land also resulted in cultivation of steep hill-sides, and problems with erosion.

In addition, excluded from the picture as it were, are large numbers of resident households who were not members of the service cooperative ostensibly because they had not paid a registration and membership fee (Ethiopian Birr $13.00). This included all newly formed households not yet allocated land, an unknown percentage of female-headed households and, in Babile, pastoralists (those involved in the sedentarization campaign and others); in short, the poorer, politically marginal households.[13]

In many instances, reallocation of holdings between households resulted in further land degradation since peasants had little incentive to invest in land they would not be farming in years to come. In addition, trees 'belonged' to government and considerable ambiguity existed over rights to trees planted by peasants on or around their houses or plots (Scones and McCracken 1989: 8–10; Admassie 1988). There has been, therefore, no impetus to conserve existing trees or plant new ones.[15]

In this context afforestation projects have at least two effects. First, relatively large areas of land have been committed to community forests (CF), organized by the MoA but planted by local PA members, which was seen to belong to government. In PAs, this meant that responsibility for maintenance was not a local concern, and that whatever benefits accrued from the CFs were not seen to belong to households. Indeed, in many cases access to CF was prevented and PA members had no rights to timber, foliage or fruits and were prevented from grazing animals there or otherwise harvesting fodder. Second, as a result of removing land from household access, greater pressure is placed on remaining land for subsistence.[16]

Continuing drought has implications for peasant subsistence other than death and displacement of rural populations. Destruction of agricultural capital, particularly oxen, but also cattle, sheep, and tools, has led to increased rural social differentiation (Hultin 1989:6–9). The corollary is that growing numbers of households become dependent on sharing, borrowing or renting oxen to plant their fields. In two highland *awraja's* in Wollo, for instance, 50 per cent of households neither owned an ox nor possessed sufficient labour to plant their fields. These households must either rent or borrow an ox, or rent out their land to someone able to plough and plant it in exchange for part of the harvest (Rahmato 1987:18ff).

The number of these 'resource poor' households – those without draught animal power or who command insufficient family labour – are increasing for four reasons. First, oxen herds decline sharply during drought (through death and distress sale) and may take years to be replenished. Second, drought and irregular rain increase household indebtedness through loss of household assets (tools, housing, seed, etc.) and inability to maintain social/kin relations based on mutual help and extended 'credit'. Third, renting or borrowing oxen often means not being able to sow at optimal times; delays in planting and reduced ploughing result in reduced crop yields. Finally, resource poor farmers are more dependent on short season *belg* rains to produce food which, with average main season *meher* rains, allow them to survive (McCann 1988a).

The necessity to produce food during the *belg* in order to ensure adequate household food stocks underlines the narrow margins within which most peasants operate: a good year is not a bumper year but rather one in which hunger is staved off. Basic subsistence is the ideal among rural households, and there is often little between the normal hunger associated with average yields, and starvation arising from the failure of *belg* rains to provide that extra 5–15 per cent of food stocks.

What happens to households unable to survive on small, unproductive plots? Rahmato's study of famine and survival strategies in Wollo points out that these 'marginal' peasants are difficult to identify, primarily because they are dependents of other households and/or because they migrate.[17] Some are absorbed, to an extent, by kin-networks, while others apparently retreat into the mountains to work steep hillsides by hand.

However, increasing rural impoverishment through reduced access to land has created a situation where many households – including both newly formed and households in areas recently incorporated into PAs – were not registered and do not have access to land. Lack of access to land and the declining size of holdings contributes to growth of regional labour migration; a phenomenon noticed particularly in Hararghe with its so called 'professional food-for-work worker', but undoubtedly prevalent elsewhere (Admassie and Gebre 1985:44–5).

Poverty contributes to increased rural-urban migration despite the loss of political/legal rights this entailed under the PDRE, i.e. not only to land but also in terms of difficulties arising from a failure to register with authorities (Abate 1985). Social surveys undertaken in Addis Ababa in the late 1980s underlined the scope of this problem with thousands of people sleeping in the open at night, and searching for work and/or avoiding the police and military conscription during the day (ETSM 1987).[18]

The overall impact of reduced access to land is, therefore, to further undermine rural livelihoods. Consequences of rural impoverishment are largely predictable for afforestation and conservation. Since government policy determined that only CF resources were to be assisted, and private use of CF was illegal, establishment of an afforestation project ensured either that a conflict of interest would develop over resources and/or that conservation work was not maintained.

Maintenance of conservation projects and the question of the enjoyment of benefits of this work are intimately linked: only with sufficient time to keep soil in place will fertility be restored. Until recently, maintenance of CFs was done by paying guards food for work to police access. Policing was generally ineffective and numerous instances occurred of people entering forest or hill-side closures to cut and remove wood and grass, or of livestock left to graze in protected areas. Guards often know the culprits but are unable to prevent illegal cutting without risking serious conflict within the community. Even with guards, seedling survival rates have been reported as low as 5–20 per cent with an average of perhaps 40 per cent for both MoA/WFP and NGOs. Overall, afforestation, bunding and terracing, check dams, cut-off drains, etc, all have poor maintenance records.[19]

The centralized organization of afforestation programmes under the MoA clearly sent the message to peasants that community forestry creates government forests. *Local people were not consulted nor were their priorities addressed through the projects*; indeed, little or no discussion was held in PAs concerning who would benefit from the trees, much less when benefits might be expected.[20] Understandably, peasants perceived that their only 'benefit' would be the possibility of working for food. The main issue for them is not whether to participate or how much land to plant in trees; that decision was taken by government. The major decision affecting peasants appears to have been whether they will have to plant the trees through paid or unpaid labour. Clearly, substantial resources have been poured into conservation projects which have poor prospects of reaching maturity or little chance of arresting environmental degradation.

Conservation removed land from households at the same time as government cut off alternative income opportunities by restricting small-scale trade and grain marketing, which functioned in the past to offset food deficits. Simultaneously, restrictions were placed on planting particular crops (including khat and some tree species); production of non-grain food staples was discouraged (tubers, ensete, etc) in favour of grains; and specified districts were designated for the export production of tea and coffee while traditional crops were discouraged or controlled. Peasants are under pressure to produce more which often means that soils are not allowed to regenerate. In the Wollo highlands, fallowing has disappeared (Rahmato 1987:84); more generally, most peasants cannot afford fertilizer, and plant and animal residue are used in place of non-existent woody fuels (World Bank 1984). While it is not uncommon for peasants to use crop rotation and traditional means of controlling water run-off, etc. land redistribution and declining plot sizes appear to have undermined peasant willingness to invest labour in such practices (McCann 1988a:12).

The single-tine plough and associated complex of tools employed by highland peasants have remained essentially unchanged for the past millennium, despite rising population pressures. McCann attributes this technological conservatism to the socio-political system's traditional land tenure and inheritance system and to claims on agricultural surplus by non-productive classes. He argues poverty and state neglect, together with

> The social and economic complexity of local farming systems, the weak market orientation, lack of credit, and economies of scale have restricted technological change (McCann 1988a:12).

One might add that the effects of policy and continued drought and impoverishment have undoubtedly reinforced traditional risk-aversion strategies. This seems to be the attitude adopted by some peasants towards improved seed and improved single-oxen ploughs (McCann 1988a; Gryseels *et al.* 1984). Accumulated experience clearly counts for a great deal in peasant survival strategies particularly where 'improved' practices have yet to be demonstrated and may well require redistribution of wealth and/or redefinition of gender[21] and household work relations to make them effective (Hultin 1989:9).[22]

POLICY OPTIONS FOR RURAL SURVIVAL AND DEVELOPMENT

Conditions and policies prior to overthrow of the PDRE directly contributed to practices detrimental to rural livelihoods and conservation. Not the least of these has been substantially increased cropping of vulnerable lands – on hill-sides, lowlands, and river basins – which causes further soil degradation and is indicative of growing levels of rural poverty. A recent review of Ethiopian food production concluded, *à propos* of conservation efforts over the previous four years, that implementation had too rigidly adhered to bunding, monoculture and afforestation (Belshaw 1989:37). Criticisms included fundamental concern over failure to place conservation on a sustainable basis by, for example, increasing outputs of food, cash and crops at household level.

Given the interconnectedness of smallholder agriculture and conservation, it is unsurprising that peasant production is stagnating if not declining (Griffin and Hay 1985; Cohen and Isaksson 1989). Crop yields are low and would require substantially increased supplies of fertilizer, improved seed, irrigation and coordinated management which peasants cannot afford. Rural policy must overcome problems of access to land, low producer prices, the absence of economic infrastructure, and rapid population growth.

The reality, however, is an agricultural policy which over many decades has promoted forms of agricultural production – whether in the guise of capitalist farms or collective enterprises – at the expense of smallholders. Throughout this period extension work either failed to reach most peasants and/or was totally inappropriate (Stahl 1989; Belshaw 1989). In addition, taxation, producer prices, production quotas, and other levies removed significant amounts of capital from rural to urban areas even at the height of drought (Franzel *et al.* 1989; Woldemeskel 1989).[23] *Without appropriate assistance to peasants and major changes in agricultural policy, the result must be increased exploitation of the total range of remaining common property resources.*

Against a backdrop of the collapse of government functions and basic infrastructure, of continuing social and political fragmentation, and probable Western indifference to calls for increased/sufficient levels of development assistance (the Horn no longer being of strategic importance) what options exist?

First, there is no single, straightforward resolution to what are a range of inter-linked issues, one of the most important is the inter-linked nature of the highlands. While some discussions suggest existence of a uniform culture and economy (i.e. of peasant cultivators) in fact cultivators, agro-pastoralists and pastoralists; Christians and Muslims; Amharas, Oromos, Tigrayans, Eritreans, Afars and others have a long history of co-operation. Neither do *the 'highlands' constitute a separate ecology; they are composed of a set of inter-linked ecologies of great variability, supporting a range of inter-dependent livelihoods, occupations, cultures, and traditions.*

There is perhaps a more effective way of underlining the magnitude of the problem. The highlands are home to 88 per cent of Ethiopia's population. If the crisis of highland agriculture continues it is reasonable to expect: (i) further exhaustion of resources, leading to substantial out-migration (with consequent degradation of more marginal lands)[24]; (ii) the collapse of agriculture, backbone of Ethiopia's economy (i.e. and of funding for development and the welfare of the cities), and the subsistence basis of rural households and for thousands of displaced persons, refugees, and ex-combatants; finally, (iii) famine.

It is also important to be realistic about external development assistance. Even if Western assistance should prove to be more generous than in the past, the record of development work – whether of the Government, bilateral agencies, or NGO's – has not exactly been a sterling success (Campbell forthcoming). In any event, commitment of sufficient resources and adequate manpower (were they available) would still require two further conditions to be effective.

The first – a lesson painfully being learned and relearned by NGO's across the Horn – is that development depends on local initiative, without which no amount of resources will be effective. This entails an obligation to strengthen local communities and their ability to cooperate for common survival in order to achieve a measure of self-sufficiency, including the ability to resolve conflicts and agree on initiatives locally (Duffield 1992). Second, isolated development initiatives, whether instigated by communities, the state or development agencies, can only result in isolated enclaves of development within a broader context of poverty. Such enclaves, no matter how well resourced, will not be sustainable in the long term because they will attract growing numbers of 'economic refugees' from elsewhere. This underlines a real need for effective coordination which in turn relies on creation and maintenance of basic economic infrastructure.

In the past, agriculture financed an infrastructure built largely to facilitate state interests[25]; now there is a profound need to reverse this process and provide adequate infrastructure and services to rural producers as an incentive to increased production and trade. While there is clearly a fundamental economic role for political (state) structures to play in socio-economic reconstruction, this must be worked out with those who produce the wealth which pays for government programmes.

This overview permits several tentative conclusions: (i) access to land and water is the basis for the survival of different cultures and the foundation on which national recovery will rest; (ii) given the range of livelihoods and their inter-linkages – through cultivation, human and animal movement, trade, seasonal migration, markets, etc. – it seems wise to pursue, in concert with local people, a plurality of approaches to development and rehabilitation; finally, (iii) given the varied ecologies and inter-linked nature of highlands and lowlands, rural and urban areas, it seems self-evident that the future of all people in the region is interwoven. One community, area, watershed, mountain range, valley, or region cannot move forward without affecting others; conversely, failure to meet needs of any one community/area will, undoubtedly, have repercussions for all.

Notes

1. An earlier version of this chapter was published in *African Affairs* (1991), 90, 5–21.
2. Ege's analysis indicates clearly that the Imperial Government invested in commercial agriculture at the expense of peasant farming, and that even combined they absorbed a relatively minor portion of the national budget (1988). In some ways this is not too different from national expenditure patterns under the PDRE (Love 1989).
3. Direct forms of state intervention affecting peasants included villagization, reduced access to fertile land (through establishing producer cooperatives and community forestry), re-settlement, and of course 'pacification' programmes. Pastoralists, on the other hand, appear to have been systematically discriminated against through the enforced loss of access to pasture and water in the highlands which has left a legacy of bitterness (this is entirely separate from state policies in the Ogaden, for example, where pastoralists were pacified, sedentarized, taxed, and denied access to pasture and water (cf: Gamaledin 1992; Dolal 1992; Markakis 1989).
4. On the issue of land and land tenure prior to the revolution, see Cohen and Weintraub 1975.
5. This is a continuing problem with survival rates of 5–20 per cent reported and an average rate of perhaps 40 per cent; NGO survival rates of 40–60 per cent are common. The MoA, through poor management/organization, poor logistics and lack of finance, has never been able to maintain the extensive amount of conservation work it initiated through Peasant Associations (PAs).
6. Much depends on the timing of the rains, local availability of adequate food stocks for distribution, adequate preparation of the seedlings, sufficient

transport, etc. The larger the project/watershed, the greater the likelihood that all these components would not be organized to miss periods of peak demand in peasant agriculture. In short, there could often be considerable overlap of afforestation and agricultural activities.

7. It seems highly likely that the unstable conditions which now prevail in the highlands would alter the 'value' of food for work wages and the potential disincentive effects of food aid on agriculture.

8. Including the choice of tree species to be planted. Peasants know that choices are limited to a few species by official emphasis on eucalyptus despite growing evidence that it is not ideally suited to the varied altitudes and rainfall conditions found in the highlands. NGO nurseries may grow perhaps ten species, but production focuses on eucalyptus and acacia with limited efforts to introduce varieties of fruit trees.

9. In many rural areas the collapse of the state, and in particular of the MoA, undoubtedly resulted in abandonment of official policy with regard to land 'ownership' and use (and possibly reversion to former practices and/or to local conflict over access to land, CF, etc). Policies of genuine benefit to local communities may need to be renegotiated with peasants, and local institutions revived or constructed to work in partnership with government to enhance rural livelihoods through appropriate forms of environmental conservation.

10. Specific evidence for this conflict of interests comes from a study in Wollo (Scones and McCracken 1989: 9–11).

11. Redistribution of plots reinforces land insecurity for peasants. Fragmentation is widely documented, see: Gebre-Kiros 1980; Woube 1986; and Rahmato 1985.

12. Sources: (a) Wello: Rahmato 1987:76; (b) Shoa and Gemu Goffa: McCann 1987b:252; Maxwell 1990. For estimates of average size of land holdings by region see Griffin and Hay 1985:42.

13. Non-membership in service cooperatives meant that households were not entitled to receive an allocation of (irregularly supplied) subsidized commodities including some food, tools, fertilizer, and agricultural credit. Most development assistance was channelled through these cooperatives.

14. Data come from visits to the area in 1988, from discussions with Service Cooperative officials and with MoA development agents and woreda officials. These statistics are merely indicative of trends as they were unable to be verified.

15. This did not mean that peasants were uninterested in trees. In Hararghe, as elsewhere, official policy forbid distribution of seedlings other than through ffw afforestation programmes. However, unofficially, at least one nursery was inundated with individual requests amounting to tens of thousands of seedlings to which the MoA turned a blind eye.

16. This applies not only to CF but also to land committed to hill-side closures which have tended to be planted with trees, thus reducing availability of badly needed fodder, see: Admassie 1988: 14.

17. Rahmato 1987; McCann 1988a, 1987c. McCann shows that Amhara traditions of ambilineal descent and partible property have, under pressure of land scarcity, shifted to one in which eldest sons inherit his father's estates. This facilitated migration from the highlands by younger siblings and the

landless.
18.   A minor business in Addis Ababa was the running of flop houses for migrants without urban kinsmen. Other migrants sheltered with kinsmen resulting in a high degree of overcrowding. Another 'invisible' group of migrants were peasants fleeing resettlement in the south who were trying to make their way back to Wollo or Tigray.
19.   Admassie 1988:34; and Wood and Stahl 1989:12, who also report that over the past 15 years perhaps 63,000 ha of wood lots, 50,000 ha of CF and 300,000 ha of land has been reafforested. 'However, even if this latter figure is correct it does little to compensate for the loss of 1.5–3.0 m ha of forest and woodland which will have been cleared during the same 15 years.'
20.   Scones and McCracken (1989: 9) cite several studies. Overt conflicts are reported in PAs where spontaneous fires were set in afforested areas and enclosures in Wollo (Hilsum n.d.:7) and in southern Shoa (the Konso development project reported in Leach and Mearns 1988).
21.   Vital research must go to gender in the context of highland society and to cultural and political factors which so effectively constrain female participation (Poluha 1987; Fellows 1987; Mama 1992).
22.   With the drastic reduction of pasture there may be too little fodder to allow herd levels to recover to pre-drought levels. Belshaw (1989:30-ff) considers factors hindering the adoption of intensification of agricultural practices as these are linked to technological conservatism by peasants.
23.   At the height of the 1984–5 famine in highland Wollo local peasants were required to pay the 'famine levy', often by selling food stocks.
24.   Indeed, one study estimated that 80 per cent of the entire country, not just the highlands, already shows evidence of substantial levels of land degradation, accelerated erosion, etc. (Kuru 1988)!
25.   There is clearly a need to prioritize development objectives and to concentrate available resources on strategic areas of production (e.g. provision of agricultural credit and inputs) and public welfare (e.g. culturally appropriate measures dealing with population growth). At the same time, an effective means of coordinating agricultural and conservation efforts at national/regional and local level must be found; one obvious possibility, despite its past history of abuse, could be a reformed and strengthened role for Service Cooperatives and PAs.

References

Abate, A., 1985. 'Urbanization and Regional Development in Ethiopia', *Geographie als Sozialwissenschaft* (Bonn), Band 18: 242–71.
Admassie, Y., 1988. 'Impact and Sustainability of Activities for Rehabilitation of Forest, Grazing and Agricultural Lands Supported by the UNWFP Project 2488', Report to UNWFP and MoA, Peoples Democratic Republic of Ethiopia (Sept.).
Admassie, Y. and S. Gebre. 1985. *Food-For-Work in Ethiopia, A Socio-economic Survey* (Addis Ababa University/IDR).
Anderson, D. and D. Johnson. 1988. 'Introduction: Ecology and Society in Northeast African History', in D. Anderson and D. Johnson (eds), *The Ecology of Survival, Case Studies from Northeast African History* (Boulder: Westview)

pp. 1–24.

Belshaw, D., 1989. *Food Production and Food Processing in Ethiopia*: Priorities for Action Within the Frameworks of the National Food and Nutrition Strategy and the Five-Year Plan 1989–94, FAO and ONCCP, Peoples Democratic Republic of Ethiopia, Addis Ababa, (May), Annex IV.

Campbell, J. forthcoming. 'Constraints on Sustainable Development in Ethiopia: Is there a Future for Improved Wood-stoves?', *Public Administration & Development*, 14(1).

Cohen, J., 1975. 'Effects of Green Revolution Strategies on Tenants and Small-scale Landowners in the Chilalo Region of Ethiopia', *Journal of Developing Areas*, 9: 335–58.

Cohen, J. and N-I Isaksson, 1989. 'Food Production Strategy Debates in Revolutionary Ethiopia', *World Development*, 16(3): 323–48.

Cohen, J. and P. M. Koehn 1977. 'Rural and Urban Land Reform in Ethiopia', *African Law Studies*, 14: 3–61.

Cohen, J. and D. Weintraub, 1975. *Land and Peasants in Imperial Ethiopia, The Social Background to a Revolution* (The Netherlands: Van Gorcum).

Dolal, M., 1992. 'Pastoral Resources, Human Displacement and State Policy: the Ogaden Case', M. Doornbos, L. Cliffe, A. Ghaffar Ahmed and J. Markakis (eds), *Beyond Conflict in the Horn* (London: ISS/J. Currey) pp. 185–8.

Duffield, M., 1992. 'Famine, Conflict, and the Internationalization of Public Welfare', in M. Doornbos, L. Cliffe, A. Ghaffar Ahmed and J. Markakis (eds), *Beyond Conflict in the Horn* (London: ISS/J. Currey) pp. 49–62.

ETSM (Ecole Technical Superior Municipal), 'Addis Ababa Higher 06 Kebele 25 Upgrading Project', vol. 1, July, 1987, (Addis Ababa).

Ege, S., 1988. 'The Agricultural Crisis in Ethiopia', in S. Ege, (ed.) *Development in Ethiopia*. Proceedings. University of Trondheim, Working Papers on Ethiopian Development, no.3. pp. 153–92.

Evans, J., 1989. 'Community Forestry in Ethiopia: The Bilate Project', *Rural Development in Practice* (May/Brighton) pp. 7–8, 25.

Fellows, R., 1987. *Background Information on the Status of Women in Ethiopia* (Canadian Embassy, Addis Ababa).

Franzel, S., F. Colburn and G. Degu. 1989. 'Grain Marketing Regulations: Impact on Peasant Production in Ethiopia', *Food Policy*, 14(4): 337–60.

Gamaledin, M., 1992. 'Pastoralism: Existing Limitations, Possibilities for the Future', M. Doornbos, L. Cliffe, A. Ghaffar Ahmed and J. Markakis (eds), *Beyond Conflict in the Horn* (London: ISS/James Currey) pp. 178–82.

Gebre-Kiros, F.,1980. 'Agricultural Land Fragmentation: a Problem of Land Distribution Observed in some Ethiopian PA's', *Ethiopian Journal of Development Research*, 4(2): 1–12.

Griffin, K. and R. Hay, 1985. 'Problems of Agricultural Development in Socialist Ethiopia: An Overview and a Suggested Strategy', *Journal of Peasant Studies* 13(1): 37– 66.

Gryseels. G., A. Astatke, A. and G. Assemenew, 1984. 'The use of single oxen for crop cultivation in Ethiopia', *ILCA Bulletin* (April) Addis Ababa. no.18: 20–25.

Hilsum, L., n.d. *The Terraces of Wello* (London: Panos Institute).

Hoben, A., 1973. *Land Tenure among the Amhara of Ethiopia* (Chicago: University of Chicago Press).

Holt, J., 1983. 'Ethiopia, Food for Work or Food for Relief', *Food Policy* (August), pp. 187–201.

Hultin, J., 1989. 'The Predicament of the Peasants in Conservation-based Development', O.D.I. Agricultural Administration Unit (London), *Pastoral Development Network*, paper no. 27c.

Hurni, H., 1983. 'Soil Erosion and Soil Formation in Agricultural Systems, Ethiopian and Northern Thailand', *Mountain Research and Development*, 3: 131–42.

ILO/Provisional Government of Ethiopia, 1986. *From Crisis to Sustained Development*, A Programme of Action. ILO Multi-disciplinary Programme Mission, vol.1. Addis Ababa.

Kohlin, G., 1987. 'Disaster Prevention in Wollo: The Effects of Food-for-Work', Swedish International Development Authority/Ethiopia Red Cross Society. Addis Ababa. (Aug).

Kuru, A., 1988. 'Accelerated Soil Erosion in Ethiopia: a Result of Strategic Policy of the Empire State', in S. Ege (ed.) *Development in Ethiopia*. University of Trondheim, Working Papers on Ethiopian Development no. 3. pp. 41–56.

Leach, G. and R. Mearns, 1988. *Beyond the Woodfuel Crisis* (London: Earthscan).

Lirenso, A., 1986. *Food Aid and its Impact on Ethiopian Agriculture*, Addis Ababa University/Institute of Development Research, Research Report no. 26.

Love, R., 1989. 'Funding the Ethiopian State: Who Pays?', *Review of African Political Economy* 44: 18–26.

McCann, J., 1987a. 'Report on Evaluation of Oxfam/Oxfam America Hararghe/Ethiopia Projects' (Oxfam, Addis Ababa) mimeo.

McCann, J., 1987b. 'The Social Impact of Drought in Ethiopia: Oxen, Households and some Implications for Rehabilitation', in M. Glantz (ed), *Drought and Hunger in Africa* (Cambridge: Cambridge University Press) pp. 245–67.

McCann, J., 1987c. *From Poverty to Famine* (Philadelphia: University of Pennsylvania Press).

McCann, J., 1988a. 'A Great Agrarian Cycle? A History of Agricultural Productivity and Demographic Change in Highland Ethiopia, 1900–1987', Boston University African Studies Centre *Working Paper no. 31.*

McCann, J., 1988b. 'History, Drought and Reproduction: Dynamics of Society and Ecology in Northeast Ethiopia', in Anderson and Johnson (eds), *The Ecology of Survival* (Boulder: Westview) pp. 283–303.

McCann, J., 1990. 'Historical Trends of Agriculture in Ankobar District, 1840–1989', in S. Ege (ed.), *Ethiopia: Problems of Sustainable Development.* University of Trondheim, Working Papers on Ethiopian Development. no. 5. pp. 201–24.

Mama, A., 1992. 'The Need for Gender Analysis: A Comment on the Prospects for Peace', in M. Doornbos, L. Cliffe, A. Ghaffar Ahmed and J. Markakis, (eds), *Beyond Conflict in the Horn* (London: ISS/James Currey) pp. 72–8.

Markakis, J., 1989. 'The Ishaq–Ogaden dispute', in A. Hjort af Ornas and M. A. Mohammed Salih (eds), *Ecology & Politics* (Uppsala: Scandinavian Institute of African Studies) pp. 157–68.

Maxwell, S., 1986. 'Food Aid in Ethiopia: Disincentive Effects and Commercial Displacement', *I.D.S. Discussion Paper* (Sussex), no. 226.

Maxwell, S., 1990. 'State or Market? Options for a Rural Safety Net in Ethiopia', RUPAG Seminar, Sussex IDS (Jan.).

Pausewang, S., 1983. *Peasants, Land and Society, A Social History of Land*

Reform in Ethiopia (Koln: Weltforum Verlag).

Pausewang, S., 1988. 'Peasants, Organisations, Markets: Ten Years after the Land Reform', S. Ege (ed.), *Development in Ethiopia*. University of Trondheim, Working Papers on Ethiopian Development no. 3, pp. 127–52.

Poluha, E., 1987. *The Current Situation of Women in Ethiopia*. A report to the World Bank. Addis Ababa (May).

Rahmato, D., 1985. *Agrarian Reform in Ethiopia* (Trenton, NJ: Red Sea Press).

Rahmato, D., 1987. *Famine and Survival Strategies, A Case Study from NE Ethiopia*, Food and Famine Monograph Series No.1, Institute of Development Research, Addis Ababa University. May.

Scones, I. and J. McCracken (eds), 1989. *Participatory Rapid Rural Appraisal in Wello*. Peasant Association Planning for Natural Resource Management (London: Ethiopian Red Cross Society/International Institute of Environment & Development).

Stahl, M., 1973. *Contradictions in Agricultural Development* (Uppsala: Scandinavian Institute of African Studies).

Stahl, M., 1989. 'Capturing the Peasants through Cooperatives: the Case of Ethiopia', *Review of African Political Economy* 44: 27–46.

Webb, P. and J. von Braun, 1989. *Drought and Food Shortages in Ethiopia*. A Preliminary Review of Effects and Policy Implications, IFRI and ONCCP, Addis Ababa (February).

Woldemeskel, G., 1989. 'Ethiopian Agrarian Policy and its Effects', *Food Policy* 14(4): 361–75.

Wood, A. and M. Stahl, 1989. *Ethiopia: Natural Conservation Strategy*, Phase I, Addis Ababa and IUCN. (November).

World Bank, 1984. *An Economic Justification for Rural Afforestation: The Case of Ethiopia*. Energy Department Paper no. 16, Washington DC.

Woube, M., 1986. *Problems of Land Reform Implementation in Rural Ethiopia*, Uppsala University/Geografiska Regionstudier Nr. 16, Uppsala.

11 Caught between Two Worlds: Eritrean Women Refugees and Voluntary Repatriation

Helene Moussa

INTRODUCTION

This chapter focuses on the decision-making process of Eritrean women refugees in Canada regarding returning to Eritrea. This process is gendered and is affected by the refugee experience, skills learned in exile, and conditions in Eritrea.

Repatriation of 400,000 or more Eritreans in Sudan is rightly a priority of the Provisional Government of Eritrea, given their numbers, impoverished conditions and Sudan's economic situation. Return of exiles in the West is nevertheless important to consider, given their education and skills, as well as their exile experience. They represent a brain-drain and a potential human resource for development. Understanding themes in the decision-making process can point to significant issues when planning for repatriation and reintegration, as well as for reconstruction and development. Tasks ahead for the Government of Eritrea are monumental. Macro-issues in creating a new and democratic state structure and development plans are undoubtedly multiple. To be effective such plans must recognize the role women play in domestic work (e.g. household tasks, care of children, family health, cooking and providing food etc.), as well as in the public sphere, such as in agriculture, industry and service industries, income generating activities, paid domestic labour among other developmental activities. Gender relations and women's rights are integral parts of the conceptual framework of current development discourse and practice (e.g. Carrillo, 1992; Davies, 1987; Sen and Grown, 1987; Smyke, 1991; Tomasevski, 1993; Wallace and March, 1991). Women must play a major decision-making role at all levels of Eritrean society.

In this chapter I raise gender related questions about reintegration of exiles with families and with respect to post-liberation social and cultural issues in Eritrea. I base this focus on feminist theory and practice which

208

clearly argues that the personal is political. Here, I am struck by the theme of the UN's Year of the Family (1994): *Building the Smallest Democracy at the Heart of the Family*. Just and equitable gender relations are essential elements of democracy and development.

After thirty years of war and living as refugees, reconstituting the family will necessarily be complex. Pressures of the refugee experience have created many family tensions, family break-ups, widowed and abandoned women and orphaned and abandoned children. Voluntary repatriation will not magically resolve these situations. At the same time, many are only now realizing that relatives who joined the liberation struggle are dead. Families are fractured and will need social support systems to recreate their family units as part of Eritrea's reconstruction as a democratic state.

This study draws on my original research which examines identity formation in terms of discontinuities, continuities, resistance and reconstruction in the lives of women from Ethiopia and Eritrea (Moussa, 1992, 1993). Now that return is possible, it is especially significant to listen to hopes and concerns of women in exile. I therefore re-interviewed most of the Eritrean women for this chapter, as well as other Eritrean women in Toronto not interviewed previously. I was particularly interested in interviewing women who had returned from visits after Eritrea's liberation. Interviews took place between August 1991 and October 1992.

Marital status of women in this study varied: married, engaged, single mothers, divorced and single. At the time of flight their ages ranged between 5 and 36; at the time of interviews their ages ranged between 22–46. In 1992 the age range of children in these families was 1–19 years. The status of their families prior to flight was: driver, farmer, civil servant, mechanic, businessman/woman, soldier and 'professional.' Younger women came to Canada with parent(s) or alone. Several had siblings and relatives in North America. All lost many family members in the war, when they were imprisoned, during the Red Terror campaign or by natural death. Gendered implications of these losses may be understood in the context of a patriarchal society. For instance, to return to their country without the 'protection' of their family and especially male heads of household would be difficult.

Several women were imprisoned and tortured prior to flight. Most came to Canada from Sudan and Italy; others were in Kenya, Djibouti, Spain and Uganda. In these countries they were vulnerable to sexual abuse and several were sexually violated in flight and when and after they crossed the border. When they first arrived in Canada (1981–6) most were employed in female-ghetto jobs. By 1991 many were employed in computer related jobs and as cashiers. A few were employed in professional or management positions. Some who came with their parents or alone attended school in Canada, as well as college and university. The range of years women were in Canada by 1991 was 1.5 to 12 years.

RESEARCH ON REPATRIATION AND REINTEGRATION

Research on and understanding of repatriation is still exploratory and regionally uneven. With the exception of work on/with Latin American exiles in Europe, research has predominantly focused on repatriation from first asylum countries in the South. While asylum in the South and the exile experience in Western countries are radically different we can draw similar themes.

Unless research is on women refugees, no distinction is made between male and female refugees in the repatriation process. If there are gender differences, the literature gives no such indication. There is also no discussion about gender dynamics among family members deciding to repatriate. A first attempt is a study comparing gendered decision-making processes of Eritreans in the US and in Canada (McSpadden and Moussa 1993). This study is based on the concept of social place of individuals in sociocultural systems and the urgent need of refugees to develop or gain a sense of belonging (e.g. Malkki 1992; Stein 1986). Concepts of power and belonging emerged as interrelated issues critical to a gender analysis of social space. While many situations and themes these men and women raised appear similar (e.g., education valued as a source of mobility, importance of taking financial responsibility for family members back home and supporting younger siblings in Canada, facing racism in Canada) the significant gender difference is that for men the social power they desire is congruent with traditional Eritrean socio-cultural understanding of masculinity, based on education, employment, family responsibilities, and social status. Women in contrast tried to maintain creative tension between aspects of their cultural identity which are fulfilling (e.g., women-centred networks) and at the same time assert their rights as women in an egalitarian sense. Women had gained something in resettlement they did not want to lose (McSpadden and Moussa 1993).

Research and experience show that refugees will not return until they perceive that conditions are safe (Akol 1987; Crisp 1984; Kibreab 1989:487–8, 1991:206; Malley 1992; Manz 1988; *Refuge* 1987; Stein 1986). Some evidence indicates that refugees will choose to return when they are less well adapted in the asylum country. Conversely refugees are likely not to return when they are more self-sufficient and culturally adapted and when they question returning to 'war devastated economies' of countries of origin (Akol 1987:150; Christensen 1985:124). Christensen's (1985) study on Burundi refugees reveals that a small number of refugees chose to remain in Tanzania because the trauma of conflicts and flight was still very much in their memory. They wanted to live among fellow refugees with whom they shared personal burdens of flight experiences, customs, and language.

Some researchers argue that repatriation plans must also include reintegration of refugees into their home countries (Akol 1987; Christensen 1990; Dupree 1988; Malley 1992; Stein 1986:265). Reintegration varies according to skills, experiences, education, physical disability, political allegiances, and perception about the life style and opportunities to which they would return. Returnees have to be prepared for changes that have occurred at all levels of societal life in their absence, as well as the fact that they too have changed as a result of the exile experience (Akol 1987:150–57; Christensen 1985:128; FASIC 1981; Malkki 1992; Thorn 1991:55–8; Zetter 1988). Research also shows that reintegration is facilitated when refugees flee and return as communities rather than as individuals and when economic assistance and employment opportunities are provided on return (Basock 1990:281–97). Repatriation of refugees, in summary, is influenced by diverse and at times even contradictory factors.

RETURNING OR STAYING IN CANADA? DECISION-MAKING BEFORE LIBERATION

The journey of Eritrean refugee women involved a series of violent encounters, threats to personal safety and challenges to their identities as women and as Eritreans. They left behind all they loved and cherished, as well as support systems that gave meaning and direction to their lives and protection as women. They made difficult choices and paid a heavy price for their choice to 'live'. They risked flight, and flight was a risk particularly because of their sexuality and gender. In asylum countries, including Canada, they experienced extreme poverty and the humiliation and powerlessness of being refugees and women refugees in particular. They also had to deal with pervasive racism, isolation, and the disappointment of not being able to continue their education because of economic reasons and lack of time due to family responsibilities including supporting younger siblings.

When I interviewed these women in 1988–9, almost all said they would definitely return to Eritrea when it became independent and when there was peace. One summarized this general view when she said, 'We can have a change in government [in Ethiopia] and Eritrea can become independent but we can still have war.' These women told me that if by the time they could safely return they would have acquired Canadian citizenship, they would still return 'home.' Nothing, they said, would stop them.

In contrast, those who said they would not return explained that they did not have the mental, physical or emotional energy to uproot themselves again. Resettlement in Canada had been very difficult and they were just beginning to feel a sense of stability in their personal life and jobs, as well as the possibility of educational opportunities. In addition, they said that too many members of their immediate family were now dead and, consequently, they would not have the same support systems they had before they fled. They still longed to be 'home' and said if they could afford it they would return on visits. One said that all her family had died and her village no longer existed as a result of the war. To return as a woman on her own was frightening.

In 1988–9 women explained that they wanted to return 'home' because they 'belonged there'. Eritrea was the source of their cultural identity, providing a sense of personal history (i.e. rooted in family and in communities where they grew up) and collective history with the Eritrean people. They also expressed an attachment to the 'land' both in a physical/ ecological sense and because of a historic attachment to it. Emily Nastrallah (1988), a Lebanese writer and refugee in Canada, expresses this attachment poetically by saying that 'my ancestors are there in the earth'. An Argentinean artist reflecting on return describes exile with a metaphor of a fallen tree with its roots in the open air; the need to be re-rooted in one's home country or in exile is vital to mental health and continuity of life plans (Vasquez and Araujo 1988:212–13). Desire to return is not a self-deceiving myth but rather a search to make meaning between home (belonging) and the world (Schwartz 1989:136). It is a process which includes the grief of uprooting and a search to belong to which the repatriation process is very much linked. Home gives meaning to the world.

Some women I interviewed in 1988–9 also said Canada was becoming their second home. They quickly added that this did not mean that they would abandon Eritrean identity. Rather, it is a recognition that the social construction of identity is not static. It is a continuous process of self-definition as people interact with their social world. It is important to note that these women had found spaces, albeit limited and gendered, in Canadian society where they felt accepted and recognized for who they are and who they want to become. A few even felt recognized as relevant contributors to Canadian society and to Eritreans with settlement needs in

Canada. They struggled to find the 'glue' that would recreate a sense of their identity as women, as Eritreans in Canada. They appeared to be developing a new identity that was enabling them to 'belong' in two countries/cultures. It is a creative way of dealing with exile/refugee identity rather than remaining stuck in the past.

I draw this analysis from Latin American researchers and therapists in Europe who have developed two concepts concerning identity deconstruction and reconstruction amongst Latin American exiles. The first concept, 'critical integration', involves ability to critique (rather than romanticize) one's country of origin, and to find spaces and relationships in the country of asylum or resettlement that are congruent with one's values and ideology, rather than becoming ghettoized. This process also includes a critique of the dominant ideology and culture of the country of asylum and/or resettlement. The second concept is 'transcultural identity'. A transcultural identity enables exiles to have multiple identities, including the possibility of feeling that they can belong to two countries and cultures (Barude 1988; CIMADE 1981; COLAT 1981; da Rocha 1982; FASIC 1981; Vasquez 1981; Vasquez, Richard and Delseuil 1979).

RETURNING HOME OR STAYING? DECISION-MAKING AFTER LIBERATION

The collapse of the Mengistu government and EPLF victory was greeted with jubilation. Women were proud of the Eritrean fighters and relieved that peace at long last was a real possibility. 'I am happiest for the people at home who can now live in peace' was voiced by many women. Since liberation, the decision-making process about returning (and when) or not returning has become a topic of daily conversation in families and among friends. The process is fraught with painful choices, contradictions and uncertainties.

When I interviewed women in 1992, I noted much ambivalence about the timing of return and whether this would be permanent. Issues they raised revealed contradictions in values, beliefs, and personal and family priorities. In contrast to the decision to flee which was spurred by persecution, repression and/or war, their decision now centres on desire to return to their homeland and their situation in exile. As one woman said 'I feel I have to return because the reason we left was that we had no country.' Yet she and others now have to weigh many other considerations. One woman laughed when she reminded me that in 1988 she had told me that she would without question return as soon as possible. Some confided they have decided not to return on a permanent basis.

After listening to the powerlessness and vulnerability women experienced during flight and refugee journeys, I suggest that some women feel that Canadian citizenship represents security. Letting go of this security is very difficult. One woman said, 'The future [in Eritrea] is still uncertain. Who knows? We may have to flee our country again or it may happen for our children. Why should we risk going through the refugee experience again? Can you imagine knowingly choosing to risk re-experiencing what I did!' This woman, like many others, was sexually violated in flight and in the first asylum country. Women also vividly remembered how many refugee women in Sudan and Djibouti turned to prostitution as a last resort to support themselves and their children (Demeke 1990; Moussa 1993:194–8).

Another woman reminded me of her response to my question three years earlier. She said, then, that she did not have the emotional, mental or physical energy to start over again. This woman was abandoned by her husband when she followed him to Sudan; their child was then eight months old. When I interviewed her in 1989, she had just completed a job training programme and was looking forward to gainful employment. Although she was unemployed in 1992, she held the same position about returning to Eritrea and added 'I have nothing [funds] to take back with me to start all over again. I can't depend on my family because they are poor and they expect me to help them. At least here I can get financial assistance until I find work and no one can pressure me to marry.' I sensed she represented the feelings of many single mothers and single women in particular. Refugee and resettlement experiences in Canada were traumatic and they could not risk uprooting themselves once more. Above all they wanted to maintain the personal autonomy they had attained as women.

Some single women, who had little memory of Ethiopia or Eritrea or who were born in exile and who had achieved college or university education in Canada said they wanted to go to Eritrea because they 'wanted to be useful ... to make a difference. It will be a challenge. Here [in Canada] jobs have a different meaning. You work for a personal achievement and goals. There I can perhaps contribute to the development of my people.' They also wanted to go to Eritrea to test 'how I would fit'. I asked if they had specific reasons as women that made it difficult for them to leave Canada as quickly as they would have liked or not want to leave at all. Their responses were strikingly similar.

Women's Rights

The tremendous strides taken in liberated areas of Eritrea with respect to equal gender relations are well known (Wilson 1991). Attitudes and values, however, are hard to change. Advances in women's status made in liberation struggles are often relinquished after liberation (Randall 1974; Urdang 1987, 1989). Lessons of the failure of other liberation movements to promote women's emancipation must be learned if history is not to repeat itself.

The most emphasized reason that makes many women question returning permanently was what they termed 'women's rights'. They recognized that liberated areas had made great strides in this respect but felt that attitudes of the general population (even among many male exiles) had not changed and would take a long time to do so. As one said, 'there are no laws yet about pay equity and against wife abuse and assault and rape. The EPLF may be more progressive than the population. I would find it difficult to live without [guaranteed] basic human rights.'

Others took a different stand. They felt the struggle for women's rights was something that women should work towards. One said, 'After all women in Canada are continuing to demand for their rights. It is our responsibility to continue in this struggle in our country.' The only factors that seemed to distinguish these women were: (1) they were actively involved in the National Union of Eritrean Women (NUEW) and therefore believed gender issues could be challenged with support of existing structures (2) they had experienced some level of independence before they fled and/or, (3) they were younger, single women who had developed a gender analysis in Canada and recognized the continuing struggle for women's liberation as a global issue.

Several married women I interviewed wondered if relationships with their spouses in the homes would revert to 'old ways' if there was house help and because of the assistance of women in an extended family. Some quickly added that many men in exile had also resisted change and still do. Resistance is not limited to men. Some women point out that attitudes against female genital mutilation are resisted by women themselves: 'It is women who do the circumcision not the men. Many women even insisted on doing it in Sudan, even in refugee camps.'

Women's rights were, for all these women, very much tied to creation of a democratic society which allowed rights to education and health services, employment equity and shared family responsibilities, as well as the right to express opinions. One woman emphatically said, 'It is not perfect here [in Canada] but you can ask for your rights.' When I asked women in 1988 and 1989, what they would like to take back to Eritrea from their Canadian experience, responses included: the human rights system, equality for women, democracy, freedom of speech, and availability of basic resources such as housing, food and medical care for everyone.

Rebuilding rural Eritrea requires what Christensen, discussing Afghan refugees, terms 'the principle of positive discrimination in favour of women' as a response to deep seated gender inequalities in Afghan society so that women will not be 'left behind' in the development process. Christensen also recommends that reconstruction plans need to establish two strategies to ensure rights of rural women. The first concerns advancement of women's conditions (social and economic) and the second is promotion of women's rights within the context of human rights (Christensen 1990: 70). Patriarchy is not limited to rural societies. Similar strategies are essential in urban areas as well.

Education

Education of children is an important consideration in the decision-making process. Three patterns of responses emerged. Some mothers said they did not want to return because they wanted their children to have the best possible education. The qualifications of teachers and the quality of the educational curriculum in Eritrea after years of war were of concern to them. One woman deplored the authoritarian teaching methods she underwent in Eritrea and did not want her children to have to endure such an intellectually and emotionally oppressive system. These mothers also wanted to ensure that their children would have the opportunity to go to university.

A few women categorically said they would not leave Canada permanently or give up Canadian citizenship for themselves or their children. They said they would still not change their position even if their spouses decided to return permanently. They were determined not to abandon Canadian citizenship. There was, however, some ambivalence about this should their children eventually decide to settle in Eritrea. They also added that if they could afford it financially (by taking a leave of absence from their jobs in Canada) they wanted to offer their services on a voluntary basis to Eritrean development. Some were looking for NGO funding to back projects they felt would be of use for reconstruction. Interestingly, these projects focused on women and children (e.g. refugee women and children returning from Sudan, disabled women and children, retraining for prostitutes, female fighters in independent Eritrea). They also hoped they could afford to send their children on visits so children could 'feel connected to our country and culture'.

The second pattern of responses came from women who said they would delay returning until their children completed high school. Children could remain in Canada if they wished to complete their education, but parents would return. These women were decisive about their eventual return. As one said, 'It doesn't make sense not to return when the reason we left was because we didn't have our country.' Mothers who had put aside their own education in Canada for economic reasons and/or family responsibilities also said they were planning to prepare themselves in a profession or for a skill that would be useful to Eritrea. The notion of working to serve their country was very strong and had underlying motivations to assert their rights as women in private and public spheres of Eritrean society.

The third pattern of responses was from mothers who were decisive about permanently returning when their young children were ready for school. The explanation one mother gave succinctly summarizes these views:

I definitely want to take my children back when they are young so that they can be socialized in our culture ... it is a very good culture ... that is why we have been able to survive and succeed here ... we know we are Eritreans ... I prefer to take them when they are young. Later on they can come to Canada if they want to go to university here.

At the same time, these families also said they would not give up Canadian citizenship. Parents were willing to live separately until children completed schooling in Eritrea. Several parents are also considering the possibility of one (usually the male partner) of them remaining in Canada and the other returning to Eritrea with the children. The timing of this return is still undetermined not merely because of the age of their children but because of uncertainties in Eritrea and the shortage of housing and work possibilities.

Many mothers wonder whether their children would want to live in Eritrea when they have spent their formative years in Canada. One mother said that her oldest daughter is quite adamant about not moving again (they were in three African countries as refugees before coming to Canada). Many of these children were born in exile or were too young when they fled to have any memory of Eritrea. They have established their own friendships, relationships, and identities in Canada. Some have conflicting views about where they 'belong'. Latin American literature on children of exiles reflects similar differences among the child population (Vasquez and Araujo 1988:83–129; Vasquez 1981:22–34).

Single women and mothers who had not yet had the opportunity to further their education also said that now that the war was over and Eritrea would be independent they wanted to put all their energies and finances towards bringing over family members and in assisting them in settlement.

They said they would not return until they had improved their educational status and developed skills that would enable them to be self-supporting and to contribute to the development of their country. In their earlier socialization in Eritrea or Ethiopia, schooling gave these women the opportunity to delay and even resist women's ultimate role as wives and mothers. Achieving higher levels of education and better still a professional education before returning, they felt, would strengthen their sense of autonomy as women.

Anticipated Dynamics of Re-adaptation

One can anticipate several levels of re-adaptation among different peoples in Eritrea: returnees and those who remained in Eritrea have to engage with each other both at personal and public levels. This interaction involves people who lived in a refugee culture and mentality in asylum countries of the South and refugees who resettled in different countries of the North, Eritreans who lived in liberated areas and those who lived under occupation. Eritreans with very different histories now face the challenge of creating a new culture based on peace and democracy. This process of re-adaptation must be based within the family and the community if democracy and development are to be rooted at the base.

Women also recognized that returning would require social and cultural adaptation between themselves and Eritreans who had remained there. There were positive feelings, as well as concerns raised about this. All those I spoke to were very clear that they had changed even though they maintained a strong sense of Eritean identity. They felt, Eritrea, as well, had changed and that it could not be the same Eritrea of five, ten or fifteen years before. How had they changed and what difference would that make in reintegration? I recalled a conversation in 1989 in Geneva, Switzerland with a group of Eritrean women. One woman despaired for Eritrea and young Eritreans who were in so many different countries. She observed that in Europe young Eritreans ('the future leaders' she added) tried to adopt the ways of host countries. As a result, in her opinion, they were neither Swiss, German, Swedish nor Eritrean. Looking ahead towards independence and repatriation, she felt these young people would be alienated in Eritrea. The diversity of cultures of returnees from the diaspora was a great concern to her. She even called it the future *maladie de notre pays* (the future sickness of our country). Others, however, did not agree. They believed young people in exile were adopting Western ways as a means of survival and because many did not have parents to guide them. Despite the changes these young people had undergone, they were, in the opinion of these women, Eritreans – a *different* kind of Eritrean (i.e. with a transcultural identity). They also believed that the knowledge that young exiles would bring back from European countries would be an asset to Eritrea. The Eritrea of the future, they felt, could not be built as a 'closed society'.

Reflecting on this dilemma shared by exiles from Latin America, Vasquez and Aruajo quote from F. Ainsa's *D'ici, de l'á-bas*. Ainsa argues that multiple identities exiles develop must be seen as the privilege of living through many identity transformations, as well as an opportunity (if not mission) to explore and share new life experiences. While exiles usually do not value these multiple identities, the richness of learning and the broadening of their perspectives as a result of exile cannot, according to Ainsi, be attained by those who have never left their place of birth (Vasquez and Araujo 1988:209). When I asked women what they had learned from their life experiences since flight, without exception they said that they never realized how 'strong' they were. One woman said:

> Now I think of myself as a heroine, because I overcame all those situations [threats to her life and sexuality in flight and in a first asylum country]. I never imagined I could do that. It makes me proud of myself. Now if I have to face [an] even harder situation, I know that I can manage it. I can help others when they are concerned about little problems and show them that they can overcome them (Moussa: 1993: 255)

As women, they all felt that the refugee experience had forced them to depend on their own resources rather than on their family. Crises had not only tested their strength but also created a new strength of character. Others pointed out that in restrospect their world view had broadened because they were exposed to many different cultures. Their resilience, often under formidable odds, can serve as a model to Eritrean women and the hurdles which will have to be overcome in reconstruction and development of their nation. This strength and resilience can as well become a resource for their reintegration should they return. Women I interviewed identified several specific differences that would require adjustment on their part, as well as 'bridges' that would have to be rebuilt with their families and others in Eritrea. They also noted positive factors in Eritrean society that would facilitate adjustment. In this respect, regular and clear information (from informal and official sources) about social and economic conditions in Eritrea is critical if their decisions are to be based on realities rather than misinformed assumptions.

One woman observed that Eritrean women who were returning on short visits since May 1991, were making sure to change their wardrobe, even buying the plastic sandals worn by the 'fighters'. These were symbolic measures to attempt to identify themselves with the struggle by being in solidarity with the 'fighters'. In contrast, another woman observed the difference in dress of many returning exiles who appeared 'wealthy' compared to Eritreans who remained in their country. She felt these differences could create barriers based on material resources returnees have been able to acquire compared to the limited resources available to those who remained in their country during the liberation struggle. She chose not to dress like Eritrean women her age (skirts and a *shama* – traditional white shawl) because she did not want 'to pretend I was not different. I just wore casual and comfortable clothes ... what I wear most of the time in Canada'.

Women who visited Eritrea also reported that they appreciated the 'simple' life people led where 'small things satisfy people [as against] the highly pressurized life and consumer-oriented and materialistic values in Canada'. One woman who returned on a visit said, 'It was like a heavy load off my back and mind' not to feel all the pressures that had become part of her life in Canada. In Eritrea, they went on to say, people are so happy to be alive and to finally have peace. Some never had experienced peace in their lives.

Another woman said, 'The most amazing thing is that doors are not locked and children can play freely in the neighbourhood.' Another said she caught herself cautioning her children in Asmara who were running out of the house on their own. For Ethiopian and Eritrean refugee women, doors which could not be securely closed in first asylum countries meant a threat to personal safety, including risk of rape. In Canada neighbours' closed doors were a symbol of unfriendliness. Child abduction in Canada had taught them that they could not leave their children unattended outside the home. Another visiting exile was shocked when a former fighter wiped the nose of a child (a stranger) as they were walking in the streets. Something that would never happen in Canada! This gesture symbolized for her a sense of caring in community as against the alienation of individualism she experienced in Canada.

One woman who had returned from a visit said:

> I suddenly realized the strangest thing after a week. I had forgotten that I ever left. It was like I never was a refugee or in Canada – I felt *really* at home. I was no longer an 'outsider' the way I feel in Canada after seven years.

When she shared this feeling with others, she found that they too had experienced a similar 'oblivion' of their existence in Canada. They no longer had to explain 'where we come from' and neither did they feel members of a visible minority. What particularly distinguished these women was that they were immediately able to make links with professionally/vocationally related activities in Eritrea. That is, they were not limited to family relationships.

Women who returned on visits also identified differences in the vocabulary of returning exiles and Eritreans at home. 'It is not the same Tigrinya we speak', said one. Another angle on differences in language expressions in Eritrea is that children in liberated areas were taught in Tigrinya and children in areas controlled by the Ethiopian government were taught in Amharic. A new vocabulary developed in Eritrea because of the occupation and war. A regular radio comedy programme in Eritrea addresses these differences. One woman said, 'They think we are strange.' It appears that this programme focuses only on exiles and not on the changes exiles observe in Eritrea. The women I interviewed felt that people in Eritrea have little understanding of the refugee experience. One woman summarized the concern of others when she explained that there appears to be a general assumption in Eritrea that:

> people get rich quickly when we come to Canada. They don't understand how hard it has been and still is for many of us no matter how long we have been here. They don't know how much we suffered ... it is only when parents have visited their children here [Canada] that they realize how hard life is ... the pressure in our life and how we can have two jobs and not have enough to live on.

Recalling interviews in 1988–9, I remembered that women spared telling their parents about vulnerability they experienced as women in flight and asylum, as well as the poverty, humiliation and racism they experienced in Canada. One woman told me that she did not write to her family from Sudan 'because I always related writing letters with good news ... what could I write about the miserable life we have here? Besides we did not have the money to buy writing paper or postage stamps.' What these women experienced is always measured against the horrors of repression and war their family and others faced daily. Feelings of guilt about their safety and level of comfort made them judge the refugee experience as insignificant compared to the suffering of those in Eritrea. Furthermore as a means of coping with the shame of being sexually violated (in flight and/or in asylum), women literally suppressed the memory of this experience.

Dupree (1988:19) suggests that lack understanding of Afghan women's refugee experience is a concern in their reintegration with families in

Afghanistan. These gaps in understanding reflect the broader cultural differences in values and perspectives which have to be bridged if Eritrean women and men are to work together to reconstruct their nation. Some women said that there would certainly be gaps between them and their family. Relationships could not be what they were before they left. All have had different life experiences in Eritrea and as refugees in different parts of the world. While they anticipated that it would be wonderful to be reunited, they would have to find ways of reconstructing these relationships. One woman illustrated it with the tensions that evolved between families who fled from Asmara at the heat of the conflict and joined relatives in rural areas.

> You can imagine what it would be like when some of us return. Many of us would have to live with the family until we are settled and with the housing shortage that may be for a long time. We are really caught between two worlds. We missed our extended family here but we also learned to live alone. We learned a different way of life.

Studies on Latin American refugees who returned to their homeland after exile revealed that exiles once again had to reconstruct their identities, as well as their physical, social, cultural and social reference points in the public realm and especially in the family sphere. Returning families and individuals were often with their families for as long as two years. This required extraordinary flexibility from all. Women had to reassert their sense of autonomy, this time within their extended family and in their own country (FASIC 1980:35–40; Vasquez and Araujo 1988:207–15). Similar 'cultural gaps' were noted in adjustment of fighters to 'civilian life'. In the 'field' they learned to make such personal decisions as to who they wanted to marry (even across ethnic and religious differences). Now they face parents wanting to arrange their marriages. Many female fighters are not accepted by their in-laws – especially if their ethnic and religious background differs. Marriage break-ups among fighters were evidenced and male fighters are marrying 'traditional women'. Women fighters, in the opinion of some women I interviewed, feel constraints on their life and activities much more than male fighters. As one women said, 'men can get away with anything in Eritrean families'.

Reflecting on the decision-making process, one woman described the difference between fleeing and returning: 'Now when we are thinking of returning we have to carefully plan it. It is a long-term plan. When we fled our country we just fled.' When refugees flee they do so to seek safety and security. Returning home is leaving a position of relative social security.

TRANSITION FROM A 'WAR CULTURE' TO A 'PEACE CULTURE'

Much discourse on repatriation only focuses on reintegration of exiles in their home countries. The changes these countries undergo during transition from repressive regimes and/or war to the promise of democratization are hardly addressed. Latin American exiles who fled dictatorships and returned to their homeland from Europe observed authoritarian state practices, so to speak, under the rubric of democratization. Popular groups who sought the fall of the dictatorship now have to learn, if not unlearn, strategies they used to oppose dictatorship (Sullivan and Opitz 1990). Strategies to build democracy are different from those used to defeat dictatorships or occupying forces. The Eritrean struggle lasted thirty years, a period in which Eritreans experienced a war that not only devastated the countryside but also their home lives. A whole generation has only known war. While peace is welcomed and energies are being devoted toward construction of the new state, the human scars (social and psychological) of living in a 'war culture' are not only issues for those who remained in Eritrea but also for reintegrating exiles. A peace culture cannot be built on a military model.

I asked women who visited Eritea since liberation if they, or their friends, had observed behaviour and attitudes that could be ascribed to a 'war culture'. They responded by saying that play activities of children, particularly orphans who lived in liberated areas, centred around war symbols and situations. They also commented that children had lost their childhood. One said, 'You think you are talking to adults. They talk politics and about war, how to shoot and what soldiers can do. How will our children fit in this?' Her last comment was interesting because it reflected a belief that children returning from exile had no choice but to accept this way of playing.

One illustration of the shift from a war to a peace culture was illustrated by a woman who said that when orphans were moved to the cities they would take fruits and vegetables from store stands. They did not see this as 'stealing'. They had no perception of having to pay for food because they had learned in liberated areas that crops and food before them were *Hafesh* (for the masses).

It is interesting to note that when these women settled in Canada they learned, as do other migrants, that they had to accept any job irrespective of prior experience and qualifications. As returnees/migrants to Eritrea they are once again internalizing a denial of their knowledge and skills, this time developed in the resettlement process in Canada. The difference between these responses lies in the sense of guilt exiles feel because they were safe from war and political repression while friends and family in Eritrea remained in danger – they would therefore not want to appear to be taking over jobs and activities, let alone being critical of values and behaviour learned under occupation.

Male and female fighters also have to undergo changes as civilians, not merely in relation to skills but, also with respect to behaviour. Reflecting on repatriation of Afghan women, Dupree (1988:19) raises an important question when she expresses concerns about where aggression of male militants will be directed when there is no war. Eritrean women were also active militarily in the liberation war. What behavioural changes must they undergo?

One woman said that on a recent visit she observed that fighters were role models for young people. 'They are heroes and heroines because of their sacrifices and their role in the liberation of Eritrea.' However, she noticed strong gender differences; whereas young boys only emulate the 'military' part of male fighters, she heard little girls singing 'I want to marry a fighter.' Female fighters in contrast are neither emulated by women nor sought as ideal future mates by boys or men.

Some women who recently returned from Eritrea were very concerned about Eritrean women and girls who were forced into prostitution by occupying forces during the war. Prostitution became a means of livelihood for many women in Asmara and in port towns of Assab and Massawa. My interviewees said prostitution continues despite the Ethiopian army's departure. They also observed that prostitutes were exploited by bar-owners who expect them to work all day without pay as waitresses in exchange for money they receive for their sexual services on the premises. My informants feared that changing the situation of these women will be very low in the new government's reconstruction and development plans and hoped the NUEW would give priority to economic reorientation of prostitutes within national reconstruction and development (Comte 1991:16)

Clearly a peace culture in Eritrea must begin by denouncing violence against women, by developing policies and strategies to ensure gender equality in public and private spheres, and by providing women with choices for economic livelihood which will not exploit them because of their gender, as well as publicly acknowledging the strengths and contributions of women in times of struggle and national reconstruction. Highlighting and putting into continued practice the innovative social, technological, medical, health and economic developmental achievements in the liberated areas (Firebrace and Holland 1987; Wilson 1991) can become the seeds of a peace culture.

CONCLUSION

Desire to return to Eritrea is unequivocal among women I interviewed. The actual decision and time of this return is, however, more complex. Women are caught between two worlds and their decision-making processes are centrally gender related. Women's questions, concerns and choices differed in emphasis and focus because of subjective and objective factors related to their refugee experience, legal and citizenship status in Canada, the economic, social and political situation in Eritrea since liberation and expectations of family members. The decision to return home is also influenced by reintegration opportunities or the lack of them. Questions and concerns in decision-making in the repatriation process are personal and political.

The reintegration process is not limited to adjustment of exiles to Eritrean society. It also involves 'reintegration' of fighters and people who lived in liberated areas with those who lived under Ethiopian military occupation. The shift from thirty years of war towards creation of a democratic state necessitates a change in world views in the family and in state structures, a transformation from a 'war culture' to a peace culture, and a shift from a patriarchal culture to a society built on gender equality. These are integral considerations in national development.

References

Akol, Joshua O., 1987. 'Southern Sudanese Refugees: Their Repatriation and Resettlement after the Addis Ababa Agreement', *Refugees: A Third World Dilemma*, John R. Rogge (ed.) (Totowa, NJ: Rowman and Littlefield) pp. 143–58.
Associated Press, 1992. 'Afghan women veil their hopes', *Globe and Mail*, 5 May, A14.
Carrillo, Roxana, 1992. *Battered Dreams: Violence Against Women as an Obstacle to Development* (New York: UNIFEM).
Barude, Jorge, 1988. 'L'utilization de l'approche systématique lors de thérapies avec des familles de refugiés politique', *Documents Refugiés* Supplement No. 46 8/17 aout.
Basock, Tanya, 1990. 'Repatration of Nicaraguan Refugees from Honduras and Costa Rica', *Journal of Refugee Studies*, 3(4): 281–97.
Christensen, Hanne, 1985. *Refugees and Pioneers* (Geneva: United Nations Research Institute for Social Development).
Christensen, Hanne, 1990. *The Reconstruction of Afghanistan: A Chance for Rural Afghan Women* (Geneva: United Nations Institute for Social Development).
Cimade, 1981. 'The Influence of Political Repression and Exile on Children', in *Mental Health and Exile* (London: World University Press Service) pp. 22–34.

COLAT, 1981. 'Towards a Libertarian Therapy for Latin American Exiles', *Mental Health and Exile* (London: World University Press) pp. 10–13.

Comte, Buche, 1991. 'Rapport de voyage en Erythrée.' *Terres des Hommes Suisse*, 15–30 November.

Crisp, Jeff, 1984. 'The Politics of Repatriation: Ethiopian Refugees in Djibouti: 1977–1983', *The Review of African Political Economy*, 30: 73–82.

da Rocha, Valentina, 1982. 'Women in Exile: Becoming Feminist', *International Journal of Oral History*, 5(6): 81–99.

Davies, Miranda. 1987. *Third World Second Sex: Women's Struggles and National Liberation* (London: Zed Press).

Demeke, Tadele, 1990. 'Refugee Women's Survival Strategies in Eastern Sudan', *Refugee Participation Network*, 7: 26–8.

Dupree, Nancy, 1988. 'The Role of Afghan Women after Repatriation', *Writers Union of Free Afghanistan*, 3(4): 19–24.

FASIC, 1981. 'A Social-Psychological Study of 25 Returning Families (1980)', *Mental Health and Exile* (London: World University Press) pp. 35–40.

Firebrace, James and Stuart Holland, 1984. *Never Kneel Down: Drought, Development and Liberation in Eritrea* (Nottingham: Betrand Russell House).

Hemispheric Migration Program Newsletter, 1990. 'HMP Research Points to Common Elements in Repatriation', *Hemispheric Migration Program Newsletter*, 4(1).

Kibreab, Gaim, 1989. 'Local Settlements in Africa: A Misconceived Option?', *Journal of Refugee Studies*, 2(4): 468–90.

Kibreab, Gaim, 1991. 'The System of Asylum in African Economies under Pressure', *'Hundred Flowers Bloom.' Essays in Honour of Botstafsson*. Kersti Ullenhag (ed.) (Stockholm). pp. 199–214.

Malkki, Lissa, 1992. 'National Geographic: The Rooting of Peoples and Territoralization of National Identity among Scholars and Refugees', *Cultural Anthropology*, 7: 24–42.

Malley, William, 1992. 'Political Reintegration of Refugee Communities: The Case of Afghanistan.' Paper presented at the Third International Research Advisory Panel Meeting, Refugee Studies Programme, Oxford University, 2–6 January.

Manz, B., 1988. *Refugees of a Hidden War: The Aftermath of Counterinsurgency in Guatemala* (New York: SUNY Press).

McSpadden, Lucia Ann and Helene Moussa, 1993. 'I Have a Name: The Gender Dynamics in Asylum and in Resettlement of Ethiopian and Eritrean Refugees in North America', *Journal of Refugee Studies*, 6(3): 203–225.

Moussa, Helene, 1993. *Storm and Sanctuary: The Journey of Ethiopian and Eritrean Women Refugees* (Dundas, Ontario: Artemis).

Moussa, Helene, 1992. 'The Social Construction of Women Refugees: A Journey of Discontinuities and Continuities.' Ed.D. Thesis University of Toronto.

Nastrallah, Emily, 1988. Radio broadcast, CBC Sunday Morning, 24 January.

Randall, Margaret, 1974. *Cuban Women* (Toronto: The Women's Press).

Refuge, 1987. 'Report on the Djibouti Refugee Situation', *Refuge*, 6(4):8–10.

Schwartz, Jonathan, 1989. *In Defence of Home Sickness: Nine Essays on Identity and Locality* (Kobenhavms: University of Denmark).

Sen, Gita and Caran Grown, 1987. *Development, Crisis and Alternative Visions: Third World Women's Perspectives* (New York: Monthly Review Press).

Smyke, Patricia, 1991. *Women and Health* (London: Zed Books).
Stein, Barry N., 1986. 'Durable Solutions for Developing Country Refugees', *International Migration Review*, 20: 264–82.
Sullivan, Rosemary and Juan Opitz, 1990. 'Dictating Democracy in Chile. An Interview with Fernando Paulsen', *Canadian Dimension*, June, pp. 25–8.
Thorn, Lynda, 1991. *From Rice Truck to Paddy Field* (Thailand: United Nations High Commission for Refugees).
Tomasevski, Katarina, 1993. *Women and Human Rights* (London: Zed Books).
Urdang, Stephanie, 1987. *Fighting Two Colonialisms. Women in Guinea-Bissau* (New York: Monthly Review Press).
Urdang, Stephanie, 1989. *And Still they Dance. Women, War and the Struggle for Change in Mozambique* (New York: Monthly Review Press).
Vasquez, Ana, 1981. 'Adolescents from the Southern Cone of Latin America in Exile', *Mental Health and Exile* (London: World University Press) pp. 22–34.
Vasquez, Ana and Ana Maria Araujo, 1988. *Exils Latino-Américains: La Malédiction d'Ulysse* (Paris: L'Harmattan).
Vasquez, Ana, Gabriella Richard and Marie Claire Delseuil, 1979. 'Psychologie de l'exile', *Esprit*, 5 Juin. pp. 9–21.
Wallace, Tina and Candida March (eds), 1991. *Changing Perceptions: Writings on Gender and Development* (Oxford: OXFAM).
Wilson, Amrit, 1991. *Women and the Eritrean revolution* (Trenton: Red Sea Press).
Zetter, Roger, 1988. 'Refugees, Repatriation and Root Causes', *Journal of Refugee Studies*, 1(2): 99–106.

12 Disaster in the Horn of Africa: The Impact on Public Health

Marion Kelly

INTRODUCTION

In past decades, the Horn has been battered by war and drought. Figure 12.1 shows some pathways by which these adversely affect health of communities. Although interactions and overlaps make any grouping of these processes somewhat arbitrary, this chapter considers three main headings: (i) direct effects, (ii) effects associated with people's attempts to preserve their usual way of life in the face of adversity, and (iii) effects associated with distress sequelae that ensue when such endeavours fail or are thwarted.

DIRECT EFFECTS OF DROUGHT AND WAR

Prolonged and severe drought has been a major factor in recent famines in the Horn. In addition to causing crop failure, lack of rain reduces availability of water and grazing, decimating livestock herds upon which pastoralists depend for survival (see Unruh, this volume, Chapter 7). However, drought is neither a necessary nor sufficient pre-condition for famine.

The view of famine as mass starvation due to crop failure has been critically re-examined in recent years. Sen (1981) explains famine by focussing not on food supply per capita but on household access to food: every household has one or (more often) several entitlements to food, based on trade, contractual or social obligations, or production of food for consumption by the producer household. To minimize risks of catastrophic entitlement failure, vulnerable households strive to diversify entitlement bases, especially when entitlements are threatened. An alternative theory questions Sen's emphasis, arguing that under stress the household gives priority not to avoiding hunger but to preserving its way of life (de Waal 1989); thus, livelihood security, rather than food security, is the household's main concern (Maxwell 1991).

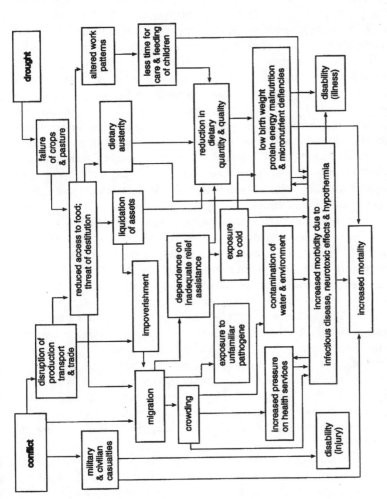

Figure 12.1   Processes by which conflict and drought affect public health

Central to both models is recognition that households and communities with a history of food insecurity have various contingency plans or coping mechanisms to avoid or postpone catastrophe. Common mechanisms include diversification of income sources, borrowing cash or food, and liquidation of assets. In Sen's view, famine occurs when entitlements collapse completely, leaving people without access to food and, therefore, starving to death. In contrast, de Waal argues that most famine deaths are attributable to disease epidemics spawned by conditions arising when people under great stress attempt to avoid destitution (de Waal 1989). Famine is best understood as the result of failure of coping strategies at all levels (national, regional, community, household) following acute reduction in access to food. It is characterized not only by excess mortality but also by abrupt and drastic disruptions of social and economic order. These often include collapse of asset prices and large-scale 'distress migration' of destitute households. Whether drought (or any event threatening food security) leads to famine depends not only on the initial coping capacity of those affected, but also on the extent to which external events affect viability of coping strategies.

To obtain alternative sources of income, household members may take up or intensify petty commodity production and trade, or leave home in search of employment. Household heads may migrate to borrow food or money from relatives, if credit cannot be obtained locally. Those unable to get credit or unwilling to go into debt may sell livestock or other possessions to purchase food and other necessities. Another strategy is dietary austerity. This includes substituting cheaper foods, replacing preferred staples with wild foods, and deliberately reducing the number and size of meals. Recent research in Sudan and Ethiopia shows that, contrary to beliefs of many outsiders, substantial reduction in food intake is not a 'terminal' or late indicator of food insecurity (Rahmato 1987; de Waal 1989; Webb *et al.* 1992; Kelly 1992). By deliberate 'belt-tightening' during acute food insecurity, vulnerable households stretch existing supplies and reduce the need to liquidate productive assets, thereby staving off destitution.

Armed conflict takes various forms, ranging from 'low-intensity' to all-out. Many wars between nations are of the latter type, whereas civil conflict is often characterized by the former. Low-intensity warfare is less concerned with acquiring territory than with elimination or suppression of organized resistance. Its perpetrators employ various tactics that intimidate communities, threaten their values and aspirations, and fragment their economies (Summerfield 1991). Injury, disability and death are the most obvious direct effects of war. Although conditions in the Horn make it difficult to quantify such casualties with precision, it is thought that over a million died in the Ethiopian civil war, including many civilians (Kloos 1992). During 1984–8, over a quarter of a million people, over 90 per cent civilians, died in the war in south Sudan (Dodge 1990). Use of land mines – as in Somaliland,[1] where over a million were planted (SCF 1991) – means that civilians continue to be maimed and killed for many years after war has ended.

Less obvious, but perhaps even more inimical to public health, is the disruption of productive activities, trade and provision of services. Injuries due to conflict increase demands for curative interventions and divert health resources from preventive care. Low-intensity warfare often involves deliberate attacks on health care facilities (Sabo and Kibirige 1989; Kloos 1992), hampering provision of all services. Also common are looting of grain stores and livestock, and disruption of farming and trade. For example, 40 per cent of Eritrea's agricultural land was unused in 1987, due to land-mines, destruction of livestock and military attacks (Cliffe 1989). Another factor constraining production is labour-shortages due to conscription, imprisonment, injury or death.

Responding to depleted household labour power, women often assume heavier work burdens. Other attempts to cope with effects of conflict also involve altering habitual activity patterns. Following livestock raiding by combatants in Somalia and southern Sudan, pastoralists and their herds moved toward urban areas, which afforded greater security but fewer and poorer pastures (Macrae and Zwi 1992). In Tigray, farmers responded to daytime aerial bombardment by working in twilight (Barnabas Gebre-ab, personal communication). Eritreans held markets at night after daytime bombing raids curtailed trading in rural centres (Cliffe 1989).

Parallels can be drawn between these responses to military insecurity and attempts to cope with food insecurity caused by drought. In comparison with episodes of food insecurity, however, it is more difficult to anticipate the course or duration of conflict; at household levels, scope for pro-active measures is more limited, and reactive responses predominate. Nevertheless, responses to conflict or drought can be classed as either coping mechanisms, by which households endeavour to preserve their way of life, or distress sequelae that people are forced into when other options are denied them.

Distress sequelae can be triggered when attacks on civilian populations force large numbers of households to move in search of safety. Examples from the Horn include movement of war refugees from the Ogaden to northern Somalia in the late 1970s; migration of war and famine victims into eastern Sudan from Tigray and Eritrea in the mid-1980s; internal displacement, due to drought and war, of people from southern and western Sudan to Khartoum and other cities, beginning in 1984–5 and continuing into the early 1990s; and the late-1980s influx of war refugees from northern Somalia into eastern Ethiopia.

Conversely, conflict can make key transportation routes (not just roads, but railways, seaports, rivers and airspace) so dangerous that movements of people, commodities and supplies are drastically constrained[2]. In addition to blocking the flow of food, fuel, spare parts and medical supplies into affected areas, isolation imposed by warfare can prevent travel, imperilling livelihoods and interfering with services such as agricultural extension and 'outreach' from health facilities. Examples are rife in south Sudan, where in recent years food and other supplies had to be airlifted into beseiged government-held towns. At the same time, people in Juba, the South's main city, were unable to venture into the countryside for fear of landmines[3] (Winnubst *et al.* 1990).

Interactions of War and Drought

When conflict coincides with food insecurity due to drought, threats to health and survival increase. War aggravates food insecurity by disrupting production, obstructing trade (leading to higher prices in inaccessible areas) and jeopardizing coping mechanisms that require free movement. These factors combine to force people into distress reactions and crisis sequelae more rapidly than would otherwise be the case. Given that many of the Horn's devastating recent disasters involved both drought and conflict, it is difficult and rather artificial to attempt to separate health impacts of these two types of event. Instead, this chapter is organized in terms of the distinction between coping responses and crisis sequelae.

HEALTH IMPACTS OF COPING RESPONSES

The coping behaviour of the Kababish people of North Kordofan, Sudan exemplifies a strategy combining altered work patterns and dietary austerity. In the early 1980s, this pastoralist group responded to drought by taking herds further in search of pasture, although this greatly reduced access to meat, milk and remittance income for household members who remained behind in dry season camps. They also reduced both size and frequency of meals, and increased reliance on wild foods, although it could take an entire day to collect enough for just one meal (Riely 1992).

The international relief and development community has shown much interest recently in coping. However, current thinking tends to emphasize the survival value of coping responses with little systematic exploration of their costs, some of which are incurred as adverse effects on health. Available evidence, much of it indirect, is considered below.

Impacts on Health of Women and Infants

Studies of several communities in the Horn show that when households practice dietary austerity, efforts are made to protect intakes of pregnant and lactating women, babies and young children (Rahmato 1987; FAR 1991). Nonetheless, evidence from Wollo, Ethiopia indicates that despite these efforts young children's diets are to some extent compromised during food insecurity (Kelly 1992). If, as seems likely, there are also limits to households' ability to protect mothers' food intakes, adverse effects on both maternal nutrition and foetal development are virtually inevitable.

Poor maternal diet during pregnancy impairs iron status and increases risk of anaemia, diminishing work productivity and increasing chances of death from post-partum haemorrhage. Iron-deficiency anaemia during pregnancy also endangers the baby by increasing risks of premature delivery (Scholl et al. 1992) and low birth weight,[4] both associated with significantly increased infant mortality (Ashworth and Feachem 1985; Victora et al. 1988). Another factor adding to the risk of low birth weight, especially among under-nourished women, is low energy intake (i.e. too few calories) during pregnancy (Prentice et al. 1987). Heavy physical work during the second half of pregnancy also contributes to low birth weight (Ashworth and Feachem 1985). Although women in the Horn are no strangers to long hours of strenuous exertion, some coping mechanisms (e.g. collecting firewood or wild foods; collecting water from distant sources; migration of able-bodied males in search of employment) might elevate incidence of low birth weight by increasing their work burdens.

Throughout the Horn and especially in rural communities, most babies are breastfed well into the second year of life, if not beyond (Rahmato 1987; de Waal 1989; Ibrahim et al. 1992). Research shows that mothers continue to produce near-normal amounts of good-quality milk even when moderately undernourished (Prentice 1991). Although enhanced metabolic efficiency during lactation (Illingworth et al. 1986) may play a part, it seems likely that maintenance of lactation in these circumstances is achieved at least partly by means of further depletion of maternal nutrient stores.

Impacts on Health of Young Children

By reducing time available for child care, home hygiene and clinic visits, coping responses that make additional claims on women's time and energy can increases incidence, severity and duration of infectious diseases in their children. Even when efforts are made to set aside sufficient food for the most vulnerable, coping responses that increase women's workloads can mean that young children, who need to eat 'little and often' to meet nutrient requirements associated with growth, are unable to consume food earmarked for them because they cannot be fed frequently enough.

To some extent, children on reduced energy intakes can compensate by limiting physical activity, thereby reducing energy expenditure. However, if not offset by reduced energy expenditure, reductions in energy intake lead to weight loss and slowing of growth in height, which can result in protein-energy malnutrition. Even in Wollo during 1987–8, when effects of drought stopped short of actual famine, deterioration in weight for length[5] of children under five was detectable within six months of the harvest failure (Kelly 1992).

Weight loss is reversible, and so too (to a limited extent) are linear growth deficits, but as long as a child remains malnourished risk of dying is increased (Pelletier 1991); this is attributable, at least partly, to reduced resistance to infection (Tomkins and Watson 1989). Following drought in 1990, prevalence of wasting malnutrition (weight for height < 80 per cent) in children in north Sudan, normally around 5–10 per cent, rose to 15–20 per cent in many areas. Since mass migration was not widespread, many outsider concluded that people had coped successfully and famine had not occurred; nonetheless, a 20 per cent rise in under-five mortality can be inferred from observed increase in malnutrition (Kelly and Buchanan-Smith 1994).

Reductions in total food intake and diminution of dietary variety can lead to micronutrient deficiencies as well as protein-energy malnutrition. Data are scanty, mainly because systematic community-level assessments of micronutrient status are rarely undertaken unless clinical signs of deficiency become obvious; however, in populations whose usual intakes are marginal, it is likely that subclinical (i.e. mild) micronutrient deficiencies become common even in early stages of dietary austerity. Vitamin C comes mainly from fresh fruit and vegetables, while important dietary sources of iron include meat and green leafy vegetables. Whole milk, foods containing milk fat, eggs, various fruits and vegetables are useful sources of vitamin A.[6] Consumption of these is often cut back when belts are tightened and livestock lost or sold.

Risk of vitamin A deficiency is highest in young children. Even mild deficiency is associated with increased risk of death from measles and diarrhoea (Sommer *et al.* 1983; West *et al.* 1991; Glasziou and Mackerras 1993; Ghana VAST Study Team 1993). Clinical vitamin A deficiency takes the form of xerophthalmia, progressive deterioration of the eyes which can culminate in irreversible blindness. Ethiopia and Sudan are classed by the World Health Organization as having very high rates of vitamin A deficiency (Humphrey *et al.* 1992). High 'background' levels are likely to be elevated by austerity measures in response to food insecurity and economic stress. Following severe drought, a survey in rural South Kordofan, Sudan found that in nearly a quarter of the villages visited young children were fed fewer than three times a day; over 13 per cent of the sample suffered from night blindness, an early clinical sign of xerophthalmia (FAR 1991).

Because traditional diets of most Somalis include large amounts of milk and milk products (Murray *et al.* 1976; Greenham 1978; Ibrahim *et al.* 1992), vitamin A deficiency is less common than in Sudan or Ethiopia. In 1987, however, surveys of villages in four drought-affected regions of Somalia revealed night blindness in 3 per cent of the young children;[7] in one region, signs of scurvy (vitamin C deficiency disease) were seen in a similar percentage (CDC 1988). This suggests that a much larger proportion had subclinical deficiencies of vitamins A and C. Although this survey did not assess iron status, there is a high background prevalence of anaemia among Somalis; if, as seems probable, this is attributable mainly to iron deficiency (Greenham 1978), it was likely exacerbated by poor vitamin C status, since vitamin C promotes iron absorption. Iron status can also be adversely influenced by vitamin A deficiency (Haschke and Javaid 1991), and might well have been so in this population, which exhibited signs of xerophthalmia. Iron deficiency in children is associated with retarded psychomotor development, impaired cognitive functions and reduced attention span; these persist even after iron deficits are corrected (Cook *et al.* 1993).

Impacts on Health of Other Population Subgroups

Ability to fall back on wild foods in times of hardship undoubtedly has been a major factor in survival of rural people in the Horn. However, some of these foods are potentially toxic and can cause illness, permanent disability and even death. Deaths attributed to overconsumption of *Euphorbia candelabrum*, a wild plant found in Wollo were reported by survivors of the 1984–5 famine (Rahmato 1987). In Darfur, Sudan, consumption of improperly prepared wild foods was said to have caused the deaths of a number of infants (Mohamed and El Bashir 1992:43). In other episodes of accidental poisoning from wild foods, men and boys were the main victims.

Ergot, a fungus that infects rye and wild oats, contains neurotoxic alkaloids which, if ingested in sufficient quantities, can induce ergotism, a condition characterized by convulsions and gangrene. An outbreak of ergotism was documented in Wollo in the late 1970s among peasant communities that resorted to eating contaminated wild oats during drought. Prevalence was only 2.2 per thousand, but 50 per cent of those affected died of the disease, which affected over twice as many males as females. There were few cases among the elderly and none in children under five (Demeke *et al.* 1979).

The lathyrus pea (*Lathyrus sativus*) is a drought- and pest-resistant legume that grows in Ethiopia. Because it contains a neurotoxic amino acid, it can safely be eaten only in small quantities; when large amounts are eaten over an extended period, a disorder characterized by irreversible spastic paralysis called neurolathyrism can result. This danger is well known to rural Ethiopians, who normally produce and consume only small amounts of lathyrus pea, taking care to reduce its toxicity by pre-soaking, then cooking it in several changes of water. However, when other food crops are scarce or expensive and only lathyrus pea is readily obtainable, epidemics of neurolathyrism can occur, especially among the very poor; typically, most victims are older boys and adult men. Such an epidemic, attributed to a combination of drought, flood and pestilence, occurred in Gondar Region in 1976. Although no deaths were reported, there were over 1350 cases, giving a prevalence of almost 10 per thousand in the area studied (Gebre-ab *et al.* 1978).

Another coping response that can have a negative impact on health of men and older boys is migration in search of work, through which they may encounter pathogens to which they have little or no immunity. Thus highlanders who are not normally exposed to malaria (owing to the mosquito vector's inability to live at high altitudes) and therefore lack resistance, may succumb to the disease if they move to lowland areas where it is endemic.

HEALTH IMPACTS OF DISTRESS SEQUELAE

If coping mechanisms become inoperable or coping capacity runs out, households can be pushed into displacement and destitution. Although these processes are often intertwined, this section considers impacts of each in turn.

Health Impacts of Displacement

Health consequences of migration vary according to numbers of people involved, their general state of health, and access to health services. Moderate numbers of able-bodied males migrating to towns in search of work may experience some ill-health, but when hundreds or thousands of people of all ages and conditions move to unfamiliar environments with few amenities or health care facilities, results are more serious. For example, many refugees from the Tigray highlands died of malaria after fleeing to lowland areas in eastern Sudan in 1985 (Toole and Malkki 1992).

Host communities as well as the displaced can suffer as a result of conditions created by an influx of migrants. Arrival of displaced persons increases demand for health services, often overstretching material resources and energies of local health care staff. Where ethnic or family ties exist between incoming migrants and host communities (as is often the case when disaster victims are displaced within their own country, or across borders straddled by a single ethnic group), host communities may experience overcrowding as they attempt to shelter increasing numbers of migrants. Crowding increases contact between those who are well and those who are ill; this facilitates transmission of diseases such as tuberculosis and measles.[8] In 1985, tuberculosis was responsible for up to 50 per cent of deaths in refugee camps in eastern Sudan and over a quarter of adult deaths in camps in Somalia (Toole and Waldman 1988).

Factors affecting measles fatality include exposure (determined by physical proximity) (Aaby *et al.* 1988) and vitamin A status (Barclay *et al.* 1987; Hussey and Klein 1990). When large numbers of undernourished and unvaccinated children are crowded together due to distress migration, epidemics easily occur, often with devastating results. In one camp for Ethiopian refugees in eastern Sudan, nearly 10 per cent of all children under five and almost 5 per cent of those aged 5–14 years were attacked by measles during a single month in 1985; about a third of the cases proved fatal.[9] Measles accounted for 40 per cent of all deaths in the camp that month, making it the single biggest killer (Shears *et al.* 1987). Since measles infection has an adverse effect on both vitamin A status (Hussey and Klein 1992) and utilization of energy and protein, survivors are at high risk for both xerophthalmia and protein-energy malnutrition.

Another way in which health is jeopardized by distress migration and overcrowding is through environmental degradation and increased pressure on basic amenities. Increased demand for water and sanitary facilities, sometimes compounded by failure to maintain water and sanitation infrastructure, may lead to water shortages and contamination of both water and environment, thereby facilitating faecal-oral transmission of diseases like diarrhoea and infectious hepatitis.

In 1985-6, Ethiopian and Eritrean refugees in camps in Sudan and Somalia experienced outbreaks of infectious hepatitis (non-A, non-B), related to onset of rains, which may have washed sewage into water used for drinking and cooking. Most cases were adults. Fewer than 5 per cent of cases proved fatal, but over half of those who died were pregnant women (CDC 1987). Two similar outbreaks, possibly related to shortages of water for personal hygiene, occurred in a camp for Somali refugees in eastern Ethiopia in 1989 and 1990 (Toole and Malkki 1992).

A more common consequence of poor water supply and sanitation is diarrhoeal disease, which accounts for much of the morbidity in crowded camps. A survey of Ethiopian refugee children in a camp in eastern Sudan found that 35 per cent had had diarrhoea in the previous 48 hours (Shears *et al.* 1987). Following floods in Khartoum in 1988, diarrhoea accounted for nearly a third of all visits to health facilities in the affected area (CDC 1989a). As well as being a major cause of illness and contributing to malnutrition, diarrhoea can be deadly: data from Ethiopian and Eritrean refugee populations in eastern Sudan's camps indicate that diarrhoea caused 25-50 per cent of all deaths (Toole and Waldman 1988).

In addition to a chronically high incidence of diarrhoea in camp populations, there were several cholera epidemics. In eastern Sudan in 1985, 4 per cent of the combined population of two camps contracted cholera over a six-week period, and 4 per cent of the cases died (Mulholland 1985). Although mortality was less than 5 per cent in most recorded outbreaks, a cholera fatality rate of 25 per cent was noted in a camp in northwestern Somalia in 1985 (Toole and Malkki 1992).

Displaced people may be prone to psychological problems as well as physical illness. Those who end up in areas where they have no kin or ethnic ties have little or no social support. They may be alienated from host populations by language or cultural barriers, while competition for scarce resources (such as water) can engender hostility. Additionally, presence of displaced people can create political embarrassment, to which host governments may respond with attempts at forcible relocation. Such conditions prevailed in the unplanned settlements that sprang up around Khartoum in the mid-1980s and are now inhabited by three-quarters of a million victims of war and famine.

It would not be surprising to find high levels of anxiety, depression and other forms of mental illness among those who have gone through the dislocation, isolation, harassment and bereavement experienced by many displaced people (Dick 1984; Summerfield 1991). Although mental health has never been systematically studied under disaster conditions in the Horn, it was observed that drought-affected Somali nomads in camps in Ethiopia's Ogaden region had many psychosomatic complaints, possibly related to lack of work and hostility of the area's long-term residents. The same authors reported neglect of needy neighbours and elderly family members, apparently due to erosion of the traditional value system by combined effects of various stresses (Murray *et al.* 1976).

Health Impacts of Destitution

Knowing they will be cut off from their usual means of livelihood, war refugees often take livestock, cash or valuables with them as a buffer against destitution when they flee their homes.[10] But unless their sojourn is very brief it is just a matter of time before they become destitute as well as displaced. Unless adequate relief assistance is available, the destitute must subsist on grossly inadequate diets. Many health workers believe that psychological stress and poor diet make women unable to breastfeed, but effects of extreme maternal malnutrition and psychological stress on milk output have never been directly assessed (Kelly 1993), and indirect evidence is equivocal. A survey of sites in central, southwestern and eastern Ethiopia reported that in the worst famine year many mothers were 'forced to wean their babies earlier than expected because their breasts had dried up' (Webb *et al.* 1992, p 57).[11] However, in Darfur and Wollo even during acute food insecurity and famine, women continued to breastfeed their infants, enhancing babies' survival chances[12] (de Waal 1989; Hassan 1991; Kelly 1993).

Even in communities with low vitamin A intakes, breastfeeding substantially reduces risk of xerophthalmia in children (Tarwotjo *et al.* 1982; West *et al.* 1986; Mahalanabis 1991). However, breastmilk of mothers whose vitamin A status is poor may have a lower vitamin A content. Consequently, their babies might enter the weaning period with supobtimal stores of this nutrient, with increased risk of developing vitamin A deficiency if dietary vitamin A is inadequate (Wallingford and Underwood 1986).

The Horn has seen alarming xerophthalmia outbreaks associated with prolonged consumption of diets lacking vitamin A. In 1984–5, high rates of xerophthalmia were observed among children of famine-stricken Ethiopian and Eritrean families, including many who had walked to eastern Sudan (Pizzarello 1986). One of the most severe outbreaks of vitamin A deficiency ever reported occurred in a village in Hararghe where people had subsisted on food aid and wild foods for several years. There, the proportion of children with signs of xerophthalmia was much higher than the national average (Wolde-Gebriel *et al.* 1991; 1993). Relief rations supplied to disaster-affected populations usually consist simply of grain, pulses and edible oil,[13] and are virtually devoid of several micronutrients (Toole 1992; Acheson 1993). However, most people who depend on food aid manage to obtain small amounts of fresh food, often by exchanging part of their rations in local markets. Severe and widespread clinical vitamin deficiencies occur when populations dependent on relief rations are denied access to fresh foods.

Following closure of local markets where inhabitants of nearby camps had been able to purchase camel's milk and other fresh foods, widespread clinical signs of scurvy, including bleeding gums, painful joints and muscle weakness, were seen among Ethiopian refugees in Somalia (Magan *et al.* 1983). Data from six camps for Ethiopian and Eritrean refugees in Somalia and Sudan for 1985–7 showed that scurvy began to appear three to ten months after the refugees' arrival. Although prevalence was higher in females, in both sexes it increased with age and duration of residence in the camps; prevalence was elevated in the dry season, in remote camps, and in desert camps (Desenclos *et al.* 1989). Refugees from northern Somalia developed scurvy after several months in camps in an arid region of eastern Ethiopia (CDC 1990), and in 1991 an outbreak occurred in former Ethiopian soldiers in eastern Sudan (Toole and Malkki 1992).

Yet another health risk faced by those who are destitute as well as displaced is exposure to the elements. In many instances, displaced destitutes inhabit flimsy makeshift shelters on sites exposed to natural hazards[14] such as dust storms or flooding. For example, occupants of unplanned settlements suffered more than the city's long-term residents when Khartoum was inundated by floods in August 1988 (CDC 1989a).

Even in the absence of natural catastrophes, displaced and destitute people often suffer from exposure to cold, wind and rain, owing to lack of fuel, clothing and blankets, as well as inadequate shelter. Need for protection is especially crucial at high altitudes[15] and in desert areas, where night-time temperatures drop to within a few degrees of freezing. Cold exposure is particularly dangerous to those suffering from undernutrition, certain diseases and psychological stress, all of which can aggravate loss of body heat (Lloyd 1986). Although deaths from hypothermia have not been documented in displaced populations in the Horn, probably some have occurred. The most likely victims are the elderly, in whom effectiveness of thermoregulatory mechanisms is reduced. Those who survive cold stress do so mainly by shivering. This adaptive response increases body heat production but also incurs energy costs. Once the ambient temperature falls below 20°C, energy expenditure may increase by as much as

1 per cent for every 1°C decrease; this is intensified by the so-called wind-chill factor (Rivers and Seaman 1988). Exposure may contribute to malnu-trition among destitute displaced, although it is probably less important than inadequate rations.

Unsurprisingly, there is an association between energy content of relief rations and rates of child malnutrition (Toole *et al.* 1988). During Ethiopian and Sudanese famines of 1984–5, prevalence of wasting malnu-trition (WFL < 80 per cent) in children under five rose from 5–10 per cent to over 25 per cent in the worst camps (Nash 1986; Shears *et al.* 1987). As mentioned, malnutrition in children increases risk of dying. The magni-tude of this risk is related both to the individual child's weight deficit and to the baseline level of child mortality (a proxy for the prevalence and severity of infectious disease) in the surrounding population (Pelletier 1991). In other words, for a child with a given weight deficit, the more pathogenic the environment, the greater the risk of death. Thus children of the destitute and displaced are not only less likely to thrive, but more likely to die once they become malnourished.

Death by starvation *per se* is rare, but not unknown, during disasters in the Horn. In April 1992, a survey in southern Somalia revealed extremely high rates of wasting malnutrition,[16] and malnutrition was the single most commonly cited cause of death (Manoncourt *et al.* 1992). At three sites in south Sudan, a 1993 investigation found roughly two-thirds of children suf-fering from wasting malnutrition, and half of all recent deaths were attribut-able to starvation (CDC 1993). Although mostly caused by conditions that can easily (in technological terms) be prevented or cured, mortality remains high among disaster-affected populations, especially the displaced and des-titute. As of early 1993, annual mortality rates were roughly ten times normal levels at the three sites in south Sudan noted above (CDC 1993). A 1992 survey in central Somalia found that at one site almost three-quarters of all displaced children under five had died over an eight-month period. Daily crude mortality rates, estimated at thirty times expected peacetime levels, were among the highest ever recorded for civilian populations (Moore *et al.* 1993). In many cases, a disproportionate number of those who die are young children (Toole and Waldman 1990).

IMPLICATIONS FOR DISASTER PREPAREDNESS AND DEVELOPMENT

It is no coincidence that the least developed countries are also least able to avoid or mitigate disasters. In fact, building and maintaining the ability to prevent and deal with disasters is so central to true development that, if it were not so difficult to measure, this capacity could be used as a yardstick of overall economic and social well-being.

At the time of writing, civil war and food emergencies still rage in parts of the Horn, while in others, the worst is over – at least for now – and rehabilitation is now the top priority. As far as public health is concerned, the most pressing needs in these areas are for removal of land-mines, repair of water and sanitation infrastructure, reconstruction of homes and farms, and re-establishment of health care programmes. It is also essential to enable and assist people to rebuild their livelihoods. Putting livelihoods on a surer footing will help to restore coping capacity at household level, thereby reducing vulnerability to future shocks. At regional and national levels, measures to strengthen disaster preparedness could include:

- Measures to achieve lasting improvements in food security and nutritional status, e.g., provision of agricultural inputs and credit; regulation of producer and consumer prices; provision of employment opportunities and protection of incomes.

- Increased attention – on a routine basis – to disease prevention measures such as immunization, support for breastfeeding, and improvement of environmental sanitation and water supply.

- Vulnerability mapping to identify communities at risk of losing their livelihoods or access to food.

- Improving famine early warning systems and strengthening links between early warning and relief response.[17]

- Contingency planning to support indigenous coping strategies, e.g., establishment of decentralized, locally-controlled food security reserves; pre-planning Food for Work programmes and livestock price support schemes.

- Contingency planning for management of emergencies, e.g., training health personnel in refugee community health care; maintaining emergency stocks of micronutrient-fortified relief foods, shelter materials, blankets, essential drugs, and water and sanitation equipment in readiness for influxes.

- Provision of adequate funding and appropriate staff training for national agencies with responsibility for refugees.

Efforts to design and implement many of these measures are already underway in several parts of the Horn. However, success in disaster reduction and mitigation requires substantial material and financial resources, technical know-how and political will. Much of the political will must come from within the countries concerned, and might be strengthened by greater democracy and press freedom, which would increase governments' accountability.[18] Much technical expertise has been acquired by those called upon to deal with past disasters; this must be retained, consolidated by further training, and shared with those who have less experience, to enhance effectiveness of relevant national institutions. Building the material and economic capacity to deal with disasters requires transfer of resources, either from one budget to another within countries concerned, or from international and bilateral sources.

Notes

1. Formerly northern Somalia.
2. Although not all de facto blockades are deliberately created, in many cases they were intentionally used as weapons of war; see Keen (1991); Macrae and Zwi (1992).
3. Juba has been ringed by two concentric circles of landmines, one laid by rebels and the other by government forces.
4. Defined as a body weight of less than 2500 g at birth.
5. Weight for Length (WFL) is an index expressing body weight relative to the average for healthy children of the same length. Weight for Height (WFH) is identical to WFL but involves measurement of standing height rather than supine length.
6. Camel's milk is unusual in that it also supplies useful quantities of vitamin C.
7. This prevalence exceeds the 1 per cent level set as the borderline above which vitamin A deficiency is considered a public health problem (WHO 1982).
8. As 'the most infectious disease known to humans' (Hussey and Klein 1992:188), measles is particularly important.
9. In contrast, measles was not a problem among refugees from northwest Somalia who fled to eastern Ethiopia in 1988, because a high proportion of this mainly urban population had been vaccinated prior to displacement (CDC 1990).
10. Refugees from Hargeisa, northern Somalia, brought electronic goods such as cameras and cassette players with them when they fled to Ethiopia in 1988. Such items were subsequently offered for sale in and around Hartisheik camp.
11. This was reported twice as often by households in the upper income tercile of the sample than by those in the lower income tercile (Webb *et al.* 1992:56–7), a finding somewhat at odds with others from the same study indicating a clear relationship between wealth and coping capacity (ibid. p. 11).
12. In normal circumstances in the Horn, death rates among infants are at least five times higher than in children aged 1–4 years. Under disaster conditions, however, the rate of increase in mortality in children aged 1–4 years is often much larger than the rate of increase in infant mortality (de Waal 1989; Toole and Waldman 1988). The difference seems related to age-related differences in consumption of breastmilk, which contains anti-infective factors as well as necessary nutrients.

13. At times, food aid donors have been reluctant to provide anything but grain (Kelly and Buchanan-Smith 1994).
14. Also, there may be man-made hazards: Hillat Shook, an unplanned settlement near Khartoum, was sited on a rubbish dump (Dodge 1990).
15. For example, Korem, site of the camp at which the BBC filmed the scenes that alerted the world to the 1984–5 Ethiopian famine and provided the impetus for Band-Aid, is situated at an elevation of 2400 metres.
16. Over 40 per cent of children in towns and 75 per cent of those in camps had mid-upper arm circumference (MUAC) below 12. 5 cm.
17. For more on this see Buchanan-Smith and Petty 1992a and 1992b.
18. Dreze and Sen (1989) argue that most African countries that have averted threats of famine are characterized by political systems that are 'relatively open and pluralist', and have 'an active and largely uncensored press' (p. 59).

References

Aaby P., J. Bukh, I. M. Lisse and M. C. Da Silva, 1988. 'Decline in Measles Mortality: Nutrition, Age at Infection, or Exposure?' *British Medical Journal*, 296:1225–8.

Acheson, D., 1993. 'Health, Humanitarian Relief, and Survival in Former Yugoslavia', *British Medical Journal*, 307:44–8.

Ashworth, A. and R. Feachem, 1985. 'Interventions for the Control of Diarrhoeal Diseases among Young Children: Prevention of Low Birth Weight', *Bulletin of the World Health Organization*, 63(1):165–84.

Barclay, A. J. G., A. Foster and A. Sommer, 1987. 'Vitamin A Supplements and Mortality Related to Measles: a Randomised Clinical Trial', *British Medical Journal*, 294:294–6.

Buchanan-Smith, M. and C. Petty, 1992a. Famine early warning systems and response: the missing link? Case study no. 1: Ethiopia 1990/91 (Draft). Institute of Development Studies, Brighton/Save the Children Fund, London. Mimeo.

Buchanan-Smith, M. and C. Petty, 1992b. Famine early warning systems and response: the missing link? Case study no. 2: Sudan, 1990/91 (Draft). Institute of Development Studies, Brighton/Save the Children Fund, London. Mimeo.

Centers for Disease Control, 1987. Enterically Transmitted non-A, non-B Hepatitis – East Africa. *Morbidity and Mortality Weekly Report*, 36(16): 241–4.

Centers for Disease Control, 1988. Rapid Nutrition Evaluation in Drought-affected Regions of Somalia – 1987, *Morbidity and Mortality Weekly Report*, 37(7): 104–7.

Centers for Disease Control, 1989a. Health Assessment of the Population Affected by Flood Conditions – Khartoum, Sudan. *Morbidity and Mortality Weekly Report*, 37(51 & 52):785–8.

Centers for Disease Control, 1989b. Nutritional and Health Status of Displaced Persons – Sudan, 1988–1989, *Morbidity and Mortality Weekly Report*, 38(49):848–55.

Centers for Disease Control, 1990. Update: Health and Nutritional Profile of Refugees – Ethiopia, 1989–1990, *Morbidity and Mortality Weekly Report*, 39(40):707–18.

Centers for Disease Control, 1993. Nutrition and Mortality Assessment – Southern Sudan, March 1993, *Morbidity and Mortality Weekly Report*, 42(16):304–8.

Cliffe, L., 1989. 'The Impact of War and the Response to it in Different Agrarian Systems in Eritrea', *Development and Change*, 20:373–400.

Cook, J. D., R. D. Baynes and B. S. Skikne, 1993. 'Iron Deficiency and the Measurement of Iron Status', *Nutrition Research Reviews*, 5:189–202.

Demeke, T., Y. Kidane and E. Wuhib, 1979. 'Ergotism – a Report on an Epidemic, 1977–78', *Ethiopian Medical Journal*, 17:107–13.

Desenclos, J. C. , A. M. Berry, R. Padt, B. Farah, C. Segala and A. M. Nabil, 1989. 'Epidemiological Patterns of Scurvy among Ethiopian Refugees', *Bulletin of the World Health Organization*, 67(3):309–16.

de Waal, A., 1989. *Famine that Kills: Darfur, Sudan, 1984–85* (Oxford: Clarendon Press).

Dick, B., 1984. 'Diseases of Refugees – Causes, Effects and Control', *Transactions of the Royal Society of Tropical Medicine and Hygiene*, 78:734–41.

Dodge, C. P., 1990. 'Health Implications of War in Uganda and Sudan', *Social Science and Medicine*, 31(6):691–8.

Dreze, J. and A. Sen, 1989. *Hunger and Public Action* (Oxford: Clarendon Press).

Fellowship for African Relief (FAR), 1991. Nutrition Survey Report: Hamadi and Debeibat Rural Councils, North Dilling, South Kordofan, 16–30 October 1991. FAR, El Obeid, Sudan. Mimeo.

Gebre-ab, T., Z. Wolde-Gabriel, M. Maffi, Z. Ahmed, T. Ayele and H. Fanta, 1978. 'Neurolathyrism – a Review and a Report of an Epidemic', *Ethiopian Medical Journal*, 16:1–11.

Ghana VAST Study Team, 1993. 'Vitamin A Supplementation in Northern Ghana: Effects on Clinic Attendances, Hospital Admissions, and Child Mortality', *The Lancet*, 342:7–12.

Glasziou, P. P. and D. E. M. Mackerras, 1993. 'Vitamin A Supplementation in Infectious Diseases: a Meta-analysis', *British Medical Journal*, 306:366–70.

Greenham, R. 1978. 'Anaemia and Schistosoma haematobium Infection in the North-Eastern Province of Kenya', *Transactions of the Royal Society of Tropical Medicine and Hygiene*, 72:72–5.

Haschke, F. and N. Javaid, 1991. 'Nutritional Anaemias', *Acta Paediatrica Scandinavica Supplement*, 374:38–44.

Hassan, B. F., 1991. Nutrition Status Survey Results in Malha, Mareiga and Mellit Rural Councils, October 1991. Save the Children Fund UK, Darfur.

Humphrey, J. H., K. P. West Jr. and A. Sommer, 1992. 'Vitamin A Deficiency and Attributable mortality among Under-5-year-olds', *Bulletin of the World Health Organization*, 70(2):225–32.

Hussey, G. D. and M. Klein, 1990. 'A Randomized, Controlled Trial of Vitamin A in Children with Severe Measles', *New England Journal of Medicine*, 323(3):160–64.

Hussey, G. D. and M. Klein, 1992. 'Measles-induced Vitamin A Deficiency', *Annals of the New York Academy of Sciences*, 669: 188–94.

Ibrahim, M. M., L. A. Persson, M. M. Omar and S. Wall, 1992. 'Breastfeeding and the Dietary Habits of Children in Rural Somalia', *Acta Paediatrica Scandinavica*, 81: 480–83.

Illingworth, P. J., R. T. Jung, P. W. Howie, P. Leslie and T. E. Isles, 1986. 'Diminution in Energy Expenditure during Lactation', *British Medical Journal*, 292:437–41.

Keen, D., 1991. 'A Disaster for Whom? Local Interests and International Donors during Famine among the Dinka of Sudan', *Disasters*, 15(2):150–65.

Kelly, M., 1992. 'Entitlements, Coping Mechanisms and Indicators of Access to Food: Wollo Region, Ethiopia, 1987–88', *Disasters*, 16(4):322–38.

Kelly, M., 1993. 'Infant Feeding in Emergencies', *Disasters*, 17(2):110–21.

Kelly, M. and M. Buchanan-Smith, 1994. 'North Sudan in 1991: Food Crisis and the International Response', *Disasters*, 17(4). In press.

Kloos, H., 1992. 'Health Impacts of War in Ethiopia'. *Disasters*, 16(4):347–54.

Lloyd, E. L., 1986. *Hypothermia and Cold Stress* (London: Croom Helm).

Macrae, J. and A. Zwi, 1992. 'Food as an Instrument of war in Contemporary African Famines: a Review', *Disasters*, 16(4): 299–321.

Magan, A. M., M. Warsame, A. K. Ali-Salad and M. Toole, 1983. 'An Outbreak of Scurvy in Somali Refugee Camps', *Disasters*, 7:93–7.

Mahalanabis, D. , 1991. 'Breast Feeding and Vitamin A Deficiency among Children Attending a Diarrhoea Treatment Centre in Bangladesh: a Case Control Study', *British Medical Journal*, 303:493–6.

Manoncourt, S., B. Doppler, F. Enten, A. E. Nur, A. O. Mohamed, P. Vial and A. Moren, 1992. 'Public Health Consequences of the Civil War in Somalia, April 1992' (letter), *The Lancet*, 340:176–7.

Maxwell, S. (ed.), 1991. *To Cure All Hunger* (London: Intermediate Technology Publications).

Mohamed, M. A. and H. El Bashir, 1992. Final Report: Coping Strategies during Food Shortages in Darfur State, Phase II (August–October 1992) (Khartoum: Save the Children Fund).

Moore *et al.*, 1993. 'Mortality Rates in Displaced and Resident Populations of Central Somalia during 1992 Famine', *The Lancet*, 341: 935–8.

Mulholland, Kim, 1985. 'Cholera in Sudan: an account of an epidemic in a refugee camp in eastern Sudan, May–June 1985', *Disasters*, 9(4):247–58.

Murray, M. J., A. B. Murray, M. B. Murray and C. J. Murray, 1976. 'Somali Food Shelters in the Ogaden Famine and their Impact on Health', *The Lancet*, i: 1283–5.

Nash, A. H., 1986. Korem Feeding Centre. (London: Save the Children Fund (UK)) Mimeo.

Pelletier, D. L., 1991. Relationships between Child Anthropometry and Mortality in Developing Countries: Implications for Policy, Programs and Future Research (Ithaca, New York: Cornell Food and Nutrition Policy Program).

Pizzarello, L. D., 1986. 'Age Specific Xerophthalmia Rates among Displaced Ethiopians', *Archives of Diseases in Childhood*, 61: 1100–103.

Prentice, A. M., T. J. Cole, F. A. Foord, W. H. Lamb and R. G. Whitehead, 1987. 'Increased Birthweight after Prenatal Supplementation of Rural African Women', *American Journal of Clinical Nutrition*, 46:912–25.

Prentice, A. M., 1991. 'Can Maternal Dietary Supplements Help in Preventing Infant Malnutrition?', *Acta Paediatrica Scandinavica Supplement*, 374: 67–77.

Rahmato, D., 1987. Famine Survival Strategies: a Case Study from Northeast Ethiopia (Addis Ababa: Food and Famine Monograph Series No. 1. Addis Ababa University).

Riely, F. Z., 1992. Implications of Household Behaviour for Famine Early Warning: a Case Study of the Kababish Pastoralists in Northern Kordofan, the Sudan (Rome: Food and Agriculture Organization of the United Nations).

Rivers J. P. W. and J. A. Seaman, 1988. Nutritional Aspects of Emergency Food Relief. Working Paper No. 5, Conference on Nutrition in Times of Disaster, Geneva, 27–30 September 1988 (Geneva: World Health Organization).

Sabo, L. E. and J. S. Kibirige, 1989. 'Political Violence and Eritrean Health Care', *Social Science and Medicine*, 28(7):677–84.

Save the Children (1991) Emergency Update, Somalia, 9 May 1991 (London: Save the Children Fund) Mimeo.

Scholl, T. O., M. L. Hediger, R. L. Fischer and J. W. Shearer, 1992. 'Anemia vs Iron Deficiency: Increased Risk of Preterm Delivery in a Prospective Study', *American Journal of Clinical Nutrition*, 55:985–8.

Seaman, J. and J. P. W. Rivers, 1989. 'Scurvy and Anaemia in Refugees' (letter), *The Lancet*, 8648:1204.

Sen, A. K., 1981. *Poverty and Famines: an Essay on Entitlement and Deprivation* (Oxford: Clarendon Press).

Shears, P., A. Berry, R. Murphy and M. A. Nabil, 1987. 'Epidemiological Assessment of the Health and Nutrition of Ethiopian Refugees in Emergency Camps in Sudan, 1985', *British Medical Journal*, 295:314–17.

Sommer, A., G. Hussaini, I. Tarwotjo and D. Susanto, 1983. 'Increased Mortality in Children with Mild Vitamin A Deficiency', *The Lancet*, 1:585–88.

Summerfield, D. , 1991. 'The Psychosocial Effects of Conflict in the Third World', *Development in Practice*, 1: 159–73.

Tarwotjo, I., A. Sommer, T. Soegiharto, D. Susanto and M. Muhilal, 1982. 'Dietary Practices and Xerophthalmia among Indonesian Children', *American Journal of Clinical Nutrition*, 35: 574–81.

Tomkins, A. and F. Watson, 1989. *Malnutrition and Infection: a review* (Geneva: United Nations Administrative Committee on Coordination/ Sub-Committee on Nutrition).

Toole, M. J., 1992. 'Micronutrient Deficiencies in Refugees', *The Lancet*, 339: 1214–16.

Toole, M. J. and R. M. Malkki, 1992. 'Famine-affected, Refugee and Displaced Populations: Recommendations for Public Health Issues', *Morbidity and Mortality Weekly Report*. 41/No. RR-13.

Toole, M. J., P. Nieburg and R. J. Waldman, 1988. 'The Association between Inadequate Rations, Undernutrition Prevalence, and Mortality in Refugee Camps: Case Studies of Refugee Populations in Eastern Thailand, 1979–80, and Eastern Sudan, 1984–85', *Journal of Tropical Pediatrics*, 34:218–24.

Toole, M. J. and R. J. Waldman, 1988. 'An Analysis of Mortality Trends among Refugee Populations in Somalia, Sudan and Thailand', *Bulletin of the World Health Organization*, 66(2):237–47.

Victora, C. G., P. G. Smith, J. P. Vaughan, L. C. Nobre, C. Lombardi, A. M. B. Teixeira, S. M. Fuchs, L. B. Moreira, L. P. Gigante and F. C. Barros, 1988. 'Influence of Birth Weight on Mortality from Infectious Disease: a Case-control Ctudy', *Pediatrics*, 81:807–11.

Wallingford, J. and B. A. Underwood, 1986. 'Vitamin A Deficiency in Pregnancy, Lactation and the Nursing Child', *Vitamin A Deficiency and Its Control*, J. C. Bauernfeind (ed.) (Orlando: Academic Press).

Webb, P., J. von Braun and Y. Yohannes, 1992. Famine in Ethiopia: Policy Implications of Coping Failure at National and Household Levels. Research Report 92 (Washington DC.: International Food Policy Research Institute).

West, K. P., M. Chirambo, J. Katz, A. Sommer and the Malawi Survey Group, 1986. 'Breast-feeding, Weaning Patterns and the Risk of Xerophthalmia in Southern Malawi', *American Journal of Clinical Nutrition*, 44:690–97.

West, K. P., R. P. Pokhrel, J. Katz, S. C. LeClerq, S. K. Khatry, S. R. Shrestha, E. K. Pradhan, J. M. Tielsch, M. R. Pandey and A. Sommer, 1991. 'Efficacy of Vitamin A in Reducing Preschool Child Mortality in Nepal', *The Lancet*, 338: 67–71.

Winnubst, P., L. Bjorkman, D. Barker, A. Nash and M. Kelly, 1990. Report of the WFP/NGO/Donors' Food Aid Assessment Mission to Sudan, 27 November–19 December 1990, (Khartoum: World Food Programme).

Wolde-Gebriel, Z., T. Demeke and C. E. West, 1991. 'Xerophthalmia in Ethiopia: a Nationwide Ophthalmological, Biochemical and Anthropometric Survey', *European Journal of Clinical Nutrition*, 45: 469–78.

Wolde-Gebriel, Z. H. Gebru, T. Fisseha and C. E. West, 1993. 'Severe Vitamin A Deficiency in a Rural Village in the Hararge Region of Ethiopia', *European Journal of Clinical Nutrition*, 47:104–14.

World Health Organization, 1982. Control of Vitamin A Deficiency and Xerophthalmia: Report of a Joint WHO/UNICEF/USAID/Helen Keller International/IVACG Meeting. Technical Report No. 672 (Geneva: World Health Organization).

13 New Regionalisms in Africa as Responses to Environmental Crises: IGADD and Development in the Horn in the Mid-1990s*

Timothy M. Shaw

The Horn of Africa is experiencing profound changes in the mid-1990s – ecological, economic, political, social and strategic – which will affect development prospects into the twenty-first century. These are exacerbated by equally fundamental shifts in the global order, notably the end of both the Cold War strategic and post-war economic systems along with fragmentation and transformation of the post-1945 Eastern bloc. If the former 'Soviet Union' and its satellites symbolize global changes then those in the old 'Ethiopian' empire and its neighbours do so for Africa. Indeed, given the close historical, structural and contemporary connections between the two, their respective transformations are not unconnected. Moreover, sequences and outcomes of their respective fragmentation, liberalization, pacification and reorientation – from economic stabilization/adjustment to political democratization/decentralization – are by no means certain.

Hence the relevance and challenge of current interest in appropriate and innovative regional programming displayed by some donors such as CIDA, notwithstanding the latter's apparent ideological conversion and commitment to otherwise neoconservative policies for the Third World: now reinforced by recessionary pressures throughout the North – *Africa 21* as well as structural adjustment cross-conditionalities – and partial withdrawal from continuous bilateral assistance to programmatic support for human rights and democratic development. The imperative of innovative forms of regional cooperation is a function not only of international economic and political changes, but also of global environmental problems and pressures. Such tensions in political economy are particularly intense in Africa because of its contemporary crises, which have led to new forms of

249

both intervention and marginalization constituted by the ubiquitous structural adjustment programme and paradigm.

In terms of *economics*, after more than ten years of policy reforms and proliferating conditionalities, Africa is both more divided (endless national policy framework papers and negotiations) and united (almost all states are now undertaking similar adjustment projects) than ever. Yet this is the one Southern continent without any Newly Industrializing Countries (NICs) or near-NICs (see Okbazghi, this volume, Chapter 5). And adjustment programmes are as much characterized by slippage as agreed sequences. Moreover, informal sectors, both local and regional, have flourished as formal cutbacks and contractions have increased.

In terms of *politics*, popular responses to adjustment deprivations – the proliferation of 'vulnerable groups' – have encouraged and emboldened democratic movements, leading to the decline or decay of classic one-party state-centric systems, even in advance of the demise of state communism in Eastern Europe. Revival of civil society in Africa is not really a function of novel adjustment cross-conditionalities, with their focus on formal aspects of governance but a grass-roots reaction to disappointment with and disintegration of the state: if NGOs do not fill the space vacated by shrinking regimes, then even fewer basic needs will be met.

Together, such economic and political shocks and opportunities have led to *'revisionist' analysis and praxis*, even if the prevailing neoclassical paradigm is reluctant to so admit. 'Triumphalism' about political and economic 'liberalisation' – democratic and market forces – may be mistaken as responses to the demise of state socialism include tribalism and racism, corporatism and authoritarianism. In short, optimism or idealism about a 'new' world order is quite misplaced.

Such global contexts inform continental and regional prospects as *Africa* seeks to redefine itself. At the official level, it has come to recognise the renaissance of democratic political forces, particularly in the landmark Arusha conference of early 1989; likewise, the Abuja summit of mid-1991 agreed in principle on establishment of an African Economic Community. However, the real dynamic behind such redefinitions comes from a mixture of international (globalization, differentiation and regionalization) and informal (civil society, informal economies and cross-border exchanges) pressures.

Such environmental, institutional, ideological and intellectual contexts constitute the background to consideration of the genesis of and prospects for a formal inter-state regional organization like the IGADD. Given its recent, specific and problematic role, it can be taken as an example of the *'new' regionalism*: distinct purpose, genesis and structure.

'New' or 'second' wave regionalisms are distinguished by their range of purposes (i.e. less economic or strategic), participants (i.e. non-state as well as official actors) and structures (i.e. less centralized, bureaucratized and politicized). In addition to IGADD, such second generation institutions include CILSS, COMESA and SADC if not ECOWAS or SACU, even if one of the latest African collections on regionalism is still stuck in economistic rather than 'new' functional or political assumptions: for Oliver Saasa the issue involved in *Joining the Future* (1991) is still the old one of trade creation versus diversion.

Aside from the multiple issues and factors treated in comprehensive regional groupings like the EU and Canada-US Free Trade Area, amongst the more relevant comparative cases for Africa are two in Asia: ASEAN's embryonic AFTA amd SAARC, although the first of these includes several NICs or near-NICs. The latter is also a late-comer, itself concerned to emulate ASEAN's dynamic economies but overly mesmerized by strategic and diplomatic manoeuvrings. Even more than SADC, it is preoccupied with the established dominance of India and, like most African regional units, it is exclusively state-centric, with little space for non-state actors, whether private sector companies or civil society NGOs.

Aside from liberalization and nuclearization, ASEAN and SAARC have yet to begin to confront issues like ecology, narcotics and religion. Nevertheless, as the parameters of the 'new' world order clarify in the late-twentieth century, Southern regimes will have to respond not only to globalization but also to regionalization, especially across the North Atlantic and North Pacific. These trends are no longer limited to economics but incorporate various contemporary 'transnational' factors, particularly environmental ones. They constitute central elements in contemporary International Political Economy (IPE) at both intellectual and existential levels, as Dennis Gayle *et al.* (1991/92:67) recently suggested:

> developments which will attract research attention include...the application of idiosyncratic models of economic growth and democracy across the 'developing' countries, and the continued combination of international economic integration coupled with sharpened sociopolitical differentiation.

AFRICAN REGIONALISM IN THE MID-1990S

IGADD was created in the late-1980s as the Eastern African equivalent to CILSS and the *Club du Sahel* to coordinate programmes for and assistance to meet ecological challenges confronting the Horn: droughts, vulnerabilities and conflicts which reinforced underdevelopment. Initially its six member states were able to augment their limited resources by appeals to multi- and bi-lateral donors but a combination of interrelated internal and regional disputes, exacerbated by global tensions at the end of the Cold War, mitigated against success. Indeed, IGADD at the turn of the decade was probably more important for its diplomatic than development functions: regional peace and security rather than environmental regeneration, food security or water conservation.

The *conjuncture of the mid-1990s*, however, may yet afford it a new start: new leadership, resources, purposes and contexts. Whether such new regionalism will be sustainable still depends on unpredictable factors, such as the possible proliferation of state members – Eritrea if not Somaliland – regional conflicts within and among countries (Southern Sudan/Northern Uganda, Afars, Oromos, Somali 'clans'); informal regional exchange of goods, monies, peoples and refugees; and novel democratic demands from both civil society and political movements.

The mixture of economic, ecological, informal, political and strategic forces informs prospects for new regionalisms elsewhere on the continent, particularly *Southern and West Africa*. The former is especially influenced by the prospect of a post-apartheid South Africa in SACU/ SADC/COMESA and the latter by ECOMOG within ECOWAS. Both are profoundly affected by shifts in the New International Divisions of Labour (NIDL) and Power (NIDP), such as *de facto* adjustment conditionalities, like the value of the rand and franc, and the end of bipolarity and hence nonalignment. I hope that this comparative and comparable case study of IGADD will provide insights, cautions and incentives for innovative regional and continental institutions appropriate for the new period, encouraged by some donors own creative and compatible responses, such as CIDA's *Africa 21* framework.

Regionalism was relatively ignored in Africa in the 1980s, because of the former's mixed record and the latter's successive economic and ecological crises, and nationally-exclusive structural adjustment programmes. Conversely, regionalism at the global level has tended to overlook African cases, even though the two are integrally-related, because of its preoccupations initially with the EU and now with Eastern Europe, North America and Pacific Rim. Moreover, both genres tended to disregard both the hitherto 'high' politics of inter-state conflicts and diplomacy and 'low' politics of civil societies, environmental, informal, and transnational relations. In short, there is a need for 'revisionist' analysis of the contemporary African situation which brings such strands together, especially given interrelated continental and global changes apparent at the start of the 1990s. This case is also relevant to more general analyses of international political economy and ecology.

REGIONAL POLITICAL ECONOMY

The regional political economy of the IGADD member states in the mid-1990s appears at first glance quite propitious: a series of apparently unresolvable regional conflicts along with unstable regimes and decaying infrastructures. Yet, on closer observation, there are signs for hope (Doornbos *et al.* 1992). First, one of two primary regional *wars* is over – the horrendous conflict in Ethiopia – even if that in Sudan lingers on; and subsequent tensions in Djibouti and Somalia are spill-overs from peace in Ethiopia/Eritrea. Second, demands for *democracy* as well as peace have begun to be heeded in Djibouti, Ethiopia, Eritrea, Kenya and Uganda, leading to revival of more dynamic and sustainable civil societies. Third, most economies in the region are now under some form of structural adjustment regime which means they are all headed in a similar direction of 'liberalization' rather than being pointed in disparate directions as when divided by Cold War ideologies – various forms of 'African' socialism and capitalism. Fourth, partly because formal economies are in such disarray almost everywhere except Kenya, *informal sectors* are thriving, including cross-border trade in foods, goods, money and people. Yet the place of the Horn in the NIDL and NIDP, dominated by the US, European Union (EU), Japan and the NICs, along with a few 'middle powers' like China and India, is problematic. Indeed, if it fails to be more integrated and pacific as well as productive in the twenty-first century it may become truly marginal in any foreseeable world order, leading to either anarchy and/or self-reliance by default.

Given such dramatic and problematic shifts in both global and regional political economies, as well as in Canada's overseas aid policy, the current period might appear a rather inappropriate time to be considering any lessons from (dis?)integration in the Horn. Conversely, such fluidity opens up possibilities not hitherto anticipated, such as incorporation of states-in-formation: Eritrea if not (yet?) Somaliland or Southern Sudan. Moreover, previous regional development policies were based on now somewhat inaccurate assumptions; e.g. not taking into account the current conjuncture of world economic stagnation and proliferation of structural adjustment programmes, with the latter's implicit contractual conditionalities of enhanced Northern finance once 'reforms' are agreed.

The new *constellation of forces* constitutes a unique and fleeting opportunity, albeit with a somewhat higher level of risk than normal, for Canada and other donors to forge links in the post-bipolar period with new regimes and actors, particularly governmental and non-governmental organizations (NGOs), which have had to evolve to facilitate parallel transitions from war to peace polities and from regulated to liberalized economies. Although the 'peace dividend' is still problematic in scale and scope in the Horn, demise of superpower interference creates opportunities for more positive interventions from (rather than short-term retreats by) other, more benign states, like Canada. Indeed, one cost of the demise of bipolarity is evaporation of the leverage which some Southern states could realise through 'nonalignment'. Given widening 'policy dialogue/coordination', few donors or sectors now stand outside multilateral conditionalities. Hence the somewhat surprising announcement of CIDA's new regionalist *Africa 21* policy framework, which seems to contradict or at least dilute the Agency's apparently theological conversion to the adjustment paradigm. In part this may be because of its own bureaucratic imperatives – to maximize gains from the integration of previously linguistically divided units into one continental branch and to salvage lingering 'decentralization' programmes despite their costliness – as well as the anticipation of some that standard adjustment packages cannot work everywhere simultaneously. It has since been reinforced by Canada's own debt and adjustment syndrome of budget cut-backs leading to the precipitous termination of bilateral programming in the Horn by the departing Conservative government in the early-1990s.

For both macro- and micro- reasons, then, the mid-1990s represent a peculiarly opportune occasion at which to contemplate appropriate, sensitive policy innovations to advance sustainable development around the Horn's coastline (see below). To be realistic and cautious, a *pessimistic* perception or scenario can still be envisaged, reflective of regional diversities and instabilities: drought, decay and conflicts will lead to further anarchy (Somalia and Sudan writ large). By contrast, a more *optimistic* view would emphazise democracy, peace, reform and stability (Eritrea and Kenya as exemplars). In between, there are presently problematic cases of Ethiopia and Djibouti in which 'national' or 'ethnic' issues have been intensified because of conflicts and changes in neighbouring states and have yet to be resolved although their respective futures are brighter now than in previous decades, as indicated in the recently-completed regional summit meeting. Such prospects for the Horn are situated in a 'new' world order in which great power interests and interventions may continue to decline.

IGADD'S GENESIS

Given the disastrous set of ecological and economic 'shocks' which this region along with other parts of Africa suffered in the late-1970s and early-1980s, members of the UN and OAU communities sought to create a regional structure within which issues of regional responses to drought and desertification could be addressed.

Following the relative success of the *Comité permanent Inter-états de Lutte contre la Sécheresse dans le Sahel* (CILSS) and its parallel donor grouping – *Club du Sahel* – IGADD was debated, designed, proposed and approved in the mid-1980s: the Eastern African equivalent of CILSS.

However, reflective of the state of the region at the time – Cold War-type divisions and wars in both Ethiopia and Sudan – IGADD was 'politicized' from the start with parochial interests. The ability of some members to interfere in everyday affairs was exacerbated by the 'isolationalist' tendencies of the Authority's first Executive Secretary, the late Dr Makonnen Kebret. Rather than serving as a regional coordination agency for UN and other donors, IGADD became in the late-1980s a rather uninvolved, unknown and underfunded inter-state grouping with minimal connections to either member governments or civil societies let alone the global community.

As indicated in an earlier institutional review which we prepared for CIDA in Addis Ababa in 1990, IGADD has considerable potential for coordination of environment, food infrastructure, water and related human resource development and information. It also has a role in the parallel promotion of peace and stability. In the Horn both desertification and diplomacy, drought and security are equally 'high politics'. But the Authority's structure of Heads of State, Council of Ministers, Technical Committee and Executive Secretariat is overly hierarchical, with no internal focal points for either members' civil societies or donor communities. Although IGADD is now encouraging national points of contact in each member government, there has been a marked absence of networking either with environmental and other groups in the six members' societies or with bi- and multi-lateral and nongovernmental organizations outside the six.

The apparent drift in IGADD affairs was halted with the timely appointment of its second Executive Secretary in early-1991: Dr David Muduuli. He almost single-handedly began to turn the Authority around, assisted by the end of the war and accession of a new regime in Ethiopia. IGADD has been reintegrated within UN and donor communities, who in turn have provided interim financing to revive its activities. Through a series of

broad-based donor-funded meetings, it reemphasized its priorities of food
security and environmental protection along with information and communication. Moreover, the new leadership has begun to provide regular quarterly and annual reports to both members and donors, as well as one- and
five-year work plans. Within one year, Dr Muduuli overcame the drift in
IGADD's programming and publicity so that post-1992 donor funding is
likely to indicate a reversal in declining levels of assistance. But undeni-
ably there are fundamental issues yet to be resolved.

IGADD'S PROSPECTS

The next months and years for the Authority will be crucial because the
institutional reforms essential for it to become a normal international organization must be decided. In addition to reviving IGADD programmes and
finances, the new Executive-Director sought UN assistance for its structures and operations. If the comprehensive report and recommendations of
a UN Sudano Sahelian Office consultant, Dr Dennis Seiner, are adopted
and IGADD restructures itself then the donor community has made it clear
that it would once again inject quick-dispensing resources to help 'kick-
start' regional coordination activities: drought control, early-warning
systems, food security, water development etc. as well as communication
and information.

Under Muduuli's leadership, IGADD was active in the run-up to the
mid-1992 Rio de Janeiro Earth Summit – the UN Conference on
Environment and Development – which reflects and reinforces its own
focus. If it is successfully restructured and revived then the post-Rio
Agenda 21 would facilitate reinvigoration and reinstatement with multilateral agencies. If, unhappily, member states cannot accept or agree on the
necessary redesign of IGAAD, which in part means learning from evolv-
ing parallel arrangements elsewhere, then some other regional agency
might have to be put in its place as a successor. Clearly, just as fish, fleets
and pollutants as well as herds, informal sector goods and monies, and
people move across borders so some regional structures are imperative for
marine as well as terrestrial development, whether fisheries, environments
or management. Already the Horn contains national participants in several
more modest, specific and overlapping interstate networks: Arab League,
COMESA, UNEP Regional Seas and OCAPAC. So if IGADD fails to
transform itself into an effective regional coordination agency of particular
utility in transferring experiences in the marine as other sectors – then
these could become functional equivalents of the Authority. In short, in

these as other development areas, scope of the issue or resource should determine regional scale and structure.

Moreover, difficulties of effecting *regionalism outside the IGADD nexus* are apparent in the extremely limited progress made by UNEP's OCAPAC in either of its Action Plans for Eastern Africa or Red Sea and Gulf of Aden. To date, despite objective need, these are the least active, institutionalized and well-funded of the ten regional seas groupings: some $100–200 000 each per annum just to keep the so-called Action Plan alive. If even a renewed IGADD cannot cope with new state members, Hussein Adam (1990:29) has proposed an alternative 'Commonwealth of Independent Horn of Africa States' of five units (Djibouti, Somaliland, Ethiopia, Eritrea and Somalia).

In brief, the current period is crucial to the Authority's future. Seiner's *Review of the Organizational Structure of the Executive Secretariat of IGADD and Proposals for New Arrangements* is comprehensive, sensitive and informed. It suggests several similar organizational structures for a revived IGADD along with job definitions and evaluations. It already has donor support. If it now receives members' endorsement then the new regime at the Authority's headquarters in Djibouti can proceed to further members, activities and reforms with greater confidence. This positive outcome is even more crucial given the end the Cold War and the relatively stable global framework it constituted for regional inter-state relations. In the more fluid, possibly unstable, post-bipolar context – symbolized by foreseeable proliferation of states in the Horn – a conducive regional system is an imperative. Otherwise, in the absence of global superpowers, emerging regional powers, such as Egypt, Libya, Saudi Arabia or Iran may influence, even impose, an outcome.

REGIONAL PEACE AND SECURITY

IGADD's crucial and developmentally-related peace and security role involves advancing peace-making communication and *confidence-building* through establishing a tradition of regional 'functional' activities. One continuing cause for as well as result of the seemingly endless cycle of environmental drought and ecological decline is the legacy and reality of inter- and intra-state conflicts. To date, IGADD is still the only regional institution which has brought major contenders together, especially in its instrumental mediation/negotiation in the late-1980s.

IGADD's member states recognized this element in its list of functions at its foundation. Neither drought nor desertification can be transcended, terminated or rolled-back unless there is sustained regional peace. Activities aimed at going beyond but also reinforcing the Authority's primary 'functional' roles could be advanced by regional 'confidence-building' measures. Moreover, stretching any 'zone of peace' or neutrality offshore would both extend and symbolize regional tranquillity, security and stability, all areas in which Canada has comparable historical experience.

This extra-functional potential is particularly apparent in the *marine sector*, one area of relatively unexplored resources in an otherwise impoverished region. Harvests from regional seas could minimize on-shore malnutrition and starvation – fish for 'vulnerable groups' and communities, including refugees – and generate foreign exchange for importing necessary capital, parts, technologies and skills for marine and other sectors. This is especially so for desert coastal communities of Djibouti, Eritrea, Somalia/Somaliland. Such a potentially high-visibility role for a post-restructuring IGADD, encouraged by disinterested middle powers like Canada (possibly including intermediation of our distinctive non- or semi- or quasi-governmental development networks like the Canadian Council for International Cooperation and Partnership Africa Canada), becomes more feasible and more essential in a post-Cold War era when no super-power or even continental organization can so facilitate, despite the demise of regional despots like Mengistu and Siad. Given Africa's marginalization and the North's preoccupations, such inter-civil society linkages are imperative. Canada's current foreign policy review might encourage such relevant and efficient aid.

Regional peace and security are, then, not only being redefined to take into account the end of bipolarity and the reality of ecological and economic 'threats' to regional communities and regimes alike, they both remain prerequisites for and correlates of development. The mid-1990s afford a unique opportunity, given the conjuncture of national, regional and global forces – notwithstanding continuing traumas of war in Somalia and Sudan or constraints of structural adjustment conditionalities – for creative developmental and diplomatic strategies amongst a like-minded group of middle powers such as Canada: confidence-building rather than the expenses and dangers of actual peace-keeping/making. If IGADD is successfully restructured and rejuvenated, its credibility and potential will be enhanced along with the status of its donors: beyond functionalism to peace-building based on mixed-actor coalitions which include NGOs.

Such institutional reinvigoration along with task-expansion into promising areas of fisheries, coastal and oceans development and management would serve to revive members' commitment to IGADD and secure *support from elements in civil society in the region.* Inevitably, patterns of official and unofficial approval for the Authority vary over time and between states, with smaller countries in general being more positive than larger ones. Renewal of donor support for IGADD in the early 1990s has rekindled members' interest and commitment, as would the proposed *de facto* extension of its coordinating role to local seas. Moreover, association with appropriate national sectoral agencies would broaden the Authority's network and reinforce members' involvement.

MARINE DEVELOPMENT AND IGADD: CASE OF NEW REGIONALISM

Since its establishment, IGADD has paid minimal attention to offshore developments and environments. Characteristically, its new five-year plan relegates fisheries to the last of its ten programme areas, warranting but one page of project proposals. Previously, IGADD did not initiate any marine sector projects although several were proposed. At the first (and thus far only) donors' conference in early 1987 three projects in coastal fisheries were proposed: (i) construction of a fishermen's settlement or refugee locations in north-east Djibouti; (ii) rehabilitation of Somalia's artisanal fishing industry; and (iii) technical support to Somalia's Ministry of Fisheries. A 1990 consultant's report by Serefaso (financed through CIDA's regional programme) identified markets in Djibouti and Somalia and proposed investing in a fishnet plant in Uganda.

Otherwise, IGADD's first serious entry into *fisheries development* was to request the FAO to field a mission to its member countries. Following visits to the region, the mission reported in August 1990. Officials from the fisheries sector were represented and fisheries further discussed at the November 1991 IGADD Forum but there has been no further discussion or follow-up to the FAO report other than the outline in the 1992–6 plan.

Indeed, the prospect for such a positive, innovative and sustainable policy direction is nowhere more apparent than in the region's coastal communities and waters, a sector previously ignored by members and donors alike, notwithstanding its profound environmental implications. Such disregard is symptomatic of the *'old' regionalism*, which focused on limited formal inter-state economic (and sometimes diplomatic or strategic) relations rather than more informal, multi-sectoral, especially environmental and social, sectors.

To date, inaccurate and misleading *myths*, propounded in both academics' and consultants' writings, have perpetuated disinterest in marine resources, with especially negative consequences at the regional level. First, most analyses propound the myth that there is little *fishing* around the Horn; yet indigenous coastal communities and foreign offshore fleets have survived, even thrived, despite wars and droughts in the last two or three decades. Second, it is commonly alleged that there are no markets for fish; yet a variety of catches are regularly sold throughout the Horn, including Kenya, especially to Coptic Ethiopians/Eritreans as well as to markets in Europe and the Gulf. Third, it is widely asserted that 'regional seas' like the Red Sea and the Gulf of Aden face few *ecological threats* as both fishing and pollution are limited; yet the state of fish stocks is not known and at the same time coral species and biological diversity are high while the 30 km Bab el Mandeb channel between Djibouti and Yemen is traversed by over 5000 vessels a year, 20–25 per cent of which are oil tankers! Fourth, notwithstanding myriad forms of international *drought relief* in recent years, fish have been ignored as a possible food source let alone a means to ease pressure on delicate terrestrial ecosystems from unsupportable livestock herds.

Historical and current patterns of interrelated inequalities and instabilities – e.g. Djibouti, Eritrea, even Somaliland as centres of quite large-scale informal sector trade, including fish – make a *regional approach* attractive, even essential. More donors have come to so recognize and encourage on condition that IGADD is reformed. Not only are coastal areas interrelated and similar, there are lessons to be learned between say, Djibouti and Kenya on the one hand and Eritrea and Somalia on the other (artisanal fisheries and marine parks, respectively). Regional coordination and cooperation would not only insulate any bi- or multi-lateral projects from local unrest, it would also reinforce promising regional institutions and networks now identified and facilitated by CIDA's *Africa 21*.

Two related lacunae should be noted which have broader implications than just the marine sector, both related to analysts' oversights and donors' preferences. First, there seems to be considerable, unrecorded, unregulated, illegal but not illegitimate *'informal' trade* in fish throughout the region, especially lobster, shark, shrimp and tuna from Eritrea and Somalia to both Yemeni and offshore fleets (Italian, Japanese, Russian, Taiwanese etc.); indeed, fishermen survive through trading fish for foreign exchange (which in turn procures manufactured inputs plus stereos, TVs, videos etc.), along with smaller levels of exports to, say, Ethiopia (white fish for 'fasting' days) and Kenya (dried shark and tuna plus fishmeal for its burgeoning meat industries). Second, the potential, positive contribution of fish to *drought relief and desertification control* has been overlooked by short-term disaster responses. A market for fish in the Horn has always existed and is growing, providing protein and minerals for consumers especially children, jobs for female processors and sellers, and environmental relief given exponential devastation caused by excessive herds and grazing.

In short, the *regional political economy* is much more hopeful and vibrant than it might at first appear, offering reasonable prospects for judicious policy interventions by sensitive donors in the largely neglected marine sector. Any such programming should, of course, be guided by local conditions and participation. Given the fragility of tropical marine environments and interrelatedness of coastal (particularly reef), communities, fisheries and eco-tourism, any foreign assistance should seek to advance both, probably through initial support for relatively productive artisanal communities, whether private or cooperative. More sizeable and continuing assistance could then be extended in more complex areas of stock assessment, protection and management, which means dealing with the controversial but vital issue of foreign, industrial fleets. In the short-term the latter take finite stocks without paying licences or taxes, which means foreign exchange losses for the states concerned; in the long-term, depletion of off-shore resources will affect in-shore catches. Moreover, where there are coral reefs and beach hotels there is potential for conflict between fisherfolk and tourists through destruction of reefs to get shells etc for sale to the latter. Ultimately, marine conservation here as elsewhere will require appropriate and sustained, multi-level and multi-media education.

PROSPECTS FOR OTHER NEW REGIONALISMS IN AFRICA

IGADD can both learn from and offer cautions to other regional arrangements in Africa whatever their range of members, sectors, structures and supports. Likewise, possible scenarios for IGADD can be informed by alternative futures derived from *other regions*.

As indicated, novel regionalisms, especially of less official and formal varieties, have begun to appear and flourish in Africa as elsewhere, partly because of the demise of more formal federalist institutions and partly because of regionalist tendencies elsewhere, especially the EU. CILSS and SADC are particular exemplars but continuing revisions to ECOWAS (Shaw and Okolo 1994) and COMESA make them somewhat more 'new' also.

Clearly, IGADD is the most recent, small, specific and impoverished of the 'new generation' organizations. While it lacks an agreed, transparent mechanism for dealing with the crucial donor community, such as CILSS' parallel *Club du Sahel* or SADC's donors' conference; it does constitute a regional inter-state negotiating forum. IGADD has had major difficulty, because of its genesis, vintage and membership in transcending its inter-governmental origins to achieve autonomy; but this may come after the proposed re-organization, -direction and -invigoration of the early-1990s. Likewise, depending partly on sector, regime and period, member support has not been particularly high; but the Authority's current attempts at a regional constituency outside state houses, in ministries, NGOs, media, professional associations and civil societies, should secure greater commitment.

Given its recency and vulnerability, there are as yet no short- or longer-term *predictions* for IGADD, perhaps also partly because of the Horn's inflammability. Likewise, there are few for either CILSS, ECOWAS or COMESA. By contrast, the *Southern African* region is littered with outmoded futures studies, focusing on national and regional impacts of apartheid. Stoneman and Thompson (1991) identify five possible post-apartheid scenarios: (i) regional fragmentation; (ii) persistence of two sub-groupings (SADC versus SACU); (iii) market-led integration; (iv) modified customs union; and (v) development coordination along SADC lines. Davies and Martin (in Viera, Martin and Wallerstein 1992) suggest three: (i) regional restabilization; (ii) regional break-up and peri-pheralization; and (iii) fundamental restructuring.

Regrettably, neither set of previews give enough emphasis to either *global changes* – NIDL and NIDP – or local *transformations*, either structural adjustment programmes or democratization or informalization processes, let alone environmental pressures. Such forces are crucial to all regional designs, including IGADD, and constitute the primary factors behind new regionalisms: transformations in (interrelated) national and global political economies which lead towards new generation or second wave regionalisms appropriate for the next century. Moreover, these innovations reinforce each other through both example and pressure: hence the proliferation of new regionalisms from EU and NAFTA to AFTA, SAARC, etc. Redefinition of functionalism and security to embrace ecology, along with rediscovery of regionalism by African institutions and foreign donors alike, points to possibilities of sustained experimentation with new regionalisms into the twenty-first century.

*(This chapter benefits from research undertaken for ICOD with assistance from Robert McKinnell and Mark Butler on potential marine development in the Horn in cooperation with IGADD in the early-1990s. However, it reflects the author's opinions only and should not be taken to represent the policy of either ICOD or CIDA.)

References

CIDA, 1991. *Africa 21: a vision of Africa for the 21st century* (Ottawa: Africa and Middle East Branch, October).

Doornbos, Martin *et al.* (eds), 1992. *Beyond Conflict in the Horn: the prospects for peace, recovery and development in Ethiopia, Somalia, Eritrea and Sudan* (London: James Currey for ISS).

Gayle, Dennis J. *et al.*, 1991. 'International Political Economy: Evolution and Prospects', *International Studies Notes*, 16(3) and 17(1), Fall 1991 and Winter 1992, 64–8

Hussein M. Adam, 1992. 'Eritrea, Somalia, Somaliland and the Horn of Africa', *CAAS Conference* Montreal, May.

IGADD, 1987. *Report on the First Donors' Conference, Djibouti, March 1987*, (Djibouti, April).

IGADD, 1990. *Third Summit of IGADD, January 1990* (Djibouti).

IGADD, 1990. *Food Security Strategy Study, Volume 1 Draft Report. Volume 2 Annexes* (Djibouti) August.

IGADD, 1990. *Document on Assessment of Progress since IGADD First Donors' Conference of March 1987 to be Considered by Technical Representatives from Member States.* (Djibouti) November.

IGADD, 1990. *Work Program of the Secretariat for 1991–1993* (Djibouti) November.

IGADD, 1991. *The IGADD Five-Year Programme, 1992–1996* (Djibouti).

IGADD, 1991. *Plan of Activities for 1991* (Djibouti).

IGADD, 1991. *Quarterly Reports 1991* (Djibouti, three quarters to September 1991).

IGADD, 1991. *Proceedings of IGADD Forum on Agricultural Research Planning, October 1991*, (Djibouti, November).

IGADD, 1991. *Review of the Organizational Structure of the Executive Secretariat of IGADD and Proposals for New Arrangements.* (Dennis Z. Steiner, UNSO/IGADD Consultant) (Djibouti, November).

IGADD, 1992. *Sustainable Development and Integrated Management of Natural Resources in the IGADD Sub-Region: a Strategy for Implementation* (Djibouti, IGADD and GTZ, January).

IGADD, 1992. *Annual Report of the Executive Secretariat for 1992 Planned Activities for 1992* (Djibouti, January).

Saasa, Oliver (ed.), 1991. *Joining the Future: Economic Integration and Cooperation in Africa* (Nairobi: ACTS Press).

Shaw, Timothy M. and Julius Emeka Okolo (eds), 1994. *The Political Economy of Foreign Policy in ECOWAS* (London: Macmillan).

Stoneman, Colin and Carol B. Thompson, 1991. 'Southern Africa after Apartheid', *Africa Recovery Briefing Paper.* 4 (New York) December.

Viera, Sergio, William G Martin and Immanuel Wallerstein (eds), 1992. *How Fast the Wind? Southern Africa, 1975–2000.* (Trenton NJ: Africa World Press).

Index

Note: In the Horn of Africa, most people identify themselves by their first names. The index has been prepared to reflect this.

265